*f***P**

THE FUTURE ONCE HAPPENED HERE

New York, D.C., L.A., and the Fate of America's Big Cities

FRED SIEGEL

THE FREE PRESS
New York London Toronto Sydney Singapore

TO ROSIE AND HER SISTERS

*f*P

THE FREE PRESS
A Division of Simon & Schuster Inc.
1230 Avenue of the Americas
New York, NY 10020

Designed by Carla Bolte

Manufactured in the United States of America

10 9 8 7 6 5 4 3 2 1

Library of Congress Cataloging-in-Publication Data

Siegel, Frederick F., 1945–
The future once happened here : New York, D.C., L.A., and the fate of America's big cities / Fred Siegel.
p. cm.
Includes index.
ISBN 0-684-82747-6
1. Urban policy—New York (City)—New York. 2. Urban policy—Washington (D.C.) 3. Urban policy—California—Los Angeles. 4. Urban policy—United States. I. Title.
HN80.N5S54 1997
307.76'0973—dc21 97-23050
CIP

Contents

LOS ANGELES

BACK TO THE FUTURE

Introduction

Former San Jose mayor Tom McEnery attended a meeting of the preeminent urban policy organization, the United States Conference of Mayors. The organization's Washington headquarters is adorned with a large picture of President Franklin Roosevelt and with framed correspondence describing his close relationship with the mayors of the great cities:

Late in the day, "as yet another speaker droned on about the pressing need for increased federal assistance to the cities," says McEnery, the host, Mayor Marion Barry, finally showed up. Barry, dressed in the "red warm-up suit he must have slept in, slumped into the chair next to [McEnery] and closed his eyes." McEnery goes on: "Suddenly, Marion Barry came alive, interrupting the speaker [to] blurt out a few non sequiturs." Jaws dropped to the sound of nervous laughter, and the conferees gazed in disbelief as Barry rambled on. Finally, he slumped back into his chair beside McEnery, apparently satisfied that he had made his point. "Politely, we all acted as if nothing happened," says McEnery. The speaker responded with, "Excellent point, Marion. Now back on the subject of block grants." McEnery concludes, "I have never shuffled my papers as intently as I did the rest of the meeting."

In a sense, what happened with Marion Barry at the U.S. Conference of Mayors meeting was not unusual. The leading lights of urban liberalism had been averting their eyes for decades. For thirty years the mayors had been defining the big city as a welter of woes whose ruin would be rewarded with financial aid from the federal government. When failure begat failure, the venerable U.S. Conference of Mayors, begun by the legendary mayors James Michael Curley of Boston and Fiorello La Guardia of New York, persisted in pursuing policies that presented the cities as the hopeless victims of racism and governmental neglect. These once great centers of commerce and innovation redefined themselves in terms of both their dependent populations and their fiscal dependence on Washington.

The upshot has been that the cities run along liberal lines have, like Marion Barry, fallen from public grace. Cities, says veteran analyst George Grier, have been "gaining more problems than voters over the past three decades." Cities have become the symbols of government policy and society gone awry. Says Mayor Michael White of Cleveland, "Big cities [became] a code name for a lot of things: for minorities, for crumbling neighborhoods, for crime, for everything that America has moved away from."

Once upon a time, big cities and their liberal ethos were at the very center of national political and economic life. Born in the big cities, modern liberalism eventually died there. It first emerged in the 1920s, a triumph of the urbane and the tolerant over the rural and the repressive, culminating in the 1933 repeal of prohibition. It came of age in FDR's 1936 landslide presidential victory, when the New Deal shifted from a rural to an urban base and big government became a permanent part of American life.

The big cities, which had successfully integrated the vast turn-of-the-century wave of immigrants, were at the heart of the coalition that remade America in the course of defeating both the Great Depression at home and dictators abroad. These are the glories former New York mayor David Dinkins spoke of when he defined the cities as "the soul of the nation."

Confusing the past with the present, Dinkins, in the early 1990s, repeatedly asserted that "like a mighty engine, urban America pulls all of America into the future." Former New York governor Mario Cuomo was unintentionally closer to the mark when he, evoking the era of Al Smith and FDR, noted poignantly that "the future once happened here."

The political rise of the cities during the New Deal coincided with the end of a century of urban economic growth. The great cities of the Northeast and Midwest had been built on the conjuncture of rail and river, which centralized everything from manufacturing to merriment. A variety of new technologies—electricity, the internal combustion engine, the telephone—had begun to distribute the city's functions over a whole region, but as early as 1923, Frank Lloyd Wright saw that "the big city is no longer modern."

In 1930 an Atlanta editor saw the future: "When Mr. Henry Ford . . . put some kind of automobile within easy reach of almost everybody, he inadvertently created a monster that has caused more trouble in the larger cities than bootleggers, speakeasies, and alley bandits." Long before race became the central issue in American politics, the automobile allowed middle-class whites to escape the clamor and congestion of the city, with its soot and saloons, for pastoral enclaves of their own. What's more, those enclaves were subsidized by the same New Deal so beloved of urban liberals. In 1934 the Federal Housing Authority began to insure low-interest long-term mortgages for new suburban single-family housing construction.

Both people and jobs began leaving the cities. As early as the 1930s, city planners worried about what was then called "blight" as manufacturing, once organized around the railroads, moved to cheaper exurban land serviced by trucks. In some cities, such as Baltimore, the changes were astounding: between 1929 and 1939, notes the historian John Teaford, Baltimore lost 10 percent of its manufacturing while manufacturing in its metro area grew by 250 percent. The dispersal of manufacturing and jobs was only hastened by World War II, when decentralization was a matter of national security. By 1950, 23 percent of the population would be suburban; today it is 53 percent.

To make matters more difficult for the postwar cities, the mechanization of Southern agriculture sent vast numbers of Southern sharecroppers, semiliterates with few salable skills, streaming north into the cities. In the 1940s and 1950s, people who led economically isolated lives in the South were shunted, often for racist reasons, into the isolation of public housing. Had there been no racial mien to this migration, absorbing the newcomers would still have been difficult—but doable. After all, at the turn of the century, many had feared that the vast wave of new immigrants from the "backward" lands of southern and eastern Europe would be unassimilable, but in a celebrated triumph the cities proved to be the great incubators of ethnic integration; the factories, schools, and political clubs of the big cities turned immigrants into Americans. The postwar cities had a harder time integrating their newcomers. The changes in technology dealt them a bad hand, which they then played badly. But while economic decentralization was and still is a salient source of city woes, the problems plaguing cities are also the product of public policy choices produced in the 1960s, a period of extraordinary prosperity.

The current plight of the cities is linked to a series of gigantic public policy wagers made three decades ago in Washington, New York, and Los Angeles. Though now forgotten, the terms of the gambles made in the wake of the Watts riot in Los Angeles were simple enough, but the consequences have been complex and unnerving.

In the mid-1960s, urban policy makers, under the influence of a dizzying mix of guilt, fear, and hubris, decided that when it came to black and, to some extent, Hispanic America, the immigrant model of incorporation through acculturation was to be abandoned. The assumptions and institutions that allowed the newcomers from eastern and southern Europe to gain their rightful place in American life were, in the face of the riots of the sixties, to be not just modified but completely abandoned. Instead, hoping to remedy the wrongs of racial injustice, policy makers boldly decided to bet the national (or at least the urban) future on an entirely different and untested set of premises. New Deal–era assumptions about the close connection between work and well-being, the need for a common culture, and the importance of public order were cast aside as either racist or inadequate to the needs of the new arrivals.

In the wake of his 1964 landslide victory over Barry Goldwater, President Johnson called the election "a mandate to unite this nation . . . to make this Nation whole as one nation, as one people, indivisible under God." His admirable aim was to bring the margins into the center, to incorporate African-Americans into the larger national community. "I see a day ahead," he would later proclaim, "with a united nation . . . one great America, free of malice and free of hate . . . bound together by common ties of confidence and affection, and common aspirations toward duty and purpose." Civil rights were for Johnson the path to a citizenship of shared values that was to be embodied in the mutuality of government-funded social insurance programs.

Integration, however, was just a brief phase between the passage of the 1964 Civil Rights Act and the rise of the Black Power movement, between the passage of the Voting Rights Act and the full-blown emergence of black separatism, between Jim Crowism and Crow Jimism, between *colored people* and *people of color.*

New Deal liberalism, that bastard offspring of a love affair between a practicing capitalist father and a sentimentally socialist mother, has always been vulnerable to attacks from both left and right. In the sixties, simultaneous attacks from the New Right and New Left laid it low. In the cities in particular, New Deal liberalism, which had built a mild economic egalitarianism on a base of social solidarity forged in the Great Depression and World War II, was replaced with a new liberalism. Sixties liberalism yoked together an antipathy to economic markets and a faith in a free market in morals to produce what might be called "dependent individualism." In an egalitarian pursuit of equality of outcome, sixties liberalism looked to spray economic regulations into every nook and cranny of the economy. Simultaneously morally libertarian and statist, it looked to judicially minted individual rights to undermine the traditions of social and self-restraint so as to liberate the individual from conventional mores.

The dependent individualists assumed they had the right to bear children and the state had the obligation to support them. The upshot, particularly in New York and the District of Columbia, was an extraordinary transfer of responsibility from the family to the state. It was a transfer that produced the worst of both worlds: fiscal failure and further family breakdown.

The social insurance so central to the New Deal makes sense to soften the effects of unforeseen disaster. We have to help each other out in times of flood or widespread economic failure. Social insurance aimed to help people caught in tragedies not of their making, but no insurance system can compensate for the predictably destructive action of unmarried teens unprepared for motherhood giving birth to children who will later be unable to become self-sufficient adults.

The two halves of sixties liberalism—social license and economic restrictions—reinforced each other. Rent, zoning, and business regulation drained New York and Washington (though not Los Angeles) of their economic vitality. It left them saddled with expensive and inefficient governments and a state-supported economy of social workers and other members of the "caring professions," who, whatever their good intentions, came to live off the personal failings of the big cities' dependent populations.

The body of this book, which is by no means intended as a comprehensive account of what happened in New York, Los Angeles, and the District, is devoted to describing how sixties liberalism, in a series of great gambles regarding work, welfare, public order, and a common culture, reshaped the three great cities.

Why New York, Washington, and Los Angeles? In part because if power lies in telling people what to think, these three cities had been setting not just the urban but much of the national agenda. Their sphere of influence is all of America. The nineteenth-century British statesman James Bryce wrote that "the conjunction of the forces of rank, wealth, knowledge, intellect . . . makes such [cities] a sort of foundry." In such cities "opinion is melted and cast"; then it "can be easily and swiftly propagated and diffused through the whole country."

Politics and policy in these three cities, each a center of money, media, and government, play an outsized role in representing both liberalism and the big cities to the rest of America. The 1965 and 1992 Los Angeles riots (bookends of sorts for this essay); the Lindsay administration's attempt to create a post–New Deal liberalism by expanding welfare and creating multicultural schools *avant la lettre;* New York's bankruptcy; the sheer collapse of day-to-day services in Washington, D.C., under "mayor for life" Marion Barry—all have had a lasting effect on American life.

Each of these three cities represents a major tendency in American life, an experiment in ideals less fully realized in other places. Los Angeles is the centrifugal city, the center of a multiculturalism that assumes it can operate without a core of shared civic values; Washington, D.C., has been an example of black nationalism in power; and New York represents the lost world of New Deal liberalism deformed by dependent individualism, the linking together of economic overregulation with a free market in morals.

Together each of these cities has lived in the shadow of what Professor David Sears called "the riot ideology," the assumption that the violence of the sixties riots and their criminal aftermath were both justified and, to a considerable extent, functional in rectifying the sins of racism. The power to disrupt became a claim against the treasury. Violence, or at least the threat of violence, became a way of extracting money from the federal government, if only as riot insurance. But with vast federal budget deficits and widespread black, as well as white, middle-class flight from the cities, this public sector approach to peddling pathology has played itself out.

This book's closing chapters look at how a new generation of mayors and administrators—Mayor Rudolph Giuliani in New York, Mayor Richard Riordan in Los Angeles, and the Financial Control Board in the District of Columbia—have tried with mixed success to remedy the ills of their cities. For all their problems, the future of these three great cities has not been foreclosed. In New York and Los Angeles, the decline of crime and the promise of welfare reform open up possibilities for economic and social renewal unthinkable only a few years ago. As upscale Americans rediscover the charm of city density and new immigrants reclaim areas that were once wastelands, these cities have become incubators of the digital revolution. Culturally wired for creativity, equipped with fiber-optic cable, they are the centers for the software, multimedia, and Web site innovations that are reshaping both communications and the postindustrial economy. As for Washington, it is by virtue of its location so naturally rich and so well endowed with talented people that replacing the current administration would do wonders for its future.

Cities live within people as surely as people live within cities. As a son of New York City, I was weaned on a pride for her accomplishments; now I am saddened by her decline, even as I hope for her renewal. If an impassioned tone occasionally appears in my writing, it's because this book is animated by my assumption that these are cities whose wealth and talents should have secured far better outcomes.

These pages were written from a New York very few nonnatives ever see—an integrated area of Flatbush, Brooklyn, graced with Victorian homes and shaded by giant maples. It's only a short subway ride in one direction from a Pakistani immigrant neighborhood and in the other from the allure and energy of Manhattan. If, as they say, you want to know where I'm coming from, it's from Beverley Road near Coney Island Avenue, a short walk from the D train.

1. The Riot Ideology

During the 1993 Los Angeles mayoral election, rivals Michael Woo, a liberal Democrat, and Richard Riordan, a centrist Republican, faced a constant dilemma. Which word should they use to describe the civil disturbances that had hit L.A. twice in the past quarter century? Black leaders and the *Los Angeles Times* sometimes referred to the 1965 Watts and 1992 South Central upheavals as rebellions or uprisings. Most whites, Hispanics, and Asians called them riots. Woo went both ways. Appearing before African-American crowds, he talked of "the uprising" or "the rebellion"; otherwise, he spoke about "the riots."

Riordan, who wasn't nearly as smooth, had trouble figuring out how to characterize Watts. Speaking before a large black congregation on a Sunday morning, he froze when the time arrived for him to choose which word to use. Looking out at the crowd, he hesitated for several seconds; when he finally let out with "rebellion," he sent the amused congregation into gales of laughter.

L.A. whites who talk about what to them are self-evidently riots and African-Americans who refer to "the rebellion" seem to occupy separate realities. The thirty-year debate over how to describe L.A.'s traumas is a shorthand for the larger debate over how to measure black America's claims against the larger society. The term *riot,* with its clear connotation of aimless criminality, seems to ignore the injustice that fueled the rage. *Rebellion,* in turn, suggests that the violence was in the service of, and even secondary to, a challenge to the injustice embedded in the social order.

The Watts upheaval of 1965 was both riotous and rebellious. Primed by the inspiring examples of African wars of independence against colonial oppression and by the Southern civil rights challenge to the rule of heavy-handed sheriffs, the violence was triggered by an incident of police brutality that suggested that blacks in L.A. were, in their own way, as subjugated as their Southern and African cousins. The anger unleashed was directed as much toward the social order that sanctioned the police as toward the police themselves. There was also a great deal of sheer criminality, as stores were wantonly looted and buildings were set aflame, all in an almost carnival-like atmosphere. But it was the aura of rebellion that gave the upheaval its larger significance.

In the early 1960s there were small riots in both the District of Columbia and Los Angeles. In 1964 there were larger, though still not major, riots in Harlem and Brooklyn; in Rochester, New York; in three New Jersey cities—Paterson, Jersey City, and Elizabeth; and in Chicago and Philadelphia. The most intense were in Harlem and Rochester. They broke out in an atmosphere of heightened expectations sixteen days after Lyndon Baines Johnson signed the 1964 Civil Rights Act. On the second day of the Harlem riot, a local militant, Jesse Gray, who had been leading a series of rent strikes, called for "a hundred skilled black revolutionaries" ready to die "participating in guerrilla warfare." Gray's call to arms came to little at the time. Given the upcoming presidential contest between Lyndon Johnson and Barry Goldwater, the 1964 riots were considered counterproductive even by many militants. Johnson's landslide reelection and the 1965 riot in Watts changed all that.

Watts was unlike any earlier riot. We are still living in its aftermath. Watts, the first major riot to be televised, inspired subsequent "rebellions" in Washington, D.C., Detroit, and Newark. The immediate damage to Los Angeles was obvious: thirty-four people, almost all black, were dead; whole blocks had been razed; and almost four thousand arrests had been made. Much of Watts was never rebuilt, and neither was the relative optimism regarding race and integration that had briefly held sway in the wake of the historic 1963 Civil Rights March on Washington.

Many of the rioters, wrote civil rights strategist Bayard Rustin, viewed the uprising as a "manifesto," an announcement that they were a force to be reckoned with. The Watts upheaval, said Sterling Tucker of the D.C. Urban League, "symbolically unleashed centuries of pent-up animosity." The politicized rioters spoke more of revenge than reform, spoke not of integration but of power. They sought not to liberalize America but to liberate themselves from America.

The immediate response to Watts, which broke out five days after the signing of the 1965 Voting Rights Act, was to see it as the work of a small group of street toughs and criminals. The toughs were involved, but the breadth of the participation suggested something much more ominous. Los Angeles was a city with an expanding black middle class, a city that, according to a National Urban League survey, ranked first among major American cities in the quality of black life. Yet post-riot surveys showed that the rioters represented a cross section of black South Central Los Angeles. What had happened for blacks of all classes was that the surge in collective consciousness flowing out of the Southern civil rights struggle broke down barriers to the expression of the rage and hostility that had built up for so long.

The "primitive rebels" of the Watts uprising, some of them gang members, were little concerned with integration and much concerned with authenticity and the power of violence to wipe away historic humiliations. "Who has not dreamed," asked James Baldwin, "of that fantastical violence which will drown in blood, wash away in blood, not only generation upon generation of horror, but will also release one from the individual horror, carried everywhere in the heart."

Paul Williams, a young participant in the riots, described their almost mystical effect on him: "Everyone felt high. It was like an out-of-memory period. . . . Before you were hoping for freedom within the civil rights movement, and when you came out the other end you hoped for liberation."

Any doubts that the rioting was far more than a protest against poverty should have been dispelled by the Detroit riots two years later. The Motor City, boasted Jerome Cavanagh, "the most progressive mayor in America," had a large home-owning black middle class. Yet it, too, went up in flames. The Detroit rioters were asserting a collective identity, not protesting against poverty. Eighty-three percent of the Detroit rioters were employed; half of them were members of the United Auto Workers, whose policies symbolized both the bread and butter and the social successes of American liberalism since the 1930s.

Militants saw Watts as both a promising turning point in the black liberation struggle and a repudiation of integrationist liberalism, and they were not alone. What might be called the riot ideology broadly took hold not only among many blacks but among opinion and policy makers as well. Post-riot surveys showed that though whites and Latinos were resentful, the riots boosted black self-esteem. According to L.A. historian Rafael Sonenshein the riots unified, mobilized, and energized the black community politically.

Policy makers at the time didn't fully embrace the argument of radical sociologist Robert Blauner, who insisted that "the liberal, humanist value that violence is the worst sin cannot be defended today if one is committed squarely against racism and for self-determination." Neither did they fully reject it. In the wake of Watts, policy makers in Washington and elsewhere were caught in a cross fire between those who insisted that more aid to the cities was essential to prevent more rioting and those who saw more aid as a reward for violence.

Speaking in the summer of 1966, Nicholas Katzenbach, President Johnson's attorney general, warned of riots in "thirty or forty" more cities if the Model Cities legislation providing funds for community renewal projects wasn't passed quickly. Critics like Bronx congressman Paul Fino denounced Katzenbach's "scare tactics," and warned that Model Cities would both reward the violence and become a "gravy train" for the "black power" movement.

As the immediate threat of riots subsided, liberals would argue that more money for the cities was essential—if not to halt riots, then to contain the still rising racial anger, which expressed itself in rising rates of often violent crime. In New York, where John Lindsay was widely praised for having avoided a riot during his tenure as mayor, robbery increased fivefold between 1962 and 1967 and then doubled between 1967 and 1972.

In 1965, only conservatives, discredited by their opposition to civil rights, and a few contrarians saw the dangers from the riot ideology ahead. A distraught LBJ saw the rioters as equivalent to the Ku Klux Klan, as "lawbreakers, destroyers of constitutional rights and liberties." Larlene Wilson, a black Congress of Racial Equality (CORE) board member from Ohio, was dismayed by activists who talked of the ghetto "as is if there was something romantic, glamorous, and exciting about it" but, warned that "those of us who have experienced the life of the poor, uneducated, exploited Negro (exploited by blacks and whites) and who really know what it means to hate all whites (and blacks who have 'made it') will tell you . . . it is a mistake to try to identify with the man in the streets by trying to become like him."

Ms. Wilson proved prescient, but the riot ideology has endured. After the 1992 L.A. riots, an expert on conflict resolution wrote the following in an article for the National League of Cities journal, *The National Civic Review,* on the efficacy of rioting: "In the 1960s mass rioting in Los Angeles, Newark, Detroit, Chicago, and Washington, D.C., generated a movement for 'black power' in the streets and precedent-breaking legislative efforts in Washington. We do not know what political energies may be unleashed in the wake of the most recent disorders." Leave aside the fact that this poor fellow got the sequence of rioting and legislation backward; his was the conventional and deeply corrupting wisdom.

In the wake of the 1992 riots, Mayor John Norquist of Milwaukee attended a meeting of the U.S. Conference of Mayors, with about half the mayors of the twenty-five largest cities being present. To his dismay, he found that they saw the riot as a potential bonanza. The country, they assumed, would have to pay attention to the cities again, and so they began to assemble a wish list for new programs to combat the violence they had officially decried. At the very least, they expected the disaster to produce a new wave of programs, as in the 1960s, for "riot insurance." These mayors had to know that the violence would scare away business, but they had come to see their cities as victims of unmet social needs and regarded their pathologies as economic assets.

Prior to the "rebellions" it was broadly assumed that blacks, newly arrived in cities like Los Angeles and Detroit, were much like earlier waves of immigrants to urban America. "Puerto Ricans today," wrote Irving Kristol in 1966 for the *New York Times Magazine,* "resemble nothing so much as the Sicilian immigrants of sixty years ago . . . one senses . . . their destiny as an immigrant group." By comparable analogy, blacks, he argued, were very much like an earlier group troubled by broken families and substance abuse, namely, the Irish, who after a long, tumultuous struggle made it into the middle class.

For those, like Kristol, who used the immigrant analogy, the similarities with earlier arrivals in the cities were what mattered. Earlier immigrants from rural Europe, so the argument went, had suffered from illiteracy, discrimination, and the lack of political clout but had nonetheless succeeded, over the course of three generations, to work their way into the mainstream of American society. They partook of a rough bargain in which they gave up some of their old ways for a new hybrid identity. With the end of legal segregation and the migrations from the economically backward South into the more advanced Northern cities, the hope was that African-Americans would follow, however haltingly, this same path.

Many of the black migrants to D.C. ("the first stop off the bus") and New York came from the backwaters of tobacco road. The most labor-intensive of the major crops, tobacco was a jealous mistress that demanded endless, painstaking labor but few of the skills useful in an urban industrial society. The long-term social yield of plantation agriculture and its sharecropping successor was a people rich in resentment. Like the Irish arriving in Boston, in-migrants to the somewhat more enlightened climes of the Northern cities could only assume that Anglo-Saxon law, a liberation for non-Irish white immigrants, was a trick imposed by the powerful to subjugate the weak. Worse yet, the black migrants from tobacco country, like the "hillbillies" in Detroit or the "Okies" who went to L.A., brought with them a tradition of violence that easily overwhelmed the capacity of city cops to contain it.

Some argued that the new black in-migrants to the Northern cities were already American and therefore didn't have to assimilate. But they did have to acculturate to urban industrial society. Rural people, as Washington, D.C., realized after the 1991 Hispanic riots there, have to learn how to live in the city. The Hispanic riots in D.C., triggered by abusive black cops, brought a torrent of complaints from middle-class blacks. Tom Porter of the left-wing Pacifica radio station WPFW summed up these feelings:

> I'm tired of seeing them leave car batteries in their yard and paper plates after they have a picnic on the front steps. The parks were created for the children of the neighborhood, but some of the young [Hispanic] men have taken over the parks for drinking or drugs. People tell me I ought to understand their culture, but I guarantee you that the culture of El Salvador is not to get drunk in public and urinate in the parks.

Porter's complaint reads like that of a true turn-of-the-century WASP decrying the filth, stench, and squalor of "Paddies," "Hunkies," and "Wops." In Chicago the arrival of the Slovak saloons sent the WASP middle class scurrying to the suburbs and made the small neighboring city of Evanston into the headquarters of the Women's Christian Temperance Union.

In the years that followed, the New Deal showed that the country had learned something about incorporating newcomers. President Roosevelt, who once began an address to the Daughters of the American Revolution with "My fellow immigrants," defined poverty as essentially a problem of cultural incorporation. Many members of his staff, influenced by the famed social reformer Jane Addams and the settlement house movement, saw incorporation as a matter of class reconciliation. They believed, with Jane Addams, that it was essential to hold all men to "one democratic standard." This meant that while the country needed to recognize the virtues of the new immigrants, the immigrants were encouraged to adopt middle-class mores.

The New Deal efforts were an enormous success. Through the growth of trade unions, immigrant political participation, and the solidarity born of war, the turn-of-the-century arrivals and their children were incorporated into American life. Between 1940 and 1965 the percentage of Americans in poverty dropped from 35 to 13 percent, about where it is today.

Schools in the District of Columbia during the 1950s were a "showcase for integration." They were also an example of the New Deal settlement house approach applied to recently arrived semiliterate tenant farmers coming from Georgia and the Carolinas. In a system where three-fourths of the teachers were already black, the old-time liberal ethos of the District's faculty meant an emphasis on inculcating "habits of orderliness and precision" calculated to create self-discipline. Applying the model once used for immigrants, the teachers tried to acculturate the largely black student body by correcting their speech, appearance, and attitudes. The school leadership assumed that they were there to help the students adapt to the demands of urban life.

Only a few years later, the Watts riot, by contrast, was aimed at the agencies responsible for absorbing newcomers in Los Angeles. The rioters' anger was directed at the socializing institutions staffed by the sergeants of city life: teachers, cops, and social workers. The L.A.P.D. with its paramilitary style and racist operating assumptions was the most hated agency, but the seething hostility to government institutions extended far beyond the police to the Housing Authority, the Department of Public Health, and the Los Angeles Bureau of Public Assistance, as well as the schools. Each institution, with its white middle-class values, stood accused of serving as a crucible of humiliation for rural blacks newly arrived in L.A. Nor was it much different in New York or D.C., where semiliterate sharecroppers discovered the frustrations of dealing with what for them was a new institution—bureaucracy. It was an encounter fraught with confusion. The former sharecroppers saw in the bureaucrats a new version of "the man," who had for so long exploited their illiteracy to cheat them out of their hard-earned wages, while the bureaucrats saw the sharecroppers (whose anxiety, born of bewilderment with the big city, made them seem aggressively uncooperative) as ungrateful provincials.

For Paul Jacobs, a 1930s leftist trying to keep up with the times, the real villain was the "system," which sought to socialize black arrivals into "white ways." "Inherent in the very process of rule-making and objective analysis, there was," he argued, "a middle-class bias that makes bureaucratic authority especially burdensome on poor people." People who had already suffered so much couldn't be expected to engage in the same bargain as the immigrants, a bargain in which they agreed to both shape and be shaped by the larger society.

Jacobs was one of many intellectuals caught up in the ferment of the 1960s who rejected the immigrant path. The eminent black sociologist Kenneth Clark, who had dismissed the significance of the 1964 Harlem riot, spoke after Watts of how "the dark ghettoes now represent a nuclear stock-pile which can annihilate the very foundations of America." Clark, like many others, had discarded discredited pre-Watts assumptions about mutual accommodation. Speaking at the 1965 White House Conference on Civil Rights, he insisted that blacks "must reject notions which demand that the Negro change himself and accept the requirement that the society itself must change." Clark complained, "We hear about the pathology of the Negro family [referring to the Moynihan report on the breakdown of the black family] instead of the sickness of American society." "The problems which face us," insisted Clark, "will not be solved by seeking to manipulate the individual Negro, seeking to have him 'shape up' and 'clean up,' or as some would have him do, join the army." Under the pressure of the riots, it was society that would have to adapt itself to the Negro, and not the other way around.

In the new post-Watts world, African-Americans were to make the jump from rural life into the mainstream of American society without having to run the gauntlet of acculturation. "This struggle to be human and civilized without submitting oneself to the *whiteness* of those words, and above all without submitting to the fear of the Law which embodies them," explained literary critic Richard Gilman, "is at the heart of much passionate activity among Negroes in America today."

This was a very big gamble. What Gilman and those like him were asking for was an American version of China's Great Leap Forward. In the Great Leap, Mao decided that through the force of Leninist will, backward China would vault over all the intermediate stages of economic development and achieve an advanced economy in one sweeping surge. Like those third-world nations that had chosen to pursue a non-Western path to prosperity, American blacks were to be given their due and offered an honored place in American life without having to make the long journey up the social ladder by gradually accumulating the skills needed for economic success.

Some black activists presented their actions as part of the Third World rebellion against colonial rule. Near the end of his life even Martin Luther King began to refer to the ghetto as a "system of internal colonialism," the counterpart to the external colonialism of Vietnam. "What the Negro *has* discovered, and on an international level," wrote James Baldwin, "is the power to intimidate." If ghettoes constitute a kind of colony, then it follows that the riots were more analogous to uprisings. Liberation meant more than securing rights, it meant taking control of the black community and liberating it from the "occupying army" of white police, social workers, landlords, and owners of small businesses.

In the wake of the 1968 Washington, D.C., riot that followed the assassination of Martin Luther King, Sterling Tucker, leader of the local Urban League, argued that the outburst was a "low form of communication by people who seek to get a response from society that seems to be deaf to their needs." Up till now the power structure, he said, had spoken with respectable, middle-class civil rights leaders, out of touch with the street. But now they would have to deal with "the street," and in D.C. its representative was the young Marion Barry. Fresh from fighting segregation in the deep

South, Barry warned that "when the city rebuilds . . . it might just get burned down again . . . if you don't let my black brothers control the process—and I mean all the way down to owning the property." White people, insisted Barry, "should be allowed to come back only if the majority of ownership is in the hands of blacks."

White leaders and intellectuals of goodwill got the message. They responded with a mix of guilt and fear. Guilt about three centuries of racial injustice and fear that black Americans might become irredeemably alienated from American life. "The Negro district of every large city," wrote *Fortune* editor Charles Silberman in his influential book *Crisis in Black and White,* "could come to constitute an American Casbah, with its own values and controls and an implacable hatred of everything white that would poison American life."

In a 1967 editorial titled BLOW UP THE CITIES, the highly respected and moderately liberal *New Republic* argued, with a mixture of guilt and fear, for "the promise of the riots": "Terrifying as the looting, the shooting, the arson are, they could mean a gain for the nation if, as a result, white America were shocked into looking at itself, its cities, its neglect . . . smugness and evasion."

The widely discussed editorial called the idea of Black Power a blessing even as it criticized the call by Student Nonviolent Coordinating Committee (SNCC) leader H. Rap Brown in Cambridge, Maryland, to "burn this town down." The editorial described the call to arson as "fascist madness." It is "the shout of the angry, exalted young Brown Shirt, called by blood to smash the shops of non-Aryans."

Written against the backdrop of the Vietnam war, the *New Republic* editorial concluded with its own madness, arguing, "The national commitment needed to bring racial justice to the cities is unlikely until New York, Chicago or Los Angeles is brought to an indefinite standstill by a well-organized guerrilla action against the white establishment." A year later, with the whiff of revolution still in the air, George Romney, governor of Michigan during the 1967 Detroit riots and then a candidate for the Republican presidential nomination, warned a meeting of GOP leaders that "most Negroes are waiting to see if we mean what we say in America, or whether they have to have a war of national liberation here."

The call to "bring the war home"—seemingly possible during the most overheated moments of the sixties—was never heeded as such, but the riots themselves never fully ended. Instead, they were followed by a "rolling riot," an explosion in crime that has only now begun to subside in some cities.

In Detroit, site of the most violent upheaval and of unprecedented increases in individual crime, the collective violence of the riot was institutionalized in Devil's Night outbursts. Devil's Night, the night before Halloween, became an annual carnival of destruction. In the worst years of the 1980s, four hundred buildings (almost as many as went up in the 1967 rebellion) were set ablaze. Instead of experiencing a post-riot return to relative peace, the cities continued to be engulfed in a "molecular civil war" often fought by "autistic youths" whose aim, wrote German author Hans Magnus Enzensberger, was "to debase everybody—not only their opponents but also themselves."

Violence and the threat of violence were leveraged into both a personal style for street kids and a political agenda based on threat and intimidation. To the young tough walking down the street a menacing style brought tribute by way of the frightened faces of those he had intimidated. To politicians it brought federal money on the threat that the Casbah might again erupt. But the most exquisite form of intimidation came in intellectual life, where cowed intellectuals relinquished their independence of judgment.

No one can date precisely when this political correctness *avant la lettre* took hold, but Richard Gilman's 1968 review of Eldridge Cleaver's *Soul on Ice* is a good bet. Cleaver was a great admirer of Marcus Garvey, the black nationalist leader of the 1920s whose Back to Africa movement was the largest political mobilization of blacks prior to the 1960s. While in a California prison for rape, Cleaver became an adherent of one of Garvey's heirs—the black Muslim leader Elijah Muhammad—and later followed Malcolm X when he split off from Elijah. After his release from prison, Cleaver became the most famous convert to the Black Panther Party.

Cleaver spent 1956 to 1966 at San Quentin trying to think through the connection between violence and black nationalism. Unlike most immigrants (except the Irish), for whom Anglo-Saxon law was a liberation, black America experienced law as an instrument of oppression. In a famous line from *Soul on Ice,* Cleaver wrote that for a black man "rape was an insurrectionary act." He admitted, "It delighted me that I was defying and trampling upon the white man's law, upon his system of values." Cleaver defined black convicts as "prisoners of war" in the battle between separate black and white cultures. Prisoners, he argued, were "the victims of a vicious, dog-eat-dog social system that is so heinous as to cancel [the prisoners']own malefactions."

One problem of black nationalism was that it could never decide which piece of land to attach itself to. Garvey's plans for a homeland in Africa had deep emotional appeal, but only a handful of African-Americans actually wanted to return. Others, inspired by Stalin's supposed solution to the nationalities question in the Soviet Union, proposed a homeland in the Southern Black Belt. But this, too, went nowhere. Cleaver understood violence as a kind of "psychological emigrationism," as an alienation from white values and an attempt, in Stokley Carmichael's words, to "smash everything Western civilization has created." The remedy for the alienation, Cleaver argued, was Black Power, understood as black "sovereignty." But sovereignty over what? Other Panthers, like David Hilliard, supplied the answer in their call for the mininationalism of black community control over the ghetto.

When a young white radical from Students for a Democratic Society objected to the potential abuse in the Panther proposal for community control of the police, Panther Bobby Seale denounced "those little bourgeois, snooty nose, motherfucking SDSs." Black control over black neighborhoods had to be total. "To decentralize . . . implement probably on just the community level—socialism. And that's probably too Marxist-Leninist for those motherfuckers to understand," explained Seale's comrade David Hilliard. "But," he went on, "we think that Stalin was very clear in this concept, that socialism could be implemented in one country; we say it can be implemented in one community."

For Richard Gilman, writing in the *New Republic* about *Soul on Ice,* the black homeland resided in the territory of separate truths, truths based on myth more than measurement. Negroes, he argued, are oppressed by the Western liberal beliefs in a shared humanity, in universal values. Cleaver's "way of looking at the world, its formulation of experience," wrote Gilman, "is not the potential possession—even by imaginative appropriation—of us all; hard, local, intransigent, alien, it remains in some sense unassimilable for those of us who aren't black." The Negro, explained Gilman, "doesn't feel the same way whites do, nor does he think like whites."

The young Marion Barry adopted Cleaver's perspective. Once an integrationist, Barry came to view black and white culture as if they were strictly separate entities sealed off in windowless rooms. "There's a black culture, and there's a white culture; there's a black psychology, and there's a white psychology," Barry argued. "You can't plan for black people like you can for white people because there is a difference." Nor, by extension, could black city government be held to the same standards as white city government.

The black writer Jervis Anderson responded to Gilman and other separatists in *Commentary.* Anderson agreed that for Cleaver blackness is an absolute standard against which all else is evaluated. But Anderson then asked why if "we judge foreign literature by the standards we know . . . we need separate standards by which to judge writing by black Americans." It was an effective response, but at a time when liberals were willing to accept that they could know nothing about nonwhites, Cleaver and his apologists carried the day.

Blacks, wrote Gilman, have chosen to live by a set of new myths. "It isn't my right to . . . subject [their choice] to the scrutiny of the [Western] tradition. A myth, moreover, is not really analyzable and certainly not something which one can call untrue," he wrote. Nor, he should have noted, do policies based on myth carry the capacity for self-evaluation and self-correction.

The myth the militants proposed to live by—a myth of cleansing, redemptive violence—was best expressed by Frantz Fanon, a French-speaking psychiatrist who was born in Martinique and had fought with the Free French in World War II only to turn violently against the French in particular and the West in general during the bloody Algerian war of independence. In his most important book, *The Wretched of the Earth,* Fanon argued that the task of the world's dark-skinned peasants, people uncorrupted by Western values, was to recover their nations and their manhood by rising up against their oppressors. He insisted that "violence alone, violence committed by the people, violence organized and educated by its leaders, makes it possible for the masses to understand social truths" and frees them from "despair and inaction."

Fanon died at age thirty-six in 1961, but *The Wretched of the Earth,* published in the United States just before Watts, became in the wake of the riots the book that seemed to explain what had happened. Don Watts, editor of *Liberator* magazine, described Fanon's impact:

> These cats are ready to die for something. And they know why. They all read. Read a lot. Not one of them hasn't read the "Bible," Fanon's *Wretched of the Earth. . . .* Every brother on a rooftop can quote Fanon.

Fanon was himself the product of a European education. His vision of a therapeutic war on whiteness was deeply derivative of European thinkers like Friedrich Nietzsche and Oswald Spengler. The latter saw Western civilization as tottering and decayed, ready to be replaced by more vital, more spiritual non-Western cultures. The French writer Jean-Paul Sartre contributed an introduction to *The Wretched of the Earth* even more inflammatory than the body of the book. It was no more possible to banish European influence than to imagine African-Americans as purebred Africans or American culture as purely white.

In the debate over the immigrant analogy, neither the black nationalist mythmakers nor those who insisted that blacks could fit easily into the old immigrant mold were willing to deal with the specificities of black history that made Negroes both deeply American and deeply different from other Americans. After noting the ways in which American Negroes were unlike black Africans and white Americans, James Baldwin concluded that "the

American Negro is a unique creation; he has no counterpart anywhere, and no predecessors." But instead of dealing with that uniqueness, instead of adapting to it, those who argued for acculturation fled in the face of racial invective, and the field was tragically left to the half-truths of the nationalists. Those half-truths, explained Kenneth Clark, were a "very real threat" to "middle-class and middle-class-aspiring blacks." Clark warned that "part of the pattern of pretense and posturing" associated with black nationalism ascribed "all middle-class values to whites while reserving for the exclusive use of blacks the uncouth and the vulgar."

Caught up in the mythmaking, the white sociologist Robert Blauner explained, "If we are going to swing with these revolutionary times, we will have to learn to live with conflict, confrontation, constant change, and what may be real or apparent chaos and disorder." Not everyone wanted to "swing," but for those who did, like New York's Mayor John Lindsay, the message was clear: Be prepared to pay up or be prepared for trouble. In the decades that followed the 1960s, the riot ideology, a racial version of collective bargaining, became part of the warp and woof of big-city politics.

NEW YORK

2. The New Deal City

It is difficult to fully convey the religious fervor attached to New York's socialist, Communist, and trade union movements of the 1930s. More than just a struggle for self-interest on the part of poor people, the moral fervor of the often Jewish socialists came from the conviction that they represented an alternative ethic to the "weakest to the wall" practices of capitalism. In pursuing the path to a higher morality, they believed that they, not the bosses, represented the highest ethical ideals of the Western world.

In the 1930s, says literary critic Lionel Abel, the city's intellectuals "went to Russia and spent most of the decade there. . . . New York became the most interesting part of the Soviet Union . . . the one part of that country in which the struggle between Stalin and Trotsky could be openly expressed. And was! And how!"

I felt the aftershocks of the 1930s when I, as a small boy in the 1950s, had the good fortune to listen to endless debates in my grandfather's apartment on topics ranging from the promise of socialism to the perfidy of Lenin—my grandfather and his friends were militantly anti-Communist socialists, members of the International Ladies Garment Workers Union (ILGWU)—and on the greatness of Norman Thomas; the moral necessity of Israel; the importance of FDR; the immorality of the profit motive; and, on one occasion, the gutsiness of La Guardia. I can still remember one of my grandfather's friends gesticulating wildly, his expression denunciatory, as he attacked La Guardia for being far too eager to do business with the Communists, then a formidable force in New York City politics and trade unions. My grandfather, a staunch anti-Communist, answered: "Morris [I think the friend's name was Morris], you're taking things out of context. In the mid-1930s the union was fighting for its life and La Guardia was there fighting for us." "La Guardia," declared another friend, "made New York into a city fit for workers." And so he did.

In the early 1940s, while the United States and the USSR were allied in the war against fascism, a trade delegation from the Soviet Union, dressed in its diplomatic finery, visited New York's legendary mayor Fiorello La Guardia. Something of a socialist himself, La Guardia looked at the Soviet diplomats and then at his own baggy paints and frayed shirt. "Gentleman," he said, "I represent the proletariat." Indeed he did. In the best traditions of European democratic socialism and social democracy, La Guardia had tried to transform New York into the New Deal city, a workers' city where government was on the side of the laboring stiffs and not the bosses.

La Guardia, a nominal Republican, had been elected in 1933 by a mésalliance of good government Protestants, newly mobilized Italians, and left-wing militants. "I am for the Republicanism of Abraham Lincoln," he explained, "and let me tell you now that the average Republican leader east of the Mississippi doesn't know anything more about Abraham Lincoln than Henry Ford knows about the Talmud." By the time he was up for reelection, La Guardia locally, and to a lesser extent the New Deal nationally, had a new base: the forces of organized labor, particularly the New York needles trade unions, energized by the New Deal and the Wagner Act.

La Guardia, who was half Italian and half Jewish, had been raised in Arizona. His Western experiences gave the radicalism of the city's immigrant masses an American touch. La Guardia issued the classic rallying cry of early-twentieth-century American reform, the majoritarian call to support the people in their struggle against the "interests." The people, understood to be virtuous and inherently democratic, were said to be threatened by the special privileges afforded the new aristocracy, the "economic royalists" whose concentrated power threatened the rights of self-government. It was a theme whose dramatic power was useful not only in spreading the message but in allowing liberals to explain their message to themselves.

"The forces of organized money," La Guardia liked to boast, "are unanimous in their hatred of me." Cheering on the city's strikers, Fiorello pledged to make New York a "one hundred percent union town." He used his mayoral powers, notes historian Thomas Kessner, to force business to the bargaining table, and when cabbies turned violent to achieve their ends, he turned a blind eye. When business threatened to bolt the city, he threatened back, promising to blacklist anyone who left. Some, tired of his bullying, autocratic ways, mocked him as a "miniature Mussolini."

In no city is the New Deal more revered than in New York. In my childhood home, as with many second-generation New York immigrant families, Franklin and Eleanor Roosevelt were household deities. And yet in no city is the New Deal more misunderstood. This is no small matter, since the policies adopted in the 1930s are still deeply embedded in the structure of politics and government.

La Guardia and Roosevelt still cast a giant shadow over 1990s New York. New York's Mayor Giuliani—who, like Fiorello, was elected as a fusion candidate—constantly compares himself to La Guardia, while Mario Cuomo, New York State governor from 1982 to 1994, saw his "New York idea" as an extension of the New Deal model.

The reasons for the reverence are clear and compelling. When La Guardia was elected mayor in 1933, the city was effectively bankrupt, in the hands of J. P. Morgan and other creditors, and suffering unemployment rates of 25 percent and more. Both the Tammany Hall political machine, which had brought on the bankruptcy, and old-fashioned capitalism were discredited. La Guardia stepped into the vacuum. He was, he said, in the "position of an artist or a sculptor" ready to reshape New York's future.

Even before taking office, La Guardia helped Harry Hopkins design Roosevelt's Civil Works Administration (CWA); then, as mayor, he turned around and took advantage of it. New York captured 20 percent of all CWA job slots. Shuttling back and forth from Washington and sharing advisers like New Deal architects Adolf Berle and Rexford Tugwell, La Guardia struck a deal with FDR: If Roosevelt, a country squire with little love for the sidewalks of New York, treated the city generously, La Guardia would make Gotham into the New Deal's model city.

Both sides kept the bargain. Roosevelt broke precedent by treating New York City as "the forty-ninth state." FDR dealt directly with city hall, bypassing Albany and ignoring the 150 years of precedent that treated cities as mere creatures of the states. FDR poured $50 million into New York during La Guardia's first one hundred days, and La Guardia and his parks commissioner, the formidable Robert Moses, made sure the money was well spent. The man La Guardia appointed to head the local CWA placed two hundred thousand men on projects in three months (and then collapsed and died). Moses whipped the city bureaucracy into shape. He fired all five borough parks commissioners, people who had been patronage appointees, and imposed new administrators, who, under his iron tutelage, refurbished streets, parks, and public buildings.

In charge of sixty-eight thousand parks workers, many of them formerly unemployed men without hope, Moses gave them uniforms and put them to work. "Within 6 months," writes historian John Teaford, "every structure in the municipal parks was repainted, every lawn reseeded, every tennis court and playground resurfaced, and thousands of trees were removed, replanted and pruned." Here was the beginning of New York's local version of public works Keynesianism. The CWA, as Harry Hopkins explained, gave the once unemployed money to spend and "brightened the retailers' tills."

La Guardia became a master at "milking money from the federal government." Twice a week he was in Washington, where he enjoyed extraordinary access to the president. Half joking, FDR said of La Guardia, "Our mayor is probably the most appealing person I know. He comes to Washington and tells me a sad story. The tears run down my cheeks and tears run down his cheeks and the first thing I know, he has wangled another fifty million dollars." In fact, from 1934 to 1938 New York City received more than 1.15 billion for public works from the CWA, PWA (Public Works Administration) and WPA (Works Progress Administration). The critics, in part responding to a long history of Tammany's make-work boondoggles, said the letters WPA meant "we plod along," since completion of a project meant people were again out of work. But under the pushing and prodding of La Guardia, who would personally visit work sites and fire people on the spot if they were loafing, the city gained acclaim for both itself and the New Deal.

A 1939 article in staid *Harpers* boasted that New York City "happens to be one of the communities in the United States where good government is measured by getting a good deal for your money." The flamboyant "Kingfish," Huey Long of Louisiana, called La Guardia's New York "the best blankety-blank governed city in the country." New York's port, the Kingfish exuded, "is the best-managed port there is, the traffic system is wonderful, and the waterworks is the goddamned marvel of the world."

Federal grants and loans literally reshaped the city. Working closely with fellow New Yorker Harold Ickes of the PWA, Moses built the East River Drive; the Henry Hudson, Grand Central, Cross Island, Gowanus, and Interborough Parkways; the Triborough Bridge; the Lincoln Tunnel; the Queens Midtown Tunnel; and Marine Parkway, as well as piers, public schools, public housing projects, public baths, parks, prisons, parkways, paved streets, Hunter and Brooklyn colleges, boardwalks, swimming pools, and on and on. Upon entering office, wrote Thomas Kessner, La Guardia had to "beg a reluctant Albany for 30 million dollars to get out of the fiscal crisis, [but] two years later he was negotiating directly with Washington for 10 times than amount." Shortly after Fiorello entered office, the city had half a million people on relief; by 1943 that number, owing to World War II, was down to seventy-three thousand, not even a hundred of whom were employable.

At the turn of the century, Tammany Hall, under the remarkable boss Charles Murphy, had begun the job of integrating the new immigrants politically. La Guardia completed the job by tutoring the new immigrants socially and by opening up city government to the non-Irish. Murphy seized upon the outrage produced by the 1911 Triangle Shirtwaist Factory fire, when 146 workers died in a burning building, to remake the city's political culture.

The appeal of socialism to Jewish trade unionists pushed Tammany to the left on social and labor issues. Murphy's formula was jobs for the Irish and a mix of anti-anti-Semitism and social liberalism for the Jews, who, employed in the needles trade, didn't need government work. Governor Al Smith, a Murphy protégé, heavily influenced by Jewish leftist and settlement house intellectuals, pioneered the safety protections for workers that would be given national scope with the New Deal. Boss Murphy's Tammany Hall, said New York Senator Robert Wagner, another of Murphy's protégés, was "the cradle of modern liberalism in America."

What La Guardia added was a distinct class, as opposed to ethnic edge, to New York liberalism. In part, La Guardia had a visceral hostility to the bosses. Even in the boom time of the 1920s La Guardia distrusted free markets and hoped to "soak the rich." Running for mayor against "Gentleman" Jimmy Walker in 1929, La Guardia, with his left-wing views, garnered only 26 percent of the vote. But four years later, armed in part by Robert Wagner's theory of the depression, La Guardia's time had come.

Wagner, author of what was probably the single most important piece of New Deal legislation, the Wagner Act, which gave unions the right to bargain collectively with government protection, believed the depression was a matter of underconsumption. An intuitive Keynesian even before Keynes's writing arrived in the United States, Wagner argued that the depression would only end when the government placed more purchasing power in the hands of the average worker. Wagner also argued that corporate power could only be contained by creating a countervailing power through trade unions.

Together La Guardia and Wagner, who had been inspired by the municipal housing in Austria's "Red Vienna," not only pioneered the first and initially very successful public housing projects but also created the Cultural Center for the Performing Arts and established public hospitals and the

Health Insurance Plan of New York (HIP) medical insurance plan for people earning less than five thousand dollars a year.

Asked why there was such emphasis on high culture, one old socialist responded, "Nothing's too good for the working class." In fact, it might have been better stated as "Nothing is too good for that part of the working class that strives to uplift itself."

The emphasis on uplift spoke to the implicit bargain at the heart of the "workers' city" ideal; that is, the city would provide the means to a decent life only to those willing to pursue their own interests through disciplined efforts. The bargain was based on reciprocity. It assumed that only if people are willing to pull their own weight can they be counted on to cooperate in sharing another's burdens. New Yorkers were quick to denounce those who could work hard but did not as bums, freeloaders, and—if they were left-wing enough—parasites.

In the workers' city, public spending came with a paternalist twist. A turn-of-the-century article in *Harper's* described the rough thrust of earlier assimilation efforts. Gary, Indiana, it said, "takes the human product of the Balkan states, brutal, unlettered, in some cases little better than a cave dweller; it gives him a white man's house to live in and hires people to teach him how to live the white man's way." New York paternalism thirty years later was far more gentle, far more a product of the settlement house ethos of tolerance and inclusion along with acculturation, but it, too, looked to uplift the new immigrants.

The nation's first public housing projects, designed, by both New Dealer Ickes and the city, to be a model for the country, carefully screened incoming tenants. The projects were designed to spur civic pride. The all-white Williamsburg projects had a kindergarten; a nursery, where mothers were given instruction in baby care; a day-care center; and a communal meeting room, where, historian Thomas Kessner explains, tenants were to be tutored on personal and civic responsibility. The young women sent by the city to collect the rent every week or two were "instructed to chat with the families and gently ascertain if they needed any help."

If the advice families were given wasn't enough, they could get plenty of suggestions from the mayor, who in a successful attempt to create a common culture out of the city's ethnic kaleidoscope devoted his radio broadcast to what foods people should buy, the best methods of child rearing, and the dangers of gambling. The mayor, a patron of proletarian theater, tried to protect his people from sin; he smashed one-armed bandits, pulled pornography off the newsstands, and punished city employees who engaged in extramarital affairs. After visiting an exhibition of Irish art, La Guardia summed up his worldview: "Any people that insist on progressive government and maintain conservative art are pretty well balanced." Solidarity and loyalty were the mayor's bywords; his was to be a virtuous city, a New York of civic-minded people.

The relentless emphasis on virtue may seem harshly constrictive to contemporary Americans, but it's why workers saw themselves as morally superior to their bosses. It's part of why New York's social democracy succeeded for a time. The workers' city was forged from the solidarity of trade union struggles and stiffened by an often religiously acquired sense of self-restraint and mutuality, essential for day-to-day life in the city's tightly knit ethnic neighborhoods. According to author David Gelernter, it was a culture of "oughts." The "oughts" instilled by society were "an all-day everyday hand on your shoulder." La Guardia's genius was to combine the disparate elements of social solidarity—the religious, the radical, and the tribal—and forge them into a higher ethos, an ethos that would for a time come to inspire the nation at large.

In the 1920s New York seemed marginal to the rest of America. Under the weight of immigration, New York, a land of saloons, was "sliding away from the rest of the country," said H. L. Mencken. "What New York esteems," wrote Mencken, "is diabolical to Kansas." Before the 1929 Wall Street crash, New York was reviled as the home of Wall Street's financial imperialism and the Delancy Street cultural invasion. But just as the crash and the depression lifted La Guardia from political marginality in his own city, so too did they enhance New York's reputation. Suddenly the city and the state traditions of settlement house social work and bread-and-butter liberalism were brought to the center of national life, offering an alternative to the failures of laissez-faire.

New York City, which had twenty-two congressmen and had cast one of every fourteen votes in the presidential elections, had become a political colossus. The Republicans' strategy for winning the 1944 election consisted of putting a New Yorker, Governor Thomas E. Dewey, at the head of the ticket while attacking another New Yorker, Sidney Hillman, president of the Amalgamated Clothing and Textile Workers and a key FDR supporter, with billboards that subtly played to both anti-Semitic and anti-Communist fears with the words "IT'S YOUR COUNTRY. WHY LET SIDNEY HILLMAN RUN IT?"

But the crowds of trade unionists from the ILGWU and other unions that lined the streets of New York for Roosevelt's campaign motorcade through the city in October 1944 felt that both the city and the country were theirs. They were cheering not only FDR, who was for many their champion against Hitler, but how far they had come in moving to the center of American life. It was a satisfying, if passing, moment.

La Guardia's New York was both a city of ethnic animosities, ancient and otherwise, and the bearer of a social solidarity rarely seen in America (outside the passing evanescence of utopian communities). But both its sense of solidarity and its economic well-being were built on shaky foundations. A little more than a decade after La Guardia's departure, one of those ethnic antagonisms, the animosity directed by whites against blacks, would shatter the city's hard-won sense of solidarity and undermine the economy to boot.

The reflected glory of the La Guardia years was so bright, so blinding, that the city, insofar as it can be said to have had a collective consciousness, was left oblivious to the way the world was changing around it. There were, in retrospect, five major misunderstandings that would have long-term consequences.

1. At the same time the cities were rising politically, they had already begun, in the East, to decline economically. The 1930s saw an end to a century of almost continuous urban growth in the major cities of the East and Midwest. In large part this was a matter of the railroads, which concentrated the economy, being displaced by the decentralizing truck. Trucking allowed manufacturers to move to cheaper land and hire the cheaper nonunion labor of not only suburban but Southern locations.

Economic decentralization was coupled with federally subsidized suburbanization. A year before the Wagner Act passed in 1935, giving labor the ability to organize, Roosevelt's Federal Housing Authority began to insure low-interest long-term mortgages for single-family homes. This, along with the automobile, encouraged new suburban development while undermining the older cities hit with rising labor costs. The military necessity to disperse production during World War II only encouraged both of these trends.

2. The crowds that cheered La Guardia never understood the price that had to be paid for his program. The vast preponderance of New Yorkers never knew that not even the avalanche of federal funds could pay for La Guardia's social democracy in one city. When La Guardia left office, city expenditures had grown by more than 40 percent over and above the 210 percent increase in federal and state monies. Gross bonded debt, noted Kessner, "grew at five and a half times the rate of population growth." New York had begun the era of fiscal philandering that continues to this very day.

After La Guardia gave a major speech in 1938 summarizing his achievements, Adolph Berle told him that he had accomplished the "last big job that could be done . . . within the existing rules of finance." His successors, said Berle, would have to be content "merely to manage" what La Guardia had set up. La Guardia himself expected a major fiscal crisis of the sort that still plagues New York.

Rexford Tugwell, the left-wing New Dealer who had worked for La Guardia, worried that "by raising the city's level of indebtedness" the mayor "had pledged [New Yorkers] to the bankers, permanently increased the cost of their utilities, and made municipal bankruptcy inevitable." He was right in the long run, but the problem was hidden because Comptroller Joseph Goldrick began borrowing from future tax collections to pay for the current operating costs of government. He would roll one year's expenses into the next year's budget, precisely the practice that would eventually produce a full-scale fiscal collapse in the 1970s.

3. La Guardia–era New Yorkers assumed that government bureaucracies were humane and responsive. Under La Guardia the city's bureaucratic government was kept on its toes by a benign democratic centralism. Felix Frankfurter, a student at Cooper Union and Columbia College, justice of the Supreme Court, and liberal New Dealer extraordinaire, praised La Guardia as a mayor who "translated the complicated conduct of the City's vast government into warm significance for every man, woman and child." It was true, but could anyone but La Guardia do it?

La Guardia weakened Tammany Hall by more than doubling the number of jobs given civil service protection. Nonetheless, by the very force of his personality he demanded "critical bureaucracy," that is, "rules *and* humane judgment." He expected his managers to set high standards, and he expected public employees to be demanding of themselves and aware of their role as working for the public good at large. For the most part, they delivered. The city was blessed with people known as "depression-era geniuses." These talented people, often Jews and Italians who had previously been kept out of government by the Irish, kept out of the corporations by the WASPs, and put out of work by the depression, turned for work to the city. Their talent and La Guardia's leadership made the city work. But future generations of civil servants would be both less motivated and, with the addition of public employee unionization, far less accountable.

4. Whites, with a few left-wing exceptions, didn't so much misunderstand as ignore the racial hostility growing in Harlem. The question, asked the young James Baldwin, was whether the antidote to the poison of white racism should be a transracialism or whether it "should be fought with [the] poison of black racism." New York's hothouse intellectual atmosphere gave birth to both answers—to a left-wing, often Communist, interracialism and to the black fascism of Marcus Garvey.

In 1943, after the city suffered its second racial riot in eight years, La Guardia, who had been praised by the black *Amsterdam News* "for appointing more Negroes to big, responsible jobs in city government . . . than all other mayors of the city combined," initiated the popular "double V campaign," for victory over fascism abroad and racism at home. But if everywhere in America blacks were despised, it was only somewhat less so in New York. The city's language of solidarity and brotherhood notwithstanding, its economy was divided into ethnic niches: the Italians at Sanitation, the Irish on the police force, and the Jews in the schools left little room for nonwhites in city government. A mayoral report concluded that business outside of Harlem could be divided into two types: "those that employ Negroes in menial positions and those that employ no Negroes at all."

Blacks were largely excluded from the discipline and self-control imposed by industrial and bureaucratic work. Instead, living in an ideological tinderbox of a city, they were largely left to cultivate their bitterness. Well before Norman Mailer wrote *The White Negro,* placing violent juvenile delinquents on a par with freedom fighters, Harlem's James Baldwin, who had experienced the 1943 riots firsthand, wrote that "in every act of violence, particularly violence against white men, Negroes feel a certain thrill of identification, a wish to have done it themselves, a feeling that old scores are being settled at last." The Harlem riot, a portent of things to come, unleashed a "blind, unreasoning fury that swept the community with the speed of lightning," said civil rights leader Walter White.

5. Finally, and almost fatally for New York's long-term prospects, New Yorkers misjudged the relationships between the New Deal and its time and between the New Deal and the rest of the country. Much of America saw the depression-era buildup of government as a temporary response to an immediate crisis, but in New York it came to be seen as the blueprint for the future.

In 1936 La Guardia and Berle, along with Sidney Hillman and David Dubinsky, the leaders of the needles trade unions, came together to create the American Labor Party (ALP) as a means for La Guardia to free himself from earlier fusion supporters and as a line for Roosevelt to use to gather votes from leftists unwilling to pull the lever for the Tammany-tainted Democrats. The success of the ALP led Berle to think of the party as the vehicle for a thoroughgoing ideological realignment, one that would place all the progressive forces in the new party and all the reactionaries in the Republican Party.

La Guardia was so certain that the future would resemble the New Deal that at war's end he drew up plans for a permanent New Deal in New York. Largely oblivious to the way rising taxes and costs were helping to drive out the printing and garment industries, he detailed plans for a massive $1.25 billion program of public works to employ the returning veterans and keep the economy going. When a 1944 Board of Trade report described "the alarming flight of industry to younger cities," La Guardia erupted. Believing such reports to be cheap propaganda, he declared them "cowardly, despicable, a malicious, deliberate lie." We were the capital of the world; who would dare leave us?

In the one-eyed view of most New Yorkers, the New Deal was the city-oriented labor–liberal axis represented by the rise of the Congress of Industrial Organizations (CIO) nationally and of the ALP at home, and Roosevelt was its champion.

But FDR, a country squire from the rural Hudson Valley with a beloved home in Warm Springs, Georgia, had other, far more salient, loyalties. "It is my conviction," said Roosevelt, "that "the South presents right now the nation's No. 1 economic problem."

Both the South and the West were underdeveloped areas relative to the Northeast. They suffered from both an absence of infrastructure and an absence of credit. The New Deal rectified both through a mix of state capitalism, extending government credit to those regions through the Reconstruction Finance Corporation, and development projects like the dams and hydroelectric facilities that made the growth of Los Angeles possible.

Similarly, Atlanta as we now know it was seeded by what historian Frank Freidel describes as the "cornucopia from which federal aid poured into the desperately Depression-ridden South." Besides the Reconstruction Finance Corporation, the New Deal's Commodity Credit Corporation, the Rural Electrification Administration, the Electric Home and Farm Authority, the Tennessee Valley Authority, the Federal Home Loan Banks, and the Federal Loan Administration pumped money into subsidizing exports, building the infrastructure, and propping up farm and commodity processes for rural America. The New Deal's state capitalism was not just reducing the role of Wall Street, it was building up New York's competitors.

By the end of World War II, summarizes historian Dan Carter, "a combination of cheap credit, cheap power and massive defense expenditures . . . transformed the South and West and made the Sun Belt the engine of American economic development." But even after the West and the South developed, the political clout of those regions turned the New Deal's state-supported capitalism into a permanent pork barrel for the no longer impoverished. The development of the South and the West was both good and inevitable; New York's nonresponse to this transformation was neither. So ingrained was the city's sense of superiority that when Texas passed a stagnant New York State in population in the early 1990s, then-governor Mario Cuomo shrugged it off as if Texas were still the sticks.

The irony is that New York's effective adaptation to the depression produced a system and a mentality subsequently unable to adapt to new conditions.

When World War II ended, New York City was on top of the world. It was the greatest manufacturing city in North America, its output exceeding both Detroit and Pittsburgh combined. Blessed with an extraordinary harbor, a public school system envied around the nation, and an art world soon to achieve international recognition, New York was a colossus. Its international rivals—London, Paris, Berlin, Rome, and Tokyo—were in ruins while its future domestic rivals, Washington and Los Angeles, were not yet great. At home, the New Deal coalition organized by New Yorkers was still vibrant politically and demographically. In the late 1940s and early 1950s, union membership, big-city populations, and mass-transit ridership all peaked. The suburb and Sun Belt challenges were still only on the horizon.

All three candidates for mayor in 1945, the year of the first post–La Guardia election, fought over who was more liberal. The winner was William O'Dwyer, who when running for reelection four years later boasted that in his first term the city had built a new school and a new housing project every month; had added 89 social centers, 11 health stations, and 28 acres of parks and playgrounds; and had spent $48 million in new hospital construction at a time when the city already had a huge excess of beds. "This country," intoned O'Dwyer, "is in the midst of a titanic struggle between progressive Democrats and reaction, between those who believe in the people's welfare and those who believe in big business and special privilege." There was no doubt which side had won in New York.

The price of total victory for the progressives was that New York became a high-cost city. New York, as one of my cousins often joked, became both "expensive and entitled." The two were related. In 1938 the city bought up all the private subway lines, creating a public monopoly. The city-run subway maintained the near-sacred five-cent fare. This meant that the rising costs of subway workers' salaries and subway operating expenses—and the subway was running a $40 million deficit by 1944—had to be paid for out of general tax revenues. At the same time, rent control laws limiting what could be charged for apartments reduced the revenues the city could collect in property taxes.

Rent control had been introduced nationally as a wartime emergency measure in 1943. By 1948 it was rescinded almost everywhere but in New York. Housing, like cheap subway fares, had become something of an entitlement (this in a city where far fewer owned their housing compared to other major cities). Tenants never saw the cost increases that had to be absorbed by landlords. Playing to the renters, "city candidates charged their opponents with being soft on landlords as national candidates accused their opponents of being soft on communism."

The price for subway subsidies, for rent control, for the vast network of social service and health institutions, and for the free public colleges created by the city-state was compounded by the growing expense and inefficiency of city government. In the bad old Tammany days, the implicit bargain was that if you got a city job, you got the low wages and impermanence that came along with it; if Tammany lost, as it did periodically, its workers would be tossed out. But with La Guardia's civil service reforms, a city job was for life, pension included, regardless of how you performed.

To pay for its generosity, New York, notes urban historian John Teaford, "was especially devoted to the increase of minor taxes." Between 1946 and 1951 the city sales tax rose from 1 percent to 3 percent, and from 1946 to 1955 the city raised the rate of the financial business tax four times (bringing it to 1 percent). It also adopted a new 5 percent tax on hotel rooms, a 15 percent levy on race track admissions, a cigarette tax, and a 5 percent amusement tax.

The city had stepped on a treadmill. Its extensive and expensive services imposed both rising taxes and a need to protect the voters from rising costs, which produced protections for both tenants and straphangers, which in turn produced higher taxes, and so on.

Robert Wagner, Sr., was the New Deal senator who sponsored the pathbreaking labor and public housing legislation that defined liberalism for both New York and the nation. His son Robert Wagner, Jr., New York's mayor from 1953 to 1965, deepened that legacy for the city. Like his father, the younger Wagner, who identified with "the little schnook," moved easily between the world of political reformers and political regulars. Having both an Ivy League education and an easy affinity with New York's street politicians, Mayor Wagner carried on the New Deal tradition on both housing and labor issues. In what would become a classic New York pattern, Mayor Wagner took the declining private investment in housing produced by the city's stringent rent control laws not as a reason to loosen regulations but, rather, as a justification to create new forms of subsidized housing. The new Mitchell–Lama housing program extended housing subsidies well up into the middle class. In the mid-seventies Mitchell–Lama mortgage problems would trigger the city's financial collapse.

Wagner's second innovation played an even greater role in the city's fiscal follies. La Guardia, champion of labor though he was, had strong reservations about public employee unions. "I do not want," he warned, "any of the pinochle club atmosphere to take hold." Worse yet, he feared that city employee unions would cease to serve the public good as he understood it and would go into business for themselves. Mayor Wagner, by contrast, insisted that the issue was "whether to carry on the tradition that made the party great or . . . retreat into reaction." In 1958 the city passed "the Little Wagner Act," becoming the first major city to extend collective bargaining to public employees (New York had 262,000 of them). A vast new political force had been created. Over time, the city would collect and turn over to the unions the dues of their members, which in turn supported political action committees organized to elect the city's leaders the unions then bargained with. During labor negotiations, the unions would be on both sides of the table.

The 1961 election marked the end of New York's political machine, Tammany Hall. On the decline since the La Guardia years, Tammany and its leader, Carmine DeSapio, were taken down by the rising band of "left liberal" reformers, ideological activists who anticipated the McGovern Democrats nationally.

In New York's overheated political atmosphere, the fight between the regulars and the reformers was depicted by the liberal thinker Arthur Schlesinger as nothing less than a fight to preserve the New Deal from the armies of ignorance:

> The essence of the know-nothing revolt, in short, is to wipe out the transformation wrought in the Democratic Party by Franklin Roosevelt and the New Deal and recreate something like the Democratic Party of the twenties . . . a party without ideas, program, energy or zeal . . . liberalism . . . implies intellectual curiosity, moral passion and a creative approach to public policy.

Tammany, which embraced rent control, social services, civil rights, and public housing, was in fact indistinguishable from the liberal reformers on most issues. Rather than a fight over policy, this was the opening shot in what would later become a national cultural war between ethnic Democrats and the newly emerging college-educated elites for the heart of the Democratic Party. "Organized liberals," said the young Daniel Patrick Moynihan, "cannot help but be suspicious of the liberalism of Irish Catholic county leaders who are at ease on city councils and who get along with police chiefs." The Democratic Party, which had not so much moved left as up on the social scale, was about to lose touch with its ethnic base.

In 1961 the city budget fell into deficit for the first time since the Great Depression, and stayed there. Even before Wagner recognized the municipal unions, his program had been beyond the city's means. The mayor built more than three hundred new schools, hundreds of new playgrounds, and five new hospitals. He also reduced class size, increased welfare payments and the number of welfare case workers, and created the largest middle-income housing program in the country.

When Wagner was faced with a huge budget gap in 1963, he considered cutbacks; faced with pressure from the municipal unions he helped create and which had helped elect him in 1961 over Tammany opposition, Wagner caved. In breaking with the machine, Wagner and the reformers unleashed the power of the municipal unions. Municipal unions and the political machine drew on the same lifeblood—government workers. But where Tammany, vulnerable to defeat at the polls, was sensitive to competing interests, municipal unions, ensconced behind their double wall of collective bargaining and civil service protections, had little reason to either compromise or consider the city's overall well-being.

Faced with continuing deficits and an insistence that "human needs are greater than budgetary needs," Wagner borrowed and taxed to close the widenings gaps. "No city," writes John Teaford, "invented taxes more readily or raised them more quickly than New York." Between 1959 and 1963 Wagner repeatedly raised the sales tax while imposing innovative taxes on bank vaults, real estate transactions, and coin-operated amusements. By imposing a general business tax; doubling the gross receipts tax on utilities, which raised the cost of energy to manufacturers; and imposing a commercial rent tax, Wagner undermined the city's economic position. Undaunted, Wagner had a survey done to see if there was some tax somewhere else the city had not yet tapped. To his dismay, little turned up.

In his last year Wagner gave up on trying to raise taxes and just borrowed to meet the deficit. In his final 1965 budget message, he laid out a credo later adopted by Mayor Dinkins. "I do not propose," said Wagner, "to permit our fiscal problems to set the limits of our commitments to meet the essential needs of the people of the city." This was all before the Great Society opened up new opportunities for local spending and before John Lindsay, moved by the plight of black America, dismantled the bargains on which the city's politics had been based.

3. The Ocean Hill–Brownsville *Kulturkampf*, or the Immigrant Option Rejected

G. W. Plunkitt, the Tammany wit, asked: "Have you ever thought what would become of the country if the bosses were put out of business, and their places were taken by a lot of cart-tail orators and college graduates? It would mean chaos." Seer that he was, Plunkitt anticipated the mischief and misfortune that would be produced by New York's first true post-Tammany mayoralty, under John Lindsay. Lindsay's reign of "the best and brightest" produced the Kulturkampf between blacks and whites, blacks and Jews, unions and black nationalists, the ethnic heirs of the New Deal and the heirs to the civil rights movement. All these tensions crystallized around the Ocean Hill–Brownsville school decentralization strife, a conflict so intense that it was described in apocalyptic terms at the time; even today, if you ask middle-aged New Yorkers which side they were on, you will see that the embers of their anger still burn brightly.

This chapter and the next are chronologically parallel chapters that discuss two of the great gambles. This chapter covers the school decentralization disaster, the next the welfare explosion.

When he succeeded Robert Wagner as mayor in 1965, John Lindsay was dubbed "America's mayor," and in a sense he was. As the leading force behind the Kerner Commission Report, commissioned by President Johnson in the wake of the 1967 riots, Lindsay helped set the civil rights agenda for the whole country. A key player in the passage of the

1964 Civil Rights Act, Lindsay projected a patrician Republicanism defined nationally by his opposition to a Democratic Party shaped by an alliance between Irish saloon keepers from the North and Southern segregationists. Locally, Lindsay became the hero of the reform Democrats, the "left liberals" who detested Tammany Hall every bit as much as they yearned for a racial reformation. New York liberals, who already experienced a local version of the Great Society under Mayor Wagner well before LBJ became president, hoped to use the issues of race to leap beyond the limits of the New Deal liberalism they had inherited.

The need to redress racial wrongs was eloquently expressed in the Kerner Report, which asserted correctly that "what white Americans have never fully understood—but what the Negro can never forget—is that white society is deeply implicated in the ghetto. White institutions created it, white institutions maintain it, and white society condones it." Lindsay was personally responsible for the Kerner Report's famous warning that America was becoming two separate societies, one black and one white.

In a widely discussed chapter of the Kerner Report, Lindsay argued that if we are to avoid becoming two separate societes, we have to completely reject the immigrant model of incorporation. Lindsay made an effective case against assuming that blacks could easily follow in the path of the immigrants: the persecution blacks had suffered was far more severe and systematic, and there was no doubt that African-Americans were owed an enormous moral debt. But while he insisted that blacks warranted special help in making the journey into the middle class, Lindsay downplayed the many similarities between, for example, illiterate immigrants from dirt-poor semifeudal southern Italy and those from the Mississippi delta. All of the new arrivals in the city from backward rural areas suffered the dislocation of migration and the need to adapt to an urban industrial setting.

For Lindsay, everything boiled down to white racism, with the ironic upshot that over time the policies produced by assuming racism was the sole cause of black suffering exacerbated the very separation he had warned about. The singular emphasis on racism served in both the short and the long run to anger whites without aiding blacks, who were cast as almost irrevocably different from other Americans and the never-ending victims of other people's attitudes.

"The bother with the premises of the Kerner Report," wrote the New York intellectual Paul Goodman in 1967, "is that if it were true, nothing less would avail than psychiatry for epidemic paranoia, probably including shock treatment—and this is, of course, the proposition of the black terrorists." Not that Lindsay would have recognized them as such. The former congressman for the Silk Stocking District was as ignorant of the people he wanted to help as he was ardent in wanting to right racial wrongs. The world of black nationalism, of Marcus Garvey insisting that he and not Mussolini was the first fascist, and of Malcolm X praying for an atomic bomb to destroy New York was (as one of his close aides acknowledged to me) simply beyond his ken.

Lindsay had no sense of the currents that saw blacks as a people apart, an inchoate nation waiting to take shape in a rebellion against not just white racism but against integrationism as well. According to Paul Goodman, he had no idea that "frustrated and deprived blacks project onto whites the put-downs and hostility that they themselves feel." "It would be too bitter," Goodman explained, "to see . . . that the sophisticated ideology of racism has been picked up by intelligent blacks from white paranoids . . . KKK, Boers, Germans."

Flying blind on a wing and the endless praise of the prestige press, Lindsay not only rejected the bargain whereby immigrants gave up something of their own traditions to become part of the larger society but also rejected the very concepts of reciprocity and restraint upon which the New Deal city had been built. He proposed to replace those concepts with the untried and, as it turned out, unworkable notion that through giving blacks community control, the inner city, like the Third World revolutionary regimes that had inspired black nationalism, could make a great leap forward, bypassing all the stages of sacrifice necessary to create a middle class.

Lindsay insisted that it was cruel to ask more sacrifice from those from whom so much had already been taken. He was in part right; government had and still has a special responsibility in regard to African-Americans. But it was crueler yet to buy into a politics that promoted separatism in the name of reducing racial separation. That was the sure path to the disaster from which we of the cities were to suffer.

In 1968 New York and the rest of the country got to see how Lindsay's assumptions worked on the ground. The logic of the Kerner Commission Report, which had been required reading for all of Lindsay's commissioners, was given form with the Ocean Hill school decentralization experiment.

Support for decentralizing some city services had been building since the late 1940s. Six "white papers" between 1933 and 1965 called for breaking up the massively unwieldy school system. By the late 1960s a *Daily News* poll found that 62 percent of those surveyed wanted "more control for local neighborhoods," 17 percent wanted less, and 21 percent wanted to maintain the status quo. Middle-class families who left the city made no secret of the fact that getting out from under the thumb of unresponsive, unaccountable city bureaucracies was part of what made leaving so attractive.

The decline of political parties, explained lawyer Ed Costikyan, one of the city's wise men, made decentralization imperative. As bureaucracies grew larger and larger, adding layer upon layer of administration between decision makers and those people delivering services, the ordinary New Yorker was, with the decline of local political organization, left without a way to influence the bureaucracy. Moving basic city services like garbage collection and road repair out of city hall and back into New York's five boroughs and innumerable neighborhoods promised to re-create the sort of "lateral access" into the bureaucracy the political parties had once provided.

Conceptually, the push to decentralize got an enormous boost from Jane Jacob's path-breaking book *The Death and Life of Great American Cities.* It was the face-to-face interaction of neighborhoods, the richness of street life, she argued, that nurtured the city both socially and economically. The best thing planners and city officials could do, she explained, was to loosen the reins of their control. City civic leaders tried to respond with proposals that put city services into the neighborhoods, created local planning boards, and (in 1961) established twenty-five local community advisory boards for the schools.

At the same time broad support for decentralization was building, there was also broad, if not always deep, support for desegregation. Seven months after the Supreme Court's *Brown* decision, New York's school board unanimously and voluntarily became the first in the country to commit itself to uphold the Court's judgment. Desegregation, however, became a moving target. Of the 1.1 million blacks in New York City in 1964, 630,000 had arrived between the end of World War II and 1954 and an additional 340,000 had arrived since the *Brown* decision.

The city responded with an effort to regularly rezone schools to maintain racial balance as neighborhoods changed rapidly owing to both black immigration and white flight. In the early 1960s the city began an open enrollment program to counter some of the demographic shifts. It allowed students in overcrowded minority schools to transfer to underutilized middle-class and largely white schools with openings, with transportation paid for by the city.

In the left-wing journal *Dissent,* Jeremy Larner wrote that New York had "done more for school integration than other cities of comparable size." Even so, the number of elementary schools containing 90 percent or more Negro and/or Puerto Rican students more than doubled between 1956/57 and

1963/64. That's because while the number of whites declined by 8 percent, the number of black students grew by 53 percent in those same years

The slow pace of integration and the lagging academic performance of black students produced a movement in 1964, led by the Reverend Milton Galamison, to bring pressure on the school board by threatening a school boycott. Galamison was always vague about his definition of integration and academic progress, so that, as Larner explained, "few people, black or white, fully understood the aims of the boycott."

Speaking on television, Galamison announced a demonstration at 110 Livingston Street, the school headquarters. He promised that his supporters would be nonviolent but warned that nonviolent actions often attract "sociopaths to the scene." Galamison, who sent his son to a private school and drove an expensive car, told a radio interviewer that he "would rather see [the public school system] destroyed" than back off from his (vaguely stated) demands for total integration. "Maybe," he said, "it has run its course anyway."

Galamison's call for total integration had no precedent. New York, as Colin Powell attested in his memoirs, was not a city divided along stark black–white lines of domination and subordination but a mélange of numerous, sometimes competing, communities whose neighborhoods and schools were usually dominated by one or two of the city's ethnic groups. New York was not "upsouth," as so many militants, from Galamison to Sharpton, would have it. There was no one white community to integrate with. In any case, even if you added up all the whites in the public schools, there simply weren't enough to make for integrated schools without the sort of massive busing that was as disruptive as it was unpopular among both whites and blacks.

While New York wasn't "upsouth," neither was it a city of equal opportunity, despite its egalitarian ideology. The city's meritocratic creed notwithstanding, public sector jobs were divided up into ethnic fiefdoms. Largely locked out, African-Americans were understandably enraged by the disparity between universalist pretensions and privileged practices. In the course of the mid-1960s, black demands moved from a call for the absolute universalism of total integration to an insistence on blacks taking control of feifdoms of their own.

Filled with righteous anger, Galamison and his followers would nevertheless hear nothing of the complexities. No honest disagreements on integration were allowed. Galamison had nothing but scorn for whites who defended the principle of neighborhood schools. "Anyone who says he's in favor of integration and the neighborhood school is a liar—he's in favor of segregation," said Galamison.

The teachers' union, a rising force in city politics since the 1958 "Little Wagner Act," was ambivalent about the boycott, but it stood strongly for Galamison's demands for both integration and increased spending on the schools. The United Federation of Teachers (UFT) was not the typical union whose sole emphasis was on meat-and-potatoes issues. Its leader, Al Shanker, worked closely with the black activist Bayard Rustin, who had organized the heroic 1963 March on Washington. Shanker, deeply involved in socialist politics, and other UFT leaders had marched with Martin Luther King in Selma, Alabama, in 1965.

School spending in New York doubled between 1956 and 1967, and the number of educational personnel grew 60 percent between 1960 and 1965. The rapidly growing school budget paid for programs in "cultural enrichment." This meant money for concerts and museum trips, as well as for extra math and reading teachers for some schools. Psychologists, guidance counselors, and teacher coordinators joined the staff.

In the name of leveling up, New York, wrote Charles Silberman, "added a staggering number of special services to schools in slum areas." At the time, the city spent some two hundred dollars more per pupil in slum schools than in white middle-class schools. Then in 1964 the United Federation of Teachers backed the More Effective Schools program, which "provided saturation-level services for ghetto schools, including reduced class sizes, two and sometimes three teachers per class, reading specialists and extended class hours."

In the tradition of the settlement houses that acculturated earlier generation of arrivals to the city, the MES program was designed to rescue children from the "culture of poverty" while remaining sensitive to their heritage. The school curriculum already included a major focus on black history. The board of education barred the use of the phrase "culturally deprived"; it was to be replaced by "children whose experiences, generally speaking, have been limited to their immediate environment."

The concept of a "culture of poverty," a concept central to the school reforms, was borrowed from the anthropologist Oscar Lewis, a socialist who studied peasant cultures in Mexico and Puerto Rico. Lewis, both deeply sympathetic to the poor and ruthlessly honest about their shortcomings, described how people subjugated by the racial hierarchies of plantation agriculture had developed traits and customs that made it difficult for them to adapt to big-city life.

The UFT was committed to what might be described as the pluralist perspective, the view that all ethnic groups ought to be given not only the opportunity but the help needed to make it in New York's mixed economy.

Teachers had a special role in promoting black social mobility, since a good education was the best and fastest way to get into the game.

Teachers were particularly sensitive to the growth in crime, for the rise in classroom violence was a threat both to them and to their mission. Disorder in a school, while not unheard of, had in the past been a relatively minor problem.

By the late 1950s, an increasing number of kids were coming to school from dysfunctional homes without fathers. In some classes, it became impossible to teach without first imparting a heavy dose of personal discipline. "It's the two to three percent who are unteachable and uncontrollable—the ones with very deep emotional disturbances—who take so much time and trouble," explained an assistant principal.

The discipline issue quickly became racialized. The UFT and the school administrators wanted to expand the so-called "600 Schools" for severely troubled kids. As one teacher put it, "What lower-class kids need right now is that somehow we conquer the chaos they live in." Educators wanted to sort out severely troubled kids so that the great majority of students would no longer have to be held hostage to the outbursts of the few, but the Reverend Galamison and his followers wanted to close down the "600 Schools" altogether.

In what would become a familiar pattern, Galamison saw racism in the disproportionately large number of minority kids sent to the "600 Schools." The African-American Teachers Association (ATA) went a step beyond Galamison. They argued, explains historian Jerry Podair, that "the very concept of the disruptive child was an expression of white middle-class cultural bias against black culture." In the words of an ATA member, "so-called disruptive children are those who refuse to bend" to repressive white middle-class values, while another called them "high-spirited nonconformists."

The issue of school discipline sent two rising forces—teacher unionism and the black nationalism of the ATA—on a collision course. The union insisted on putting a provision in its new contract giving teachers the right to suspend seriously disruptive children from their classrooms. The teachers were so serious on this score that in 1967 they went on strike for two weeks largely on behalf of the "disruptive child clause." The strike quickly led to a clash in the Ocean Hill–Brownsville areas of Brooklyn between the UFT and local activists who wanted to keep the schools open.

The activists argued that it was the teachers and not the disruptive kids who were the problem. Where the teachers saw the pathologies of an emerging underclass, the activists—like Garveyite Al Vann, now a New York State assemblyman—saw middle-class minds unable to recognize the "culturally rich" black street culture.

The ATA insisted that black kids could not be reached by white teachers, who imposed their middle-class norms and failed to recognize the creativity of black city life. This argument was very different from the one made just a few years earlier by Galamison and other integrationists. Galamison had complained that white teachers had low expectations for black kids, expectations that blinded them to the talents, as conventionally understood, of minorities. But Vann and his allies—who, like the Black Panthers, tried to meld Marxism and black nationalism—were making a very different case: they denied the very existence of a common culture.

The ATA's mixture of Marxism and racial nationalism was far less contradictory than it appears. In late-nineteenth-century eastern Europe, peasants who had lived an isolated rural existence only became aware of themselves as Poles when they went to work in what were usually German-owned factories and discovered how much they had in common with their fellow peasants and how much they differed from and disliked their German bosses. For blacks who moved to the North, the civil rights movement was their moment of collective consciousness, and if they worked in the vast New York public sector in general and in the schools in particular, their boss was likely to be a Jewish liberal. Many Jewish liberals would in turn recognize in black militancy some of the mixture of class and race ideology they associated with the fanaticism of ignorant peasants and fascists.

The upshot was in part a case of mutual misidentification. Many blacks saw Jewish liberals as just another version of "the man," located this time "upsouth," and expected the Jews to bear the full burden of all the wrongs that had been historically heaped on African-Americans. For their part, many liberal Jews, committed to the idea that blacks were just white people with dark skin, felt betrayed by the attack on their universalist principles; worse yet, they were bewildered by blacks who pointed to their universalism as something parochially Jewish in its origins.

Damaged and disoriented by their experience as slaves and then sharecroppers, some blacks grew to distrust whatever was offered them—like New York City schooling, which was vastly superior to what they received earlier—on the assumption that anything given to them must be second-rate. Racist whites resented the black cry for recognition, but even liberal whites raised in the city's labor tradition were so puzzled by black claims of being exploited as to dismiss the condescension and contempt toward blacks that had become an integral, if generally unspoken, part of white assumptions.

UFT pluralism preached the virtues of a hyphenated Americanism, which both celebrated our separateness and insisted that above and beyond our distinct heritages there could be a shared American tradition. The UFT defined pluralism as Americanism and therefore supported a strong black history component in the curriculum. But it was a component with an integrationist vision that featured, well before his death and martyrdom, the study of Martin Luther King as its centerpiece.

At the height of the civil rights movement in the 1960s the promise of integration was that blacks would become full participants in American life. It is in part as a consequence of the civil rights movement that I can now live in a highly integrated neighborhood in Brooklyn. But over the past thirty years black nationalists and white radicals have redefined integration as a form of white supremacy.

In the 1960s the Black Power radical Stokely Carmichael argued that "integration is a subterfuge for the maintence of white supremacy." Here is how his argument went: If the common culture is defined as white, then integration means submitting to white culture. Given the existence of two different and independent cultures, two nations, in effect—one black and one white—each group has to negotiate with the other as if it were sovereign. Thus, admitting even vast numbers of blacks into American society one by one is a form of cultural and political genocide. According to Carmichael, "You integrate communities, but you assimilate individuals." The problem is that because black and white cultures are so thoroughly intertwined in America, having influenced each other so completely, the notion of independent cultures, outside of the most isolated inner-city neighborhoods, is an absurdity, but an absurdity, as the Million Man March suggests, that has gained currency over time.

The ATA wanted what amounted to publicly financed black nationalist schools organized around the ideas of Marcus Garvey and Malcolm X. Like Cleaver, the ATA wanted to assert pure blackness unsullied by the need to hyphenate into an African-Americanism. They wanted to eliminate the second half of the hyphenated term, to speak not of African-American but of Africans in America. The ATA, notes Jerry Podair, a historian of Ocean Hill, saw universalism as a Jewish liberal trick, a means by which Jews who did better academically by white standards would continue to hold on to jobs in the board of education. They pitted "that which is private and ethnic as against that which is public and culture-blind." They insisted that racial cultures were so separate that only black teachers could teach black children effectively.

Individualism and personal merit, the ATA argued, was a "myth" perpetuated by whites to create "black versions of the white middle class" or "black Anglo-Saxons." The ATA called for an "alternative black value system" based on principles of "collective work and responsibility," "cooperative economics," and unity; giftedness in black children could be measured by a willingness to challenge authority. The ATA wasn't alone: even so thoughtful a voice as Kenneth Clark argued at the time that blacks shouldn't have to adjust to a "sick" white middle-class world and that rebellion against such a world was "evidence of health" and the path to a brave new one.

The social science evidence stood firmly on the side of the UFT. The Coleman Report found that "when poor parents are trained to behave toward their children in the way that middle-class parents do, the children's level of achievement rises." And the notion that bigoted teachers kept black students down was belied by the fact that "differences in achievement are of roughly the same magnitude at Grade 6 or 9 as they are at the time children enter school."

No matter the evidence, Mayor John Lindsay was more than anxious to do battle against the ethnics, the children of the immigrants whose racism he despised, and in favor of the rising tide of black racialism that he embraced without understanding.

Not that Lindsay didn't have more narrowly political motives for setting off the fray. He began well by appointing blacks to a school board that lacked a minority member even though minorities were 75 percent of the school population. Then Lindsay called on Ford Foundation president McGeorge Bundy, a former Harvard dean and one of the architects of President Kennedy's nation-building program in South Vietnam, to recommend ways of decentralizing the system. Lindsay couldn't have made a worse choice. In a city where there was widespread support for decentralization and a growing fear of racial polarization, Bundy undermined support for the former while wildly exacerbating the latter.

At the time Lindsay commissioned the Bundy Report, there were a variety of school reform ideas being proposed, all of which are still current. Kenneth Clark, seeking to break the power of the white middle class over the schools, looked to what would now be called the "charter school," run perhaps by the colleges or the army. Milton Friedman, from the right, and Christopher Jencks, from the left, called for school choice. Vouchers, they argued, would open up the schools to what we now call multiculturalism. Bundy, too, wanted to break the power of the white middle class but by decentralizing the schools. By itself the proposal to decentralize wasn't a problem. The UFT was willing to sign on in principle, although it worried about the Balkanization that might be produced by creating too many districts. The problem was the assumption behind Bundy's version of decentralization. Bundy didn't just want to decentralize the schools; he wanted to use the concept of community-controlled schools to support a miniaturized version of black nation building. In Vietnam, Bundy and his administration had failed at nation building and ended up, as he saw it, on the wrong side of a guerrilla war. This time, siding with the "colonized" and not the "colonizers," he thought he could succeed.

Bundy's approach had enormous appeal to Lindsay, who, facing a tough reelection campaign, hoped to create a new political machine by mobilizing black activists in an alliance against the remnants of the old ethnic machine. Here was a chance, noted Charles Morris, a Lindsay administration welfare commissioner, "to put black militants on the community action payroll and use them as a battering ram." Similarly, liberal foundations like Ford, Taconic, and New World saw a chance to both reform education and create a new political alliance of the top and the bottom against the middle. Here were the seeds of the Democratic Party's decline.

Bundy and Lindsay selected three districts for demonstration projects. Two came off without controversy. The third was in Ocean Hill–Brownsville, where the teachers' union and nationalist militants had already clashed over the problem of violent and disruptive students.

For the black nationalist teachers and administrators, the clash was an unprecedented opportunity for both self-advancement and a partial answer to the land question that had always plagued them. "Black nationalism," explained Bayard Rustin, "offered a system of ideas which seemed to correspond with the interest of the emerging class of black professionals." Integration promised a torturous struggle in unfamiliar institutions with uncertain rewards. But community control promised black professionals immediate "concrete gains long overdue—jobs and promotion to administrative and supervisory positions without the accompanying discomfort of venturing into foreign schools and neighborhoods—under the ideological aegis of one's own community." It was a coincidental and perfect union of ideology and interest.

Ocean Hill was the place to carry out their program. There the hope was not so much to respond to community demands as to create a political community and, not incidentally, a jobs fiefdom by making the schools into the center of the struggle for a separate black identity.

In consultation with Bundy, local activists and parents chose Rhody McCoy, a veteran principal and ardent admirer of Malcolm X, as the superintendent for the experimental district. McCoy wanted to bring in his own staff, and initially UFT president Albert Shanker extended a helping hand. Shanker expedited the voluntary transfer of some of the teachers McCoy wanted removed so that they could be replaced by a more ideologically congenial staff. But then McCoy proceeded to dismiss thirteen UFT teachers and two supervisors who were unwilling to leave but deemed unsympathetic to community control. The teachers then walked off their jobs citywide.

The UFT continued to support the principle of decentralization, but then things turned ugly when black nationalists invited into the schools by McCoy distributed anti-Semitic leaflets insisting that black children should be taught by black teachers and not by "the Middle Eastern murderers of colored people"—this in the wake of the Six Day War between Israel and the Arabs, which generated both a recurrence of old fears and a new sense of pride among American Jews, the largest single group in the UFT.

At one school striking teachers were shoved cowering into an auditorium where politicized toughs flashed the lights on and off, shouting, "Some of you will be going out in pine boxes." For some on the New Left, the thuggish behavior of men like Sonny Carson toward the teachers was justified as part of an internal war of national liberation. But even in those fevered times it was possible to see that the violent energies released by black nationalism were a close cousin to those more general sentiments of young men around the world, from Ireland to Bosnia, who find power and pleasure in intimidating their tribe's enemies, as well as their own, with guns. For the New Left, black nationalism was the forerunner of a more general movement to liberate America, but for the kids on the streets of New York it was, in part, an excuse to give their gang activities a political patina.

The teachers, bucking harsh criticism from the prestige press, won a court order reinstating them, but Mayor John Lindsay, backed by the Ford Foundation and the ACLU, refused to have the police enforce the law. Lindsay, proud of the fact that New York had escaped a major riot, asked Shanker time and again, "Do you want the city to burn down?" For his part, Shanker said Lindsay had capitulated to "blackmail."

McCoy had no interest in compromise. It might have been possible to modify the union concept of merit based on objective universalist criteria with a balancing concern for racial representation (this was the sort of compromise Justice Powell weakly attempted in the *Bakke* affirmative action decision a decade later). But McCoy's interests weighed against compromise. His was the power of disruption. As long as McCoy kept the union teachers out, it was he who held sway.

The battle was joined, sides were chosen up, and tempers exploded in what became a fratricidal war of the political left. In Ocean Hill older rational/universalistic/professional criteria of authority were replaced by what amounted to a politically correct test of loyalty. Two rising forces—public sector unionism and black nationalism—were joined in battle (with overtones of anti-Semitism) while the energies that flowed into the antiwar and New Left movements were temporarily diverted into the fray. The situation became so overheated, so invested with the energy from other battles, including the New Left revolt against bourgeois values, that Jason Epstein, an editor at the *New York Review of Books,* wrote that "the city is now faced with a classic revolutionary situation." It was nothing of the kind, but so much was at stake that Epstein went on to argue that "the alternatives left to the white majority" were "capitulation or genocide."

Both Epstein and the black nationalists yearned for an imaginative freedom, a freedom unconstrained by the draft horse of the middle class and the bureaucratic institutions of the New Deal. The theme of community control, explained Daniel Patrick Moynihan, united left and right "in a kind of particularist alliance against the national ideals of the liberal center." Moynihan had seen the future.

Even after a series of citywide teacher strikes, Lindsay refused to enforce the law, so it was left for the state education commissioner to depose McCoy. But that was by no means the end of it. New York's civic culture was shattered into the fragments of an exploded consensus. One of the city's great assets, a first-class school system, never recovered.

De facto Afrocentric schools were created, but they failed to improve student performance, a consequence that went largely unnoticed. The very sensible move to decentralize city government and city schools was derailed. Even today as other cities experiment with decentralized charter schools, New York, its memory of the Ocean Hill strife still strong, lags far behind. Yet these were by no means the only disasters to follow.

Embittered by the strike, the UFT became exactly the kind of self-serving, rule-mongering organization decentralization was designed to deter. The UFT, along with other municipal unions, became, with the decline of political parties, the true political power both in the city and in Albany.

The school reform that followed in the wake of the Ocean Hill confrontation produced the worst of both worlds: a system that was both decentralized and unaccountable. Control over nonprofessional hiring was decentralized to local school boards, which became patronage pits, at the same time that professional hiring was centralized through the teachers' contract, which made it virtually impossible to fire even deranged, let alone merely incompetent, teachers. The local school boards became, particularly in poorer areas like the Bronx, educational institutions last and sources of contracting and patronage first.

Lindsay so angered so many that the mayoralty was stripped of its control over the schools by the state legislature and power was placed in the hands of a board of education unable to handle it. This produced divided authority and endless strife. Over the next twenty-five years the average schools chancellor lasted less than two years in office. Even worse was the strife within the schools. Angry and embittered, many teachers lived by their contractual obligations alone. They punched their time clocks but ceased to play a role in enforcing the rules that had undergirded school discipline. Whereas teachers once provided informal examples of adult authority for children who lacked stable families, their withdrawal helped produce schools where rules were enforced by metal detectors and a growing array of security guards.

Black militancy and the militancy of white unions played off each other as New York's tolerant liberalism was remade into a streetfighting pluralism. The anger at Lindsay ran so deep that when John DeLury, president of the overwhelmingly Italian sanitation workers, presented to his members a proposed contract that he had negotiated with the mayor, he not only was "hooted off the platform [and] pelted with eggs" but required police assistance to get out of the crowd.

According to political historian Chris McNickle, the anger of the sanitation workers was more toward the city than toward DeLury: "[enraged] at the apparent preference shown minorities, they felt like second-class citizens and wanted to strike almost for catharsis." The anger produced a two-week garbage strike and a sizable pay increase. The sanitation men, like teachers and members of other city unions, insisted on being indemnified for their grief.

Lindsay had hoped to pay for his social programs by reducing the power, and thus the pay, of the city unions. Instead, encountering first an early defeat by the transit workers and moving on to a defeat at the hands of the UFT, Lindsay found that the unions, increasingly hostile and well aware of his presidential ambitions, insisted on pay and pension increases far beyond what the city could afford.

4. The Welfare Explosion

A Case of Malign Intentions

While I was writing this book, I ran into a former key aide to former mayor Lindsay, a bright and thoughtful guy. We quickly got into a discussion of which had been the biggest calamity of the Lindsay years. I pointed to the Ocean Hill–Brownsville affair; he said it was close but picked instead the push to expand welfare. You can make the case either way.

Talk to intelligent urbanites in New York, Los Angeles, or Washington about welfare, and almost the first thing they'll tell you is that people are on welfare because of an absence of jobs. When you point out that the welfare explosion in America not only began in New York but also coincided with the great economic and jobs boom of the 1960s when black unemployment in the city was running at 4 percent, about half the national average for minorities, they look puzzled and tend to change the subject. This chapter might be described as an account of what people who don't want to change the subject should know.

In the mid-1960s New York City and the federal government took a great gamble. Not only did they throw out the time-honored distinction between the worthy and unworthy poor that the New Deal had clung to, but they refused to recognize that there were many different ways to be poor.

Virtue does not correlate with class, income is not a proxy for character, and hard work is not necessarily an indicator of income, but certain vices, like desertion and violent crime, do have distinct class correlates. In an act of principled ignorance, liberal activists, anxious to erase the invidious distinctions that held poor people back, argued away the essential differences between those who suffered from only a lack of money and those who suffered from far more. Liberals in New York and Washington gambled that what makes people poor is simply a lack of money and that the fastest way to eliminate poverty is to get more people on the welfare rolls while increasing what recipients are entitled to.

We are living with the results of that gamble. Under the best of circumstances, the legacy of racism and federal foolishness aside, the vast immigration to the Northern cities from the American South after World War II was bound to have been unsettling. Antipoverty policy in the 1960s not only made a tough situation worse but left a long-term legacy the cities have yet to overcome.

In the years between 1945 and 1960, the mechanization of Southern agriculture marginalized unskilled farm labor. Sometimes lured by the promise of a better future and sometimes driven off the land, a vast number of at times cruelly displaced black and white sharecroppers migrated to the Northern cities. The number of black and white sharecroppers dropped from 776,000 in 1930 to 122,000 in 1959. Some 2.75 million blacks left the South between 1940 and 1960 while the black population of New York City increased two and a half times in those same years—to 1.1 million, or 14 percent of the population.

The sheer size of the migration meant that the newcomers, black or white, would be hard to absorb. But of the migrants, blacks in particular were moving from the semifeudal world of Southern agriculture to a modern industrial setting. Richard Wright said of the black migrants: "Perhaps never in history has a more utterly unprepared folk wanted to go to the city." Much the same was true of the whites who went north. A visitor to the hillbilly areas of Detroit or Chicago in the 1950s would have found all the elements of social pathology associated with the worst elements of the black underclass.

Despite the dislocations produced by the mass migrations, welfare grew slowly until the late 1950s. In New York City and Los Angeles, where welfare was far easier to obtain than it had been in the South, the rolls increased by only 16 and 14 percent, respectively.

Welfare was kept in check by both the public attitudes inherited from the New Deal and the private attitudes of potential recipients. President Franklin Roosevelt feared that anything more than a short-term safety net would become a "a narcotic, a subtle destroyer of human spirit." His social insurance plans were designed to build civic solidarity by allowing government insurance to help people over the rough spots in the business cycle. People who received support during the downswings in the cycle were expected to contribute to the insurance pool when they were back on their feet.

The danger that social insurance might inadvertently promote dependence or illegitimacy was in the forefront of New Deal concerns. Frances Perkins, FDR's secretary of labor, who had been a volunteer in a home for unwed mothers, vehemently opposed Aid for Dependent Children payments being given to mothers with illegitimate offspring. Roosevelt said that relief aimed "to preserve not only the bodies of the unemployed from destitution but also their self-respect, their self-reliance, courage and determination."

For their part, many minority relief recipients in New York of the 1950s saw welfare as a temporary bridge. Newly arrived Puerto Rican workers used welfare as a kind of unemployment insurance for low-wage jobs in the health, hotel, and garment industries. Similarly, arriving blacks talked of welfare as a "bank," a loan made against future tax payments or against past payments they had made while working. As late as 1957, while welfare was growing, the problem of a welfare explosion was nowhere on the horizon.

For all their differences from earlier arrivals, blacks and Puerto Ricans were, until the 1958–1959 recession, getting a foothold in the cities. The steep recession, combined with the impact of newcomers still pouring into the city and looking for jobs, sent blacks and Puerto Ricans into a tailspin. Their illegitimacy rates began to rise, as did crime and the welfare rolls, and they continued to rise even after the economy recovered.

Michael Harrington's *The Other America,* the 1962 book that reintroduced the country to the question of poverty, was written in the wake of the recession. Harrington, unlike the romantic radicals soon to dominate the scene, had no illusions about the pathological nature of some of the poverty that had taken hold in his New York and elsewhere. He said that poverty got inside some of those on welfare; the new poverty, he wrote, "twists and deforms the spirit." Of those trapped in the culture of poverty, Harrington wrote: "Their entire environment, their life, their values, do not prepare them to take advantage of new opportunity." He was right. What was most extraordinary about the growth rate of both welfare and illegitimacy in the early sixties was the fact that they were both rising while the economy was creating a booming demand for labor. Black male unemployment declined sharply during the first half of the 1960s.

Between 1945 and 1960 the welfare population of New York City grew by 47,000, but between 1960 and 1965 it grew by more than 200,000 to 538,000. And then the expansion accelerated, growing in the midst of the greatest economic boom the country had ever seen. The welfare population grew by another 630,000 to a staggering 1,165,000 in 1971. New York's welfare population was larger than the population of fifteen states and more than twice the size of the state's second-largest city, Buffalo.

New York wasn't alone in this expansion. Sixty percent of the growth in welfare in the 1960s occurred in five big-city states: New York, Illinois, California, Pennsylvania, and Ohio, with New York and California representing 44 percent of the increase. Only in New York, where the ideological rationale for the welfare explosion was generated, was the character of the city fundamentally transformed, as the city was forced to take on the responsibility of 600,000 children on relief, 445,000 of them fatherless.

Looked at in perspective, LBJ's Great Society was, in large part, a belated attempt by the federal government to aid in the absorption of the millions of semiliterate farmers who moved north after World War II. In New York, where, unlike the rest of the country, the New Deal had never ended, that attempt began almost a decade earlier under Mayor Robert Wagner, Jr., heir to his father's New Deal legacy. Spurred on by his massive 1957 election victory—he won by more than a million votes—Mayor Wagner, like LBJ after his 1964 landslide victory, accelerated the city's social efforts. Wagner, speaking of the "slumless city," built hundreds of new schools, playgrounds, and health centers in poor neighborhoods. He opened new hospitals in poor neighborhoods; reduced welfare caseloads while expanding social services (even as he increased the number of cops), decreased crime, and built the largest middle-income housing program in the country.

By the end of the 1950s, a 721-page book was needed to list all the public and private social services that had grown first to integrate an earlier generation of immigrants and then to acculturate the newcomers of the 1950s. New York pioneered antipoverty law, funding innovative lawyers like Edward Sparer of the Henry Street Settlement House to sue the city itself for higher grants on behalf of welfare clients. "Social work," wrote Charles Silberman, "is one of the city's major industries. In Harlem–upper Manhattan alone there are 156 separate agencies serving about 240,000 people, roughly 40 percent of the total population."

Still, by the early 1960s expectations were already outrunning Wagner's accomplishments. The *New York Herald Tribune* accused Wagner of "indifference to the poor" and of attacking poverty with "a cap pistol." New York was already primed for a further expansion of social spending when Lyndon Johnson's 1964 landslide election broke the twenty-five-year grip Republicans and conservative Southern Democrats had held on government activism. Under Johnson the Department of Health, Education, and Welfare and the Office of Economic Opportunity encouraged states and localities to increase their social welfare spending.

Not surprisingly, New York was receptive, in part because many of the architects of the emerging federal poverty programs were themselves New Yorkers. A group of social work theoreticians and pioneering antipoverty lawyers, including Sparer, mostly affiliated with the Columbia University School of Social Work, initiated a series of innovative programs on the Lower East Side of New York through an organization called Mobilization for Youth. The MFY programs then served as a model for the Johnson antipoverty program. Realizing that many more people were technically eligible for welfare than were receiving it, MFY lawyers and antipoverty workers used court cases and social outreach to bring more people on the rolls. Under the Great Society's Community Action Programs, the federal government paid for antipoverty workers, lawyers, and community action agencies to push nationally for expanding welfare eligibility.

In a break with the New Deal perspective, the dangers of dependency were dismissed while antipoverty advocates exulted not because social insurance was being extended but because justice was finally being given to those who had been so miserably treated by their country. The initial target of the antipoverty lawyers was the elaborate and sometimes arbitrary system whereby people initially qualified for welfare and then qualified for specific grants for furniture, rent, and clothing. Caseworkers visited people's homes to check up on them and to see if a man was living in the house (if so, he was expected to contribute to the support of the family even if the children were not his own). Similarly, welfare mothers, at the risk of their own benefits, were expected to identify putative fathers of their children so that the government could collect support. This put enormous discretion in the hands of caseworkers, who generally saw themselves as helping newcomers adjust to the city. These caseworkers were denounced by antipoverty activists as dignity-demeaning "welfare colonialists"—or, worse yet, were denounced for their prurience about black sexuality if they persisted in trying to locate fathers.

One of the early New York antipoverty advocates, journalist Richard Elman, was outraged by the way the system urged and cajoled clients to restore themselves to productive citizenship and break the cycle of dependency, a condition, he argued, "that may be problematical to everybody but [the clients]." In his 1966 book, *The Poorhouse State,* Elman denounced a concern with dependency as a "bogeyman." In fact, he argued that America needed to "make dependency legitimate" so that the dependent could "consume with integrity."

The Poorhouse State was one piece of a larger cultural shift in which older ideas about shame were starting to be replaced by a new concern for self-esteem. Christopher Lasch wrote that formerly "shame was the fate of those whose conduct fell short of cherished ideals." But in the 1960s, the new age of moral deregulation and therapeutic ethics, shame came to refer to whatever prevents us from feeling good about ourselves.

In his book Elman, contemptuous of the traditional virtues of self-discipline, modesty, and hard work, concludes with this ringing call for more dependency: "We of the rising middle classes must somehow dispel our own myth that we are not dependent and do not wish to become dependent. We must try to create even more agencies of dependency, and we must make it possible for all to make use of them equally."

The vehicle for Elman's transvaluation of values was to be the marriage of antipoverty and civil rights law. On the conceptual level, poverty was to be attacked as a form of racial discrimination. On the day-to-day level, antipoverty lawyers tried to make it both easier to get on welfare in the first place and harder to be terminated once on.

Traditionally, court-appointed lawyers for the poor, like those of New York's Legal Aid Society, were temperamentally close to those who had worked in the settlement houses that helped Americanize earlier immigrants. But, as antipoverty advocate Martha Davis explains, "the poverty law of the 1960s was a radical departure from the earlier idea that legal aid to the poor would encourage newcomers to assimilate into American society." Instead, antipoverty law, as developed by Sparer in a series of strategic court cases financed first with New York City and then federal funds, was designed to create a separate, subsidized existence for the poor.

Sparer believed, and the courts came to agree, that imposing conditions on receiving welfare violated the recipient's right to privacy and the right "to choose one's own standard of morality." Clients, he argued further to a receptive judiciary, had the right to refuse work without penalty. Any insistence on work carried echoes of racial injustice in the South, where debt peonage and other forms of forced labor had lasted long into the twentieth century. Further, in an age of sexual liberation, an age of moral deregulation when the middle classes were no longer willing to put fetters on their own appetites, this was an enormously attractive approach—combined as it always was with an appeal to racial guilt.

Welfare in the new dispensation was no longer a form of social insurance for those who were part of the economy but reparations paid out by enlightened governments looking to make amends for past evils. In other words, people whose ancestors had been obliged to work as slaves and who themselves may have been subjects of a semifeudal tyranny could not now be asked to work for the uncertain and limited rewards offered by low-and entry-level jobs. And so the enormous opportunity offered by the sixties' boom to integrate the newcomers into the economy was lost.

Under the schemes suggested by Sparer and his colleagues at Columbia, Professors Richard Cloward and Frances Fox Piven, the traditional assumptions about just reward and economic mobility were reversed. Leftists traditionally argued, often with good cause, that injustice resided in using a competitive labor market to underpay workers for their efforts. The Columbians disagreed. They wanted to sever the connection between economic effort and outcome; they wanted, instead, to guarantee a high level of living to all as a matter of right. Similarly, while the traditional assumption had been that peasant newcomers attained middle-class habits like discipline and punctuality through modern, routinized work in the struggle to rise socially, that assumption was reversed by the Columbians. They contended that by guaranteeing people a middle-class income, middle-class habits would follow.

The beauty of it, argued George Wiley of the National Welfare Rights Organization (NWRO), was that "generosity now would reduce dependency later" without the need to violate the recipients' "fundamental [civil] liberties" through an intrusive and judgmental welfare system. For Wiley and the Columbians, welfare clients had a right to behave as they chose and the rest of the population had an obligation to support them.

The advocates' compelling cry for justice led many at the time (and even subsequently) to downplay the disaster of welfare dependency as "the cost of good intentions." Some of the welfare radicals, however, saw the future all too clearly. "When attachments to the role of work deteriorate," wrote Piven and Cloward, "so do attachments to the family, especially the attachments of men to their families." They foresaw "the resulting family breakdown and . . . spread of certain forms of disorder," like "school failure, crime, and addiction." For most, this was a description of disaster, but for those like Piven and Cloward, who saw welfare recipients as the cat's-paws of the coming revolution, breakdown promised to unleash the furies of rebellion. "Unfortunately," wrote Roger Starr, a former member of the *New York Times* editorial board, "the exploitation of the Negro in America has been so thorough that a strain of it even runs through the movement to liberate him."

No one, not even the preternaturally brilliant Daniel Patrick Moynihan, saw the concinnity between the emerging social breakdown of the cities, welfare, and the new politics of crime and violence more clearly than Cloward and Piven, the brilliantly original thinkers and activists. Moynihans in reverse, they welcomed the decline of the inner-city family as an opening to radical change. "From our perspective," they wrote in 1966, "the weakening of the family signified a weakening of social control, especially over the young, and it was the young who were most prominent in the disorders of the 1960s." Disorder, in turn, was a critical force in producing more liberal relief practices.

Cloward and Piven viewed the riots as a response not to injustice per se but, rather, to the ways that the old "patterns of servile conformity were shattered" in the Northern cities. The riots, they argued, were an extension of the already rising rates of violent crime, juvenile delinquency, vandalism, and drug addiction—"the litany of urban disorders in the wake of declining occupational and family controls." "Eventually," they explained, the "disorder took the form of widespread rioting, and rioters, too, were predominantly young, single, and marginally related to the occupational structure." The riots opened up the opportunity for more crime, more rebellion.

Piven and Cloward supported the efforts of Cloward's colleague Edward Sparer and of Cloward's writing partner, Richard Elman, as they did the political organizing of George Wiley. But they thought the courts too slow and the political potential of disorganized welfare clients too limited. They devised a strategy inspired by the violence of the sixties, a strategy that drew on the very disorganization of the welfare clients to end poverty by bringing down "the system." Their logic, as presented in a May 1966 *Nation* article, "The Weight of the Poor: A Strategy to End Poverty," was simple. For every one of the eight million people already on the welfare rolls nationally, there was another person who was eligible but not yet on the rolls. If eight million more could be brought on welfare, it "would precipitate a profound financial and political crisis" that might change the very nature of American society. Here was an innovative reworking of the classic far left vision of "the worse, the better."

The real power of the poor, argued Piven and Cloward, came from a street-smart version of self-help—their ability to menace and riot. "Rent strikes, crime, civic disruptions are," they argued, "the politics of the poor." In order to fend off the violence or threat of violence, local government would have to open up the welfare rolls. They assumed this would mean "procedural turmoil in the cumbersome welfare bureaus" and "fiscal turmoil in the localities where existing sources of tax revenue were already overburdened." The aim was to "generate severe political strains, and deepen existing divisions among elements in the big-city Democratic coalition: the remaining white middle class, the white working class, ethnic groups and the growing minority poor." If the system could through threat and intimidation be overloaded, if New York City was faced with "welfare bankruptcy," then, it was assumed, Mayor Lindsay and Governor Rockefeller would become "lobbyists for change in Washington."

President Johnson declared 1965 "the year of the cities." That same year, even before he took office, the national media, led by *Newsweek,* proclaimed newly elected New York Mayor John Lindsay the hero of the cities. The cities, said one pundit, are "where the action is." Lindsay agreed. He saw urban issues as a possible stepping stone to the White House. With a national audience in mind, Lindsay made welfare a central theme of his mayoral campaign. Elected by a narrow margin in a three-way race, Lindsay named Mitchell Ginsberg, MFY board member and Cloward's Columbia colleague, as his first commissioner of social services.

Ginsberg made it clear from the start that he saw it as his mission to bring more people on the rolls. First, he quickly announced plans to publicize the availability of welfare benefits, something that had been rigorously avoided till then. Then he announced his intention to replace the strict scrutiny of the system's eligibility process with a simplified system of self-declaration, leading the *Daily News* to mock him as "come-and-get-it Ginsberg." Further, he promised to eliminate the home visits antipoverty advocates had denounced as demeaning. Ginsberg was unconcerned with the price of welfare, explaining, "I have always viewed the cost of welfare to be whatever it is."

Praised in the prestige press for making welfare a serious topic for national discussion, Ginsberg went on closed circuit TV urging caseworkers to "locate people eligible for welfare who were not yet on the rolls." Explained Ginsberg, "There are nearly as many families *off* the relief rolls as there are on." Ginsberg energized the caseworkers, as did Piven and Cloward's influential *Nation* article. In the new crusading regime, explained welfare expert Blanche Bernstein, "it became something of a badge of honor for caseworkers to manipulate the regulations to build the largest possible grant for a client." Speaking in solidarity, the caseworkers' union made welfare liberalization one of their collective bargaining demands.

Catholic Charities ran workshops on how to help bring more people on the rolls, but most of the organizations recruiting new welfare clients (in about two hundred storefront centers citywide) were direct creations of federal funding from the War on Poverty. One of these, the United Welfare League, used money from the misnamed Office of Economic Opportunity (OEO) and local community activists and federally funded Vista workers to run their storefront outreach centers.

The *OEO Trainers' Manual for Community Action Agency Boards* adopted the Piven and Cloward arguments wholesale. Discussing various strategies to win power for the poor, the manual cited "threat power" and explained that "the ultimate threat power" was the riot. Riots were "clearly against the law," the manual explained, but then it went on (in Moynihan's words, "with a wink") to speak of why it was important that board members recognize "the *threat power* of rioting as a very real power and possibility."

In early 1968 the NWRO, a quarter to half of whose national membership was in New York City, decided to direct the Piven and Cloward and OEO strategy of disruptions at the caseworkers themselves in hopes of winning a guaranteed income. By the spring and summer of 1968, sit-ins at city welfare centers and at Ginsberg's office brought both chaos and an increase in special grant money. Ginsberg responded by replacing separate grants with a simplified system of enhanced basic grants. But rather than calming matters, this enraged the NWRO, which had lost its favorite issue, namely, the sometimes arbitrary nature of special grants.

By the fall of 1968 the protests swelled to more than two hundred incidents a month. The overwhelmed welfare department had to establish a "war room" to keep track of the daily "actions," as demonstrators ripped phones from the walls and trashed welfare offices. When the protesters were joined by local members of the Black Panthers, caseworkers increasingly stayed home.

The Lindsay administration had a slow learning curve. In the next year, NWRO activists disrupted a National Conference on Social Welfare meeting in New York and demanded money to build a new revolutionary organization. A Lindsay administration spokesman present responded, "Our experience is that some good can come of confrontation politics." Disruption, he explained, was "time well spent." It's not clear whether the official was speaking, as Moynihan has suggested, from a liberal "seizure of self-doubt"; whether he had adopted the new-left position that right-wing repression would bring on the revolution; or whether he was simply cowed. It mattered little, as most of the city looked on with dismay.

To make matters worse for Lindsay, in January of 1969 the *Times* broke a major scandal with this headline: MILLIONS IN CITY POVERTY AGENCY LOST BY FRAUD AND INEFFICIENCY. A group of social service administrative staff employees, the so-called Durham gang, had rigged the computer to write checks for imaginary workers. This led to a federal investigation and the conclusion by Willard Wirtz, Johnson's labor secretary, that New York "had the worst administrative problems of any antipoverty program in any city in the U.S." Lindsay responded by saying the system was "pretty good" but needed improvement. Washington auditors, however, said that the city's

Human Resources Administration was "not fiscally responsible and should not be the custodian of federal funds."

Many in the press, particularly at the *New York Times,* where the editors were part of Lindsay's "kitchen cabinet," continued to think of the mayor as a heroic, Kennedyesque figure. *Village Voice* columnist Jack Newfield spoke of Lindsay's "noble Periclean vision of New York as a modern Athens." Newfield's chief complaint was that Lindsay wasn't in touch with his own deepest feelings.

But most New Yorkers were. In 1969, a mayoral election year, it was impossible to get into a conversation with a cabby, a clerk, a waitress, or any of the other workaday people in the city without listening to them vent on the subject of Lindsay and "welfare cheats." Taxes had risen, services had declined, and the city was caught in a deep recession. Surveys showed that 60 percent of the city thought New York had become "a welfare dumping ground" for the rest of the country.

By any measure, the Piven and Cloward plan for "extreme polarization" was a success. But it wouldn't have worked nearly as well if Lindsay hadn't been the perfect mayor for their script. Lindsay's contempt for the middle class was so palpable that his planning commission made a movie about its master plan using Pete Seeger's song about "ticky-tacky" middle-class houses as its sound track to describe the kind of one-family homes in Queens the commission found aesthetically offensive.

Lindsay was saved from his own self-deceptions for a time by the peculiarities of both New York politics and the 1969 election. For one thing, although Lindsay was defeated in the Republican primary and was not yet a Democrat, he was able to run on the Liberal Party line. The Liberals were the remnants of the left-wing anti-Communists who had worked with La Guardia and FDR to redefine American politics in the 1930s and 1940s. For another thing, 1969 was the year of a bitter backlash against urban liberalism. In Los Angeles, Sam Yorty ran an ugly racist campaign to defeat Tom Bradley; in liberal Minneapolis, where Hubert Humphrey had once been the mayor, cop Charles Stenvig won on a law-and-order platform; and in Philadelphia, tough guy police chief Frank Rizzo emerged as a political force. The Liberal Party leader Alex Rose was determined not to let a white backlash defeat Lindsay. With the hyperbole typical of the 1969 campaign, Rose insisted that New York had to become "a political Stalingrad like the city where the forces of Hitlerism were turned back . . . the backlash had to be turned back."

Lindsay had the good fortune to face a divided Democratic Party. The crazy-horse mayoral candidacy of Norman Mailer running against the "boredom" of a Democratic machine that no longer existed took enough votes away from the strongest Democrat—the Puerto Rican borough president of the Bronx, Herman Badillo—to throw the primary to Mario Procaccino. Procaccino, the "law 'n' order" candidate of the outer boroughs, is now best remembered for coining the apt phrase "limousine liberals" to describe Lindsay and his Manhattan admirers. Although almost two-thirds of the electorate voted against him on either the Democratic or the Republican lines, Lindsay squeaked by with a narrow plurality in one the tightest races in New York history. It was a bitterly divisive campaign and the first to be fought over racial issues.

The election behind him, Lindsay, facing both intense middle-class hostility and a deep and growing budget deficit, began to express second thoughts on the expanding of the welfare rolls. In 1960 the ratio of people employed to those on relief was almost 10 to 1; as Lindsay began his second term in 1970 the ratio was approaching 5 to 1. In those same years welfare, broadly defined, had quadrupled to 28 percent of the city's costs.

Lindsay, a pioneer in the game of victimization, quickly blamed the feds: "We are sick to death" of the state and the federal government "ramming down our throats the cost of a program which does not work." Damning the state and federal mandates that he had previously encouraged, Lindsay, who had never been much interested in the economy, discovered that "the power to tax involves the power to destroy." New York Governor Nelson Rockefeller, who had earlier systematically supported the expansion of welfare, chimed in, declaring that the existing welfare system "will ultimately overload and break down our society."

At that point Piven and Cloward must have felt like master puppeteers. Faced with an impending welfare-driven fiscal crunch, both Lindsay and Rockefeller became ardent proponents of national welfare reform, whereby the feds would pick up the full cost of the program. For all his warning of fiscal doom, Rockefeller nonetheless proposed a sharp increase in welfare spending for his executive budget, and Lindsay wasn't so shaken that he could conceive of putting some welfare clients to work.

When Lindsay testified before the Senate Finance Committee hearings on Moynihan's proposed guaranteed minimum income, Senator Abraham Ribicoff, a liberal Democrat from neighboring Connecticut, noted that New York was "without question, one of the filthiest cities anywhere." Ribicoff then asked Lindsay and Ginsberg for the number of able-bodied people on welfare and suggested that those of the 180,000 recipients capable of work might "help make New York sparkle." "How much training do you have to have," he asked, "to have a stick, a broomstick with a spike on it to pick up a piece of paper?"

Lindsay and New York Senator Robert F. Kennedy were repulsed by Ribicoff's regressive suggestion. Kennedy compared the very limited work requirements of 1967 federal legislation to the "punitive attitude reminiscent of medieval poor law philosophy." Lindsay thought that the "coercion" of work requirements could "alienate" the poor and might even lead to an "explosion" of violence.

New York and California carried a disproportionate burden of national welfare costs. Together they had 19 percent of the country's population and 22 percent of personal income but 46 percent of state and local spending on welfare. Lindsay hoped that the Moynihan–Nixon proposal for a guaranteed income, the Family Assistance Plan (FAP), might be used to lessen that burden without reducing New York City's generous welfare scheme. But the defeat of FAP by a simultaneous opposition from the left and the right in Congress ended that possibility. Washington did grant New York limited help in reducing welfare costs. In 1972 the federal government assumed the cost of programs for the aged and disabled with the Supplemental Security Income (SSI) program. Spending was further slowed in 1974, when New York State froze the basic welfare grant, a freeze that was to last for a decade. The problem was that most of the damage had already been done.

The FAP and the National Welfare Rights Organization, each in a different way, wanted to establish a guaranteed income, but in effect New York already had one. The net income of a welfare family of four living in public housing was $5,665 (not in public housing, $5,245), that is, roughly at the level of the NWRO organizers' aim of a $5,550-a-year guaranteed income. According to Nathan Glazer, the preeminent sociologist of the city, New York had already gone "beyond welfare" to an income maintenance system. If money were the sole source of poverty, New York should have eliminated it by the end of the sixties.

Many of the criticisms directed at welfare elsewhere didn't apply to New York. Clients in New York were allowed to retain a percentage of their earnings and their children's earnings without deductions from welfare; in New York it wasn't necessary for a husband to desert his wife in order for the family to receive welfare.

By 1968 the value of welfare plus Medicaid exceeded the value of a minimum wage job. "Welfare is getting to be the best job there is!" exclaimed a Brooklyn welfare client. She was right. A late 1960s field study conducted by the Wharton School's Racial Practices in American Industry Project found that while welfare was growing, employers complained of worker shortages.

Black workers were dropping out of garment work, never to return, even as "apparel employers were searching for workers as never before."

The "other deinstitutionalization"—the release of men from their families—did immeasurable damage. Many families broke up *after* going on welfare because government payments made the father less important. In other cases, families were never formed in the first place, as Aid to Families with Dependent Children (AFDC) allowed men to opt out of the labor market and marriage. Illegitimacy soared, rising regularly regardless of the economy. In 1970, 445,000 of the 600,000 children on welfare were fatherless amid an explosion of desertion, divorce, and out-of-wedlock births. Other factors were clearly in play—the sexual revolution and middle-class moral experimentalism in the Age of Aquarius—but welfare was a key ingredient in the toxic brew that devastated vast sections of the city.

New York had detonated a disaster of unprecedented proportions and had helped bankrupt itself in the bargain, and yet the social work community never saw fit to reexamine its assumptions. In fact, as Blanche Bernstein, a former New York welfare commissioner, has described it, a small industry of judges, legal aid lawyers, and antipoverty "experts" grew up to defend what had been wrought. Too many had invested too much in the revolutionary hopes of the sixties to turn back.

The alibi industry had a justification for everything. The biggest and most important alibi was that the poor were so disadvantaged by their environment, which in turn was simply a reflection of racism, that all responsibility for their fate was shifted to government. In the words of William Ryan, author of *Blaming the Victim,* recipients were "trapped in conditions beyond their control which our nation has failed to overcome." It was on these grounds that the venerable Community Service Society abandoned casework. The assumption that some individuals might be even partly responsible for their actions was, they insisted, entirely outdated. They might have quoted Diderot playfully arguing that "the word 'freedom' has no meaning . . . we are simply the product of the general order of things."

In the 1970s the "high priests" of welfare, as Blanche Bernstein described the community activists, interest groups, and judges who drove policy, added several twists to Diderot's argument. Influenced by feminism, they questioned the importance of marriage, steadfastly refused to recognize the impact of fatherlessness, and generally demonized Daniel Patrick Moynihan. They had an army of excuses to explain why it wasn't important to bring the father back into the picture: the fathers of illegitimate kids didn't have any money anyway or any attempt to force mothers to aid in finding the fathers would violate the privacy rights of the mother. The two-parent family was, after all, just a white middle-class "hang-up." The whole "hunt for fathers," it was asserted, was just an expression of "racism and sexism." In fact, over the course of the 1970s the growth of female-headed black families accounted for almost the entire increase in poverty.

Under the leadership of Ginsberg and his successor, James Dumpson, work—particularly entry-level work—was, like fatherhood, placed in the trash can of history. Again an array of arguments was deployed to undermine the obvious: either people on welfare were incapable of working or they wanted to work but there were no jobs available or, yes, there were jobs available but there was a mismatch between the skills required and the skills of the people on welfare.

The concept of dead-end jobs was the most innovative explanation pioneered in these years. The concept probably originated in the early 1960s with the New York intellectual Paul Goodman, who raised the hurdle on what constituted satisfactory employment. Goodman explained that while "there is nearly full employment . . . there are fewer jobs that can be done keeping one's honor and dignity." Goodman's theme was taken up by Richard Elman, a coauthor with Columbia professor Richard Cloward on some of the key articles arguing that there is a right to welfare. Elman complained that the middle class wants poor people "to go the hard route, to be . . . taxi drivers, restaurant employees . . . and factory hands." Instead, he argued, the middle class ought to recognize that poor people are entitled to dignity and a decent income through welfare.

Elman's idea in turn was taken up by a member of Lindsay's Manpower Commission who said that he wouldn't try to place minority workers as taxi drivers because that "dead-end job has no future" and, besides, it "involves too little pay for too much work." Anyway, the idea that the poor should be encouraged to work was more generally dismissed as reactionary, the Northern equivalent of the forced labor and debt bondage of the South.

Congress tried to encourage work through the WIN (Work Incentives Now) program, but the program was systematically subverted in New York. Lindsay strongly supported job training, but to the exclusion of job placement, for welfare clients. The assumption was that job training would prepare welfare clients for the high-paying jobs in which minorities were underrepresented. Typically, welfare workers received more credit for placing people in job training programs than for actually getting them a job. In time, the original idealistic motives for keeping poor people out of low-paying jobs was replaced by a new motive; job training programs became a rich source of both patronage and votes in minority areas.

What stood behind the welfare revolution was a new conception of liberalism that would begin to play itself out in a variety of areas, from the idea of victimless crimes to the rights of the homeless, but that first appeared in connection with welfare. Dependent individualism yoked together the ACLU's conception of an absolute right to privacy and to the lifestyle of one's choosing (regardless of the social cost) with an equally fundamental right to be supported at state expense.

Former *New York Times* editorial board member Roger Starr tells about an encounter between Lindsay and an angry welfare mother at a public hearing. "I've got six kids," the mother shouted, "and each one of them has a different daddy. It's my job to have kids, and your job, Mr. Mayor, to take care of them." The mother was a dependent individualist. Not only was she entitled to public support, but she was entitled to that support on her own terms. With the arrival of dependent individualism, New York gave up on the idea of the city as an engine of minority mobility. Not surprisingly, and for the same reasons, an increasing number of New Yorkers began to give up on the city.

Of New York in a healthier time Jane Jacobs wrote, "A metropolitan economy, if it is working well, is constantly transforming many poor people into middle-class people, . . . greenhorns into competent citizens. . . . Cities don't lure the middle class, they create it."

Labor leader Victor Gotbaum, one of New York's most influential liberals during the 1970s and 1980s, was typical of those who would have none of Jacobs's view. He denounced those members of the school board who were "enamored of middle-class, two-parent families with children who don't have sex." He also told the *Times* that middle-class values were "contrary to the environment and lives of students in the school system." Gotbaum's New York had invested in failure, as had a dependent individualist welfare mother who had refused to either look for a job or even enter a job program, explaining, "It's my career. I can't get any old job. . . . If they want me off welfare, give me what I want to take."

The irony of New York's welfare revolution was that in the name of redressing old injustices that treated African-Americans as less than full citizens, it recreated their second-class standing through liberal paternalism. In the name of antipoverty, it trapped people in dependency; in the name of eliminating invidious distinctions, it effaced the importance of character; in the name of the old Leninist dogma of "the worse, the better," it left the city far worse.

THE DISTRICT OF COLUMBIA

5. SNCC in Power

When viewed from a distance, it's hard to understand how the District of Columbia—the center of the most prosperous metropolitan area in the United States, the city with the highest black median income in the country, an area where until very recently government spending had all but eliminated the conventional business cycle—could be morally and functionally bankrupt.

By what flaws has prosperity produced a city with a doctor-to-population ratio nearly twice that of comparable populations and yet with the highest infant mortality rate in the United States, a city with the highest ratio of public employees to population where there is no money to repair the roads and where emergency medical service is a sometimes thing while police crime is a constant menace? By what exception is D.C., the most heavily subsidized city in America, almost the sole major city with both falling employment and a still rising crime rate?

It's hard to remember the enormous hopes that were once vested in a city where the heroes of the civil rights movement came to power collectively. Like the Third World revolutions that inspired the civil rights soldiers of SNCC (Student NonViolent Coordinating Committee), the struggle for D.C. home rule was invested with all the significance of a struggle for national self-determination. And as in Ghana, home to Stokely Carmichael's hero Prime Minister Kwame Nkrumah, the promise was to not just imitate the white West but transcend it. D.C. civil rights veteran Kojo Nnamdi, now of WHMM-TV, explains: "We were not looking to run business or government the way white folks did. We were looking for the opportunity to run the government at a higher level of integrity and morality."

The District's second mayor, Marion Barry, became the incarnation of the hopes aroused by the movement for home rule. Barry, who saw himself as having successfully merged his personal ambition with the principles of the black liberation movement, thought of his new government as a light unto Africans at home and abroad. Herbert Reid, Barry's legal counsel, spoke of the new administration as a model for emerging peoples, "an example of pride to D.C., to the nation and especially to the international community." Barry himself talked a great deal about the mayor's role in international affairs. He hired the city's first director of protocol to better greet visiting diplomats, and shortly after his election he took a triumphal tour of West Africa, hailed in the *Washington Post* accounts as an example of "spiritual awakening."

With the exception of Detroit's Coleman Young, who had been a labor radical, Barry was different from earlier black mayors, who had been judges, policemen, bureaucrats, or career politicians. He was the first product of sixties radicalism to achieve executive authority, and he brought his old comrades into government with him. Stokely Carmichael's pace-setting book *Black Power*, written with Columbia professor Charles Hamilton, was dedicated to Ivanhoe Donaldson, who was a SNCC veteran; an adviser to the first black mayor of a sizable city, Richard Hatcher of Gary, Indiana (elected in 1967); and right-hand man to Marion Barry. In power with Barry, Donaldson brought together the mix of black nationalism and economic leftism that looked so promising to so many a quarter-century ago. "The District," wrote Sam Smith, a white supporter of SNCC's Free D.C. campaign for home rule, "is leaving behind assimilationist integration, it's testing a new path." And so it did. But what remains to be explained is how some of the very people who brought America up from the depths of segregation were also responsible for bringing the District and its residents down.

It is wrong to blame the disaster of D.C. on Marion Barry alone. To be sure, Barry has played the leading role in his adopted city's tragedy, but he has had a vast cast of supporting players, black and white, few of whom ever questioned the script. Barry, his personal peccadilloes aside, was the carrier of a broad political consensus that emerged in the late 1960s and early 1970s out of a mix of Great Society liberalism and the movements for home rule and black separatism—all of which were leveraged by the threat of renewed rioting.

There are a variety of arguments to explain the District's fall. Mayors Barry and Sharon Pratt Kelly have tended to see the limitations imposed on the city by the home rule charter of 1974 as the source of the problems. This is a matter I'll take up later. Suffice it to say here that there was nothing imposed about home rule that led to the collapse of the well-funded D.C. school and police systems. Local activists have pinned much of the blame on Congress. They may be right, though not in the way they assumed. For twenty years Congress, in the hands of liberal Democrats, turned a blind eye to shenanigans by both Barry and the city's fiscal managers. When Representative Ron Dellums became chair of the House District Committee in 1979, he paid a call on Barry, promising to be "an advocate, not an overseer, for District affairs." The District Committee was, like others with close connection to their clientele, such as Agriculture, an advocate of the interests it was supposed to be monitoring.

In 1995 a long series in the *Washington Post* by Blair Harden came closer to the mark. He blamed demography, particularly a black middle class outmigration to the Maryland suburbs (much of the white middle class had already left) after the 1968 riots. But Harden failed to see that the riots were central. Not only did they hasten the exodus of some of the black and remaining white middle class, but they showed that violence or even the threat of violence paid. To the extent that the riot and the politics that derived from it were the founding event in the current regime, the city's current failures were encoded in its origins.

The city that was reshaped by the upheavals of the 1960s owed its very existence to the fear of riots. Unlike London and Paris, which were great cities before they were capitals, Washington was literally created by Congress. Congress chose a swampy site on the Potomac River in part as a compromise location between North and South and in part to insulate the nation's capital from the urban mobs the Founding Fathers feared. They knew that every form of government had its weakness, and the Democratic disease, as Adams and Madison understood it from their study of history, was mob rule. It was Shays' Rebellion in Massachusetts, an uprising of farmers running whisky to avoid state taxes, that inspired the Constitution. It was the Gordon riots in London, the French Revolutionary mobs, and the march by disgruntled veterans on the temporary capital in Philadelphia that produced the new city of Washington. The capital, laid out in 1792 by an African-American surveyor, was not to be a city but a federal district insulated from both popular passions and the politics of any particular state. Federal supremacy is laid out in the very first article of the Constitution, Section 8, which gives Congress the right "to exercise exclusive legislation in all cases whatsoever" involving the capital district.

The summer 1968 riot that erupted following the assassination of Martin Luther King was preceded, beginning as early as 1962, by a series of smaller outbursts and a rising crime rate in the District. It was followed by another small riot in 1969 and an even more rapidly rising crime rate. Nevertheless, in conventional terms Washington seemed like an unlikely location for riots in either fast or slow motion.

Washington, the first major American city to achieve a black majority, enjoyed both a long history as a center of black bourgeois culture and unprecedented African-American prosperity. Home to the great black abolitionist Frederick Douglass, the District had the largest free black population in the United States before the Civil War. It was the location of the first black bank and the first black college, Howard University, established in the wake of the Civil War. With its large black professional class, Washington was, said sociologist E. Franklin Frazier, at "the center of Negro society."

Duke Ellington; William Hastie, a 1930s civil rights leader and later a federal judge; and prominent social scientists Hylan Lewis and Thomas Sowell were sons of what Leadbelly described in a song as "a bourgeois town." In the 1950s, the District became a leader in integration. Stalwart liberals like Eleanor Roosevelt, Hubert Humphrey, and Walter Reuther pushed through an early end to segregation in the capital, and in 1948 President Truman's executive order banning discrimination in federal agencies opened the door for black advancement. Catholic schools had desegregated before the Supreme Court's landmark *Brown v. Board of Education* decision in 1954. For their part, the biracial public school board quickly moved to implement *Brown,* and by the end of the 1950s, *Commentary,* then a liberal journal, dubbed the city's schools "a showcase of integration."

By the 1960s, Washington was more bourgeois than ever. Demographer George Grier notes that the number of black families in Washington with incomes of more than $8,000 doubled during the course of the 1960s while the number with incomes of more than $16,000 almost tripled. By 1970, reported Grier, there were "actually more black families [in Washington] at these higher income levels than there were white families with the same incomes in 1960." Further, although there was considerable black poverty and the city suffered from the same dislocating effects produced by in-migration as other cities, an Urban Institute Survey comparing the District to eighteen other big cities found that it was blessed with having the smallest proportion of low-income households.

A model for integration in the 1950s, the District became in the 1960s a showcase of a different sort for the young leaders of the Southern civil rights movement looking to make a mark on the big cities. In 1964 SNCC, the shock troops of the Southern struggle against segregation, lead by New York's Stokely Carmichael, began its first major effort at organizing poor blacks in the North. Inspired by rent strikes in Harlem, SNCC began agitating against local landlords in D.C., but Carmichael, who would have been the natural leader, broke with "this nonviolent bullshit" and left both the District and the United States to become a revolutionary touring Hanoi, Havana, Moscow, and Conakry.

During Carmichael's absence SNCC's first chairman, Marion Barry, gave up the Manhattan cocktail and fund-raising circuit to take up the organization's franchise in D.C. Like Barry, a long list of other SNCC activists, including Ivanhoe Donaldson and future city council chair John Wilson, became active in D.C. politics.

Marion Barry, the future "mayor for life," began building his political operation in the District with PRIDE, an organization he began with his second wife, Mary Treadwell, who handled the finances, and his connection to the streets, Rufus "Catfish" Mayfield. Funded by the feds in the wake of the 1967 rioting in Detroit, which left forty-three dead, PRIDE's aim was to use "the hard core of the hard core," the "street dudes." Mayfield, who had a record for auto theft, supplied the young juvenile delinquents and ex-cons. Secretary of Labor Willard Wirtz, fearing more riots, supplied the start-up money. Operating under the banner of instilling self-discipline and self-respect in young toughs, PRIDE bought some peace by putting people to work cleaning parks and killing alley rats. Barry, with his genius for publicity, attracted attention from Senators Humphrey, Brooke, and Kennedy, and after a five-week initial run Wirtz came up with an additional $1.5 million to keep PRIDE going.

In early 1968, Barry's rapid rise to prominence brought Stokely Carmichael, who had become a media star, back to D.C., where he tried to reassert his preeminence. Barry and Carmichael soon clashed. Carmichael, derided as "Starmichael," tried to use the Black Panthers to take over the Barry-run SNCC headquarters in a comic-opera coup complete with an armed attack. The takeover failed, thanks in part to the "street soldiers" Barry supplied, though the SNCC headquarters would later be firebombed.

Barry and Carmichael, both former chairs of SNCC, had a great deal in common. They both identified deeply with the Third World revolt against white capitalist society. Barry at one point took the middle name Shepilov as a token of his identification with the Soviet foreign minister, while Carmichael allied himself with the Black Panthers. Both mastered the rhetoric of roasting "capitalist pigs."

A few years later, when Barry ran for the school board, he pledged to get rid of those teachers who claimed that you can "get rid of unemployment in the U.S." without getting "rid of capitalism." Both of these highly educated men took on the menacing street style that paid enormous dividends at the time and has been institutionalized in popular music ever since.

Carmichael's ideological infatuation with violence separated him from the far craftier Barry, who hedged his bets by giving up nonviolence (without issuing an open call for taking up the gun). In 1967, a year before the Washington riots, Barry threatened that unless D.C.'s housing problems were dealt with, Watts-like violence might erupt. Barry learned to walk the line between threatening violence and presenting himself as the alternative. He explained: "Like I believe, as far as blacks are concerned, we should use all and every means we want to, and those persons who want to go out and shoot policemen, that's their thing. You know it's not mine."

In the revolutionary summer of 1968 that played out against the backdrop of the American defeats in Vietnam and the previous year's rioting in Detroit and Newark, Carmichael took the role of the rhetorical Trotsky to Barry's organizationally masterful Stalin. When violence erupted in the wake of Martin Luther King's death, as it did in many cities, Marion Barry laid low while Carmichael egged it on. "White America killed Dr. King last night," Carmichael told the young men who were about to touch off the D.C. riot. "[They] declared war on us. . . . There no longer needs to be discussion. Black people know that they need to get guns."

Washington's riot was not terribly deadly, as far as conflagrations go: there were twelve deaths, all fire-related. But there was more property damage than in any other riot except those in Watts and Detroit. Almost 90 percent of the rioters had jobs, and of those arrested 80 percent were employed; many worked for the federal government. This was a riot, befitting a city of government workers, against private property, not against people.

King's death released the dammed-up rivers of bitterness that had been built up over three centuries of oppression. But the riot was also, as Sam Smith noted, something of a carnival in the classic sense of the term, a day in which the old roles were reversed or obliterated. In the old order, Washington had been a white city run by the federal government primarily for its own purposes. In the new order, glimpsed during the rioting, the black political awakening would begin to redefine local politics.

The riots cost the city five thousand jobs, as hundreds of burned-out businesses chose not to reopen. It also cost D.C. the new immigrants, who headed for the safer satellite cities of Alexandria and Arlington. Worst of all, it set off middle-class black flight. But this was also a "famous victory" for black militants. A federal government acutely embarrassed by pictures of troops on the Capitol steps and rioting just ten blocks from the White House decided to put more money into local antipoverty efforts, as if poverty per se had been the primary issue.

Looking back, in a 1988 *Washington Post* interview, Carmichael said, "My role would be to properly coordinate [the riot], to inflict as much damage as possible on the enemy and then to receive as much concessions [as possible] from the enemy on behalf of the people." Carmichael never stayed around to collect the concessions, but Marion Barry did.

Carmichael's inconsolable anger frightened liberals, some of whom would have been only too happy to appease him were it possible. Many liberals were willing, even eager, given the opportunity, to surrender their old civil rights principles to a black militant willing to offer partial expiation and the promise of restraint.

Barry, who would later take a bullet from the Hanafi Muslims, was every bit as willing as Carmichael to employ violence. He drove Rufus "Catfish" Mayfield out of PRIDE at the point of a gun. Still, he was different. It's difficult to sort out the mix of idealism and opportunism that drove Barry, but he clearly understood the emerging "race game." "I know for a fact that white people get scared of the [Black] Panthers," Barry explained, "and they might give money to somebody a little more moderate." In a staged scene for a cinema verité movie made by a liberal filmmaker with an Office of Economic Opportunity grant, Barry and a young boy dramatized the riot ideology: Barry, his arm draped around an engaging lad, tells him: "We've got to try to create some love and feeling." But the kid will have none of it and erupts in anger. He calls the police pigs—"nothing but pigs"—his anger escalating each time he repeats the expression. The film ends, wrote Nicholas Lemann, with the suggestion that a great deal of work needs to be done by the Marion Barrys of the world if this cute kid's anger is to be held in check.

Comfortable in both "the streets and the suites," as the line went, Barry was a charming rogue who in a July 1969 interview told the *Washington Star*, "I don't dislike white people. I do dislike white institutions." Barry knew how to both intimidate and entice. By alternating threats and the promise of defusing those threats through payoffs and deal making, he offered liberals a chance to surrender their old color-blind ideals while keeping both a modicum of dignity and their self-image as progressive people. In Barry's version of the protection racket, people could benefit businesswise and keep their consciences clean. A number of supermarkets were looted during the 1968 riot, but Giant Foods, owned by an early PRIDE contributor, went untouched. The donor, a liberal Jew, no doubt had has own mix of idealistic and self-interested motives for supporting PRIDE. In the new Washington, backing Barry paid.

Accounts differ, but it seems clear that in the three years following the riot, Barry received at least $3.8 million in additional federal, largely Labor Department, grants to expand PRIDE. PRIDE moved into job training, ran a garden apartment complex, and opened a half dozen gas stations, as well as candy, gardening, and maintenance companies. "PRIDE," said the director of a would-be competitor, "has an absolute monopoly in the business it's in; its business is the dudes."

All of the PRIDE business except the apartments, which became a cash cow for Barry's second wife and business partner, Mary Treadwell, lost money. But that didn't matter to the "dudes" who went into business for themselves. One of the PRIDE gas stations became a fencing operation for stolen goods; other PRIDE workers, sometimes operating out of the group's offices, according to Barry biographer Jonathan Agronsky, were involved in armed robbery, murder, and drugs. "In 1969 PRIDE employees," notes Agronsky, "were indicted by a federal grand jury for misappropriating $10,000 in federal funds." This produced investigations by the General Accounting Office, the FBI, the Justice and Labor Departments, as well as by grand juries and congressional committees.

All the investigations came to naught. It appears that indictments were never handed down for fear that prosecutions would produce political unrest. When Nixon's OEO withheld some money, Barry intimidated the director, Donald Rumsfeld, into releasing it. According to Agronsky, Rich Adams, a black TV producer with long experience in covering Barry, described how his mau-mauing kept the authorities at bay. If someone questioned Barry's good intentions, his response, said Adams, imitating Barry, was as follows: "Don't ask, honky motherfucker, because if you do, we're going out on the street, and we're going to start a riot and say that the white man is trying to destroy black economic progress." Adams concluded, "This scared the living shit out of these liberals who didn't want any trouble."

It wasn't just liberals who were intimidated. Barry had the police buffaloed as well. "The ghetto," argued the Urban League's Sterling Tucker, "is now occupied territory." The first step in ending the occupation, he argued, was turning over welfare and the police to community control. As long as whites ran the police department, even drug dealers, said Tucker, were just "prisoners of war." But by turning policing over to the healing power of black community control, he expected a therapeutic process to begin that would salve the suffering that had produced the criminality in the first place.

Barry agreed. In the late sixties the OEO funded a Pilot Police Precinct Project, designed to improve police–community relations. The project was supposed to create a measure of community control by establishing locally elected citizens' review councils. It appears that Barry, who had a working relationship with the local (the thirteenth) precinct in Shaw that in effect gave him immunity from parking tickets, wanted a coequal role in running the precinct. In the midst of this dispute, Barry's cars were ticketed by cops from outside the precinct. An angry Barry, assuming he had been double-crossed, reportedly told the cops, "If you write a ticket on that car, I will kill you."

A series of melees between the cops and PRIDE people followed, leading to Barry's announcement on the steps of the District Building that he had "just declared war on the police department and the city." It was a war Barry would win as mayor when he both suborned the department and left it demoralized in the face of rising crime.

Barry's statement on the District Building steps, complete with Black Power salutes by his supporters, again almost resulted in another mini-riot. Barry clearly had the loyal following needed to make good on his threats of disruption. In anticipation of things to come, when Barry was finally brought to trial for the original brawl, he beat the rap with a jury split nine to three for conviction. As both the 1960s and the trial came to a close, Barry was riding high, probably convinced that there was almost nothing he couldn't get away with.

Barry's capacity for investing blackmail and intimidation with the higher moral purposes of the civil rights movement was by no means unique. It was precisely that combination of qualities, packaged as revenge for past injustices, that gave the Black Panthers their appeal. What made Barry special is that he, almost alone among those in the sixties who mobilized what Marx called the *Lumpenproletariat* (the criminal classes Eldridge Cleaver rhapsodized about), was able to harness them to his purposes over an extended period.

In the long run, the willingness of the country to fund the federal government depended on Washington's ability to do good works. In that sense the rise and fall of Washington as a city was not only a barometer of how the federal government was judged but also in part the basis for that judgment. We can measure the fate of American liberalism by the distance between the high hopes raised by the promise of home rule for Washington, D.C., in the late 1960s and the current disdain for the District and its government.

In June of 1996, Harry Jaffe, the coauthor of *Dream City,* an influential book on the District's decline, appeared on Jesse Jackson's TV show, *Both Sides.* There was a lot to talk about. The District's financial collapse had compelled Congress to effectively take budgetary power away from Barry and put it in the hands of a presidentially appointed Financial Control Board, similar to the boards that had helped restore fiscal health to New York city in the 1970s and Philadelphia earlier in the 1990s. Bankrupt, bedeviled by a collapsing public infrastructure, the District had taken three weeks to clear a 1996 snowfall cleared by other cities in three days. The District was losing population at an astounding rate. Between 1991 and 1993 the city suffered a net population loss of thirty thousand, almost as great as the loss for the entire 1980s. In the past, said Washington watcher George Grier, people have been *pulled* out to the suburbs but now people were being *pushed* out by high taxes, high crime, and a lowlife government.

Jaffe tried to put some of these issues on the table, but each time he did, Jackson, who had been elected "shadow senator," the District's unofficial representative in the upper chamber, waylaid the discussion. Jackson insisted that the District couldn't be held accountable for its own decline since it had, by dint of racist opposition, been denied the status of a state. Hard as it is for most people to imagine how a city that receives five times more from the federal government than it puts in could be designated a victim, the claims of victimization are the common currency of District political life.

Councilman Kevin Chavous says, "No one exploits our colonial situation better than Marion." This is true in a way, but a lot of others sure try. Sharon Pratt Kelly, mayor for a term after Barry's jailing for cocaine, with the Reverend Al Sharpton of New York at her side, blamed the city's crime problem on a capitalist conspiracy by the cocaine cartel and gun manufacturers; the more Kelly lost control of the city's finances, the more she campaigned for statehood. Or take the Reverend Walter Fauntroy, the city's former nonvoting delegate to the House, who accused Barry of being the white candidate in the 1978 mayoral election; Fauntroy ran for mayor himself against Kelly and John Ray in 1990 by accusing Ray, who is black, of being "the great white hope of real estate developers."

D.C. suffers worst from a democratic deficit. Its politics have variously been described as "motionless," "stillborn," and "nonexistent." It is a city that lacks a civic life despite its many colleges and intellectuals. Debate on public policy is as unusual as an incumbent mayor or council member faced with a competitive election.

Some have mistakenly attributed this condition to the city's black majority status. But Atlanta, the home of Martin Luther King, and New Orleans—both comparable in size, history, and social composition—have competitive political systems. Yet for all their failings—like the District, both are beset by crime, poverty, and out-migration—neither has had its civic culture suffocated by a cult of personality.

The District difference derives from what's doubly unique about Washington. First and foremost, as the nation's capital, D.C. alone among major American cities lacked its own government until recently.

In countries such as Switzerland and Canada, where the capitals, Bern and Ottawa, respectively, are located in a particular province, the national interest can be held captive to local demands. In the United States and Australia (whose capital is the little-known city of Canberra), special federal districts under direct federal control were created to free the national government from provincial interests in both senses of the term. The problem is that when such districts are created, the local residents are deprived of their democratic rights.

In D.C. the denial of the right to vote in either local or national elections led to a long history of local residents petitioning the federal government for suffrage. An 1846 petition for retrocession to Maryland spoke of Washingtonians as "a disenfranchised people, deprived of all those political rights and privileges so dear to an American citizen." Here was a clear case of taxation without representation. But the locals, notes historian Steve Diner, didn't press too hard on home rule because they were afraid that the capital might be moved out of the Potomac swamps to a more salubrious western city.

The protests, which persisted well into the twentieth century, would likely have come to naught if it weren't for the fact that in the years after World War II they became intertwined with civil rights issues. President Truman (pushed by Hubert Humphrey, Eleanor Roosevelt, and Walter Reuther) endorsed both home rule and representation for the District in Congress. Ratified in 1961, the Twenty-third Amendment, granting the District the vote in presidential elections, began as an extension of the movement to outlaw the poll tax.

In the dynamic that developed, federal antidiscrimination laws for the District, well in advance of comparable reforms nationwide, made the city a magnet for African-Americans. In turn, the growth of the African-American population intensified the support for local control.

Home rule, the election of a local government, and representation—separable issues—were, despite widespread support, repeatedly blocked in the 1950s and 1960s by Congressman John McMillan, the segregationist chair of the House District Committee. If McMillan, a South Carolinian, had been willing to relent after 1961, the District might have achieved home rule, however dubious an idea that is, relatively painlessly. But McMillan refused and in so doing inflicted his greatest damage on the District by engaging it in something of a mock struggle for local liberation, a struggle that, on the surface at least, mimicked both the antisegregation struggles of the South and Third World liberation movements.

According to journalist David Plotz, both the District's business leaders on the Board of Trade and the National Capital Planning Council "directed planning for the entire city—not just the federal areas—between 1926 and 1974." Both vehemently opposed home rule. The two organizations functioned like a shadow government working hand in hand with the District congressional committees and the three commissioners appointed by the federal government to oversee a city that for the most part was well run. Still, under their reign urban renewal had unfairly displaced poor blacks without relocating them. The quip "Urban renewal means Negro removal" was coined to describe the situation in Washington.

Barry and his SNCC allies mocked the Board of Trade as "moneylord merchants" in bed with Southern segregationists in Congress to keep D.C. in "political slavery." Barry threatened merchants with a boycott if they didn't contribute to his "Free D.C." movement. Senator Robert Byrd accused Barry of Capone-like "extortion" and even Joe Rauh, the liberal's liberal, criticized Barry's tactics as blackmail and an obstacle to home rule. Nonetheless, a cause was born.

In 1967 LBJ, unable to grant home rule because of segregationists in the House of Representatives, appointed a black "mayor" and a black majority to the newly created offices of "mayor" and "city council." In 1968 Congress provided for a popularly elected District of Columbia Board of Education. In 1969 it allowed for the election of a nonvoting delegate to the House of Representatives, a post won by Reverend Walter Fauntroy in 1971. Then in 1972, in an act of poetic justice, South Carolina Congressman McMillan was defeated in the Democratic primary by a mobilization of black voters. The path was clear for home rule.

Even with home rule achieved, the rhetoric about D.C. as "the last colony" of the federal government lived on in the new movement for D.C. statehood. "It is not rhetorical whimsy," wrote the often sensible Sam Smith, one of the many white advocates for home rule, "to describe Washington, D.C., as a colony. It is a colony—a lonely and forgotten colony." Here was a municipal case of mistaken identity.

No matter. By 1974, D.C. was—until the spell was partially broken by Barry's fall from grace—bound together in a community of error. The citizens, black and white, of the country's wealthiest city had the pleasure of both living well off other people's money and nursing a great grievance. It was this sense of collective grievance that connected D.C., superficially at least, to newly liberated Third World countries and, more substantially, to Coleman Young's Detroit of the 1970s and 1980s and James Michael Curley's Boston of the 1920s and 1930s.

Probably the most widely used metaphor for D.C. is "Third World city." Initially this was a largely positive reference, as when Barry talked about throwing off "the colonial mentality" and when on his trips to Africa he encouraged comparison between the District and its "sister cities" there. But this was not the case by the mid-1980s, when British leftist Christopher Hitchens wrote in *Harpers* that "the corruption of the Barry entourage is at once so exorbitant and so pitifully small time that it generates routine comparisons to that of some shifty, sweltering Third World kleptocracy." By March 1996 *Newsweek* summarized the city's swing from high hopes in the 1960s to the current morass by saying that Washington was "running a parallel course with some Third World countries" that tried "to put the jobless on the public payroll" and ended up effectively in receivership.

D.C. AND DETROIT

In some ways the black majority city most like Washington is Detroit, where the strong man regime of black nationalist Coleman Young left the city in ruins. Young, like Barry a heroic figure in his younger years, was a member of the Tuskegee Airmen, the famed black fighter pilots forced to fly in a segregated unit during World War II. A veteran of Detroit's fierce labor struggles, Young courageously stood up before McCarthyism, but later in life he, like Barry, reinvented himself as a man "who could talk to the streets." Famous for his lumpen language, Young swore profusely in public; evidently he thought this a sign of his authenticity. And, like Barry, his fellow mobilizer of "dudes," Young was the repeated target of corruption investigations.

Both cities were essentially one-industry towns whose political institutions reflected the insularity and arrogance of their giant bureaucracies. Detroit, a city dominated by the Big Three automakers, was in the sixties as ill prepared to face the challenge of Japanese competition as the federal government has been to face the far more muted federalist challenge to its monopoly arising from enterprising state capitals. Neither city suffered from an excess of the entrepreneurial spirit.

In the sixties both Detroit and Washington were liberal beacons, cities where social programs were initiated in advance of federal action and settings where black workers were able to achieve a middle-class standard of living well ahead of most of the country. Both were rocked by riots in the sixties that slowed down but never fully stopped. Unlike Washington, Detroit, however, never recovered economically. Detroit's descent, dating to both the riots and the onset of Japanese auto competition, has been so steep that large sections of the city have been returned to prairie.

Detroit paid a heavy price for Young's black separatism. Mayor Young made no secret of the fact that he despised the white suburbs that ringed Detroit. The bitter black–white conflicts of 1960s Detroit were in the seventies transferred into the mutual hostility between the city and its suburbs. Richard Sabaugh, a county commissioner of neighboring Warren County, made his contempt clear. "We view the values of people in Detroit," he said, "as completely foreign."

Young's Detroit, wrote journalist Ze'ev Chaefets, a native of that city, had "all the trappings of a third world city—showcase projects, an external enemy and the cult of personality . . . even a quasi-official ideology that regards the pre-Young era as a time of White Colonialism ended by the 1969 insurrection." Detroit may have been beleaguered, but it was independent. In Washington, however, at least as preached by the advocates for full home rule and then statehood, colonialism never ended.

BARRY AND CURLEY: MAYORS-IN-ARMS

But for all the similarities with Detroit, the city Barry's Washington most closely resembled was James Michael Curley's Boston, where another struggle against "colonialism" looked like it would never end. "For the Boston Irish," writes Curley's biographer Jack Beatty, "like peoples emerging from colonialism around the world, Who governed them would be more important to their group pride than How they were governed." Curley is often invoked by Barry's apologists as an example of another charming rogue of a mayor who went to prison and yet came back to be successful—so successful, in fact, that he was immortalized in Edwin O'Connor's novel *The Last Hurrah.* Barry himself has invoked the Irish machines as his model for governing, but clearly neither he nor his apologists have looked very closely at either Curley or his legacy for Boston.

First elected to Congress in 1911 and first elected mayor of Boston in 1914, Curley dominated Boston politics and the political imagination of that nation-within-a-nation, the Boston Irish, from the period just before World War I to the period just after World War II, when, again a congressman, he won his fourth and final term as mayor despite having been convicted of mail fraud. A man of compelling contradictions, Curley cared for the Irish poor even as he had contempt for their helplessness. He made a career of acting out the Irish hatred of the English even as he aped the manners and mores of the British aristocrat. And he made lawlessness almost lovable, as when with typical charm he explained, "I never stole from anyone who couldn't afford it."

The first generation of prominent Irish politicians—such as the first Irish mayor of Boston, elected in 1884—were, like the early leaders of the civil rights movement, actively integrationist. In 1876 Patrick Collins, the first Irishman elected to the Massachusetts State Senate, denounced

> any man or body of men who seek to perpetuate divisions of race or religions in our midst. . . . I love the land of my birth but in American politics I know neither race, nor color, nor creed. Let me say that there are no Irish voters among us. There are Irish-born citizens. . . . but the moment the seal of the court was impressed on our paper we ceased to be foreigners and became Americans.

Curley and his cohort reversed that integrationist emphasis after a bruising battle with a Brahman elite unwilling to make an accommodation with the newcomers. Delivered from their deference to the Boston Protestants, the closest thing in America to the English elite still holding back Ireland's independence, the Boston Irish issued their own declaration of independence. Quoting Boston's Cardinal O'Connell, Curley taunted: "The Puritan is past; the Anglo-Saxon is a joke; a newer and better America is here."

A virtuoso of ethnic indignation, Curley was a master of playing both the bully and the victim at a time when the worst of Irish suffering was well past. If the Irish couldn't climb the economic ladder, they could, under Curley, redefine the rules and revise the past. Curley attacked standards and the merit system as anti-Irish. "In Curley's version of historical revisionism," writes Beatty, "there was an Irishman at the bottom of everything American." The Irish were to be both separate and the best Americans.

If the Catholics couldn't compete with Protestants in the economic arena, declared Cardinal O'Connell, they could win politically through sheer numbers. O'Connell even drew on Booker T. Washington to suggest the need for accepting one's limitations. Beatty argues that this mix of political assertiveness and economic resignation was a formula for envy and hostility, sentiments that found expression through Curley's capacity to conjure up anti-Irish and anti-Catholic conspiracies behind every turn of events. There was always someone else to blame.

Waving the shamrock, Curley, the best accuser of the Yankee, became the voice of "Irish power." He forged a new order in Boston based on the simultaneous distrust of Protestant legal authority (outcomes, not integrity, were what counted) and dependence on government (he would first succor and then snare the Irish with a local welfare state).

"Government," claimed Curley, "was not created to save money and to cut debt. But to take care of the people. That's my theory of government." And take care he did, at least in the short run. According to the Municipal Research Bureau, by 1948 "the number of city employees on Boston's payroll was 45 percent larger than the average for the eight largest cities. . . . One of every 14 residents—some 55,000 people—lived in public housing." It was the highest proportion in public housing of any city. Moreover, by padding the payrolls, Curley's welfare state produced the highest per capita expenditure for police and fire of any major city. As Steve Erie noted in *Rainbow's End,* the upshot was that "with the highest tax rate in the country, the city's property owners groaned under the weight of the local welfare state, Irish-style."

According to a respected contemporary observer, the consequence of Curleyism was "a creeping paralysis which [was] slowly destroying Boston as a business center." To avoid the crushing weight of Curleyism, downtown property owners sometimes chopped off vacant upper stories so as to reduce confiscatory assessments, and not a single new "office building was constructed in the downtown area between 1927 and 1958."

But as the city budget swelled, the economy shrank, and the property owners weren't the only losers. "Many Bostonians," Beatty acknowledges, "were worse off in 1950 than they or their families had been in 1914 and Curley was a major reason why." In the long run, government workfare had, like the dole itself, produced a people entitled to their poverty, but little more. Politically, it reproduced the resentments that Curley used to cadge votes time and again. Says Beatty, "Curley had a stake in leaving basic problems unsolved, the better to manipulate the frustrations that meant votes to him." At the hands of Curley's cunning, the sweet salve of righting past injustice foreclosed the future of a people whose leaders were more interested in spite than in success. Beatty concludes, "Curley emerges as a contemporary, a prince of our disorder."

Curley's Boston was very much a preview of Barry's Washington, except that the politics, as the systematic organization of hatreds, was in D.C. organized around the city's supposed colonial status. Like Curley fighting the Yankees as the most recent incarnation of British tyranny, Barry fought the opponents of home rule and then statehood as latter-day segregationists.

6. The Great Society City

In the mid-1960s the District of Columbia became the proving grounds for Great Society social experiments. Most failed, but federally funded social programs succeeded as a training camp for future minority leaders. In the District the absence of a local government made the poverty programs—many of which drew on the political talent that had been developed by the civil rights movement—a government in waiting.

Social scientist Sar Levitan observed that the "expansion and proliferation of federal social programs" in the District was "staggering." From 1965 to 1972, D.C. received grants from more than three hundred federal programs. It had eleven manpower development projects alone. According to Levitan, a Great Society supporter, D.C. received "three times as much assistance as other areas" and almost twice as much when the direct federal annual payment was not counted. Federal matching formulas moved money away from basic city services and toward "human renewal" programs like job training and community development, which were carried out with "maximum feasible participation" on the part of the poor who were to be helped.

In the early 1970s the *Washington Post* described the already littered landscape of all the programs that had been created:

> The War on Poverty is now 6 years old. Six major offensives have been launched against the problems of mid-city Washington residents. . . . Each added another layer of neighborhood organization to the political map of the inner city. . . . Each federal policy decision . . . created a new generation of federally funded local organizations in central Washington, each designed to remedy the faults of its predecessors, each placed on top of its predecessors like geological strata. . . . The

citizen of the inner city may find himself to be the constituent of four or five major organizations.

Even before the city achieved home rule, even when everything the District did was subject to the whims of its de facto administrator, Congressman Jim McMillan, the segregationist from Florence, South Carolina (population twenty-five thousand), its payroll kept expanding to match the federal growth.

For most other cities—except New York and, to some extent, L.A.—the growth of this array of federal community action, or antipoverty, programs threatened the (largely white) Democratic Party political organizations. But in D.C. direct federal rule meant that there was no local political organization to put up a fuss, as Mayor Daley had done in Chicago. In Washington, the new social programs could proliferate virtually without opposition. In a city united in its support of the Great Society, a city without either a white working class or Republicans, there could be a program for every problem.

The infusion of Great Society money encouraged the District to take on large new functions. The city began delivering a vast array of social services to those on welfare—teaching skills to the unskilled and the unemployed; directly delivering health services; building and restoring homes; and even, as in New York, establishing an undergraduate college and a law school. At the time, this all seemed promising.

Many of the services were intended for "Mr. Jones," the prototypical displaced agricultural worker. In 1963 the Urban League drew up his profile:

> Born and raised in rural Georgia, with only a ninth grade education, the 33-year-old Mr. Jones sought work in other Southern cities before coming to the District. He moved in with his uncle and found work as a $45-a-week hospital orderly—one of the city's many service-industry jobs that required no special skills.

"Mr. Jones" was lucky to find work; many like him didn't.

Faced with a large population of displaced agricultural workers with few of the skills needed for a modern economy, Sterling Tucker of the Urban League saw a chance to give the new arrivals a foothold in the urban economy. He envisioned turning each of the city's problem areas into arenas for employment. Tucker proposed, for example, to have welfare investigators "hired right out of the ghetto, indeed from the welfare rolls," and put on the payroll. "Illegitimacy," he argued, "is a fact of life. Middle-class moralizing won't make it disappear. . . . Ghetto residents, welfare recipients, should be given the chance to teach and administer programs to deal with the problem." Tucker argued for the creation of a variety of new job titles in social work and teaching, such as teacher's aid, teaching assistant, and supervising teacher, to provide a mobility ladder for the new workers brought into the social service and school systems by federal money.

Much of what Tucker called for was implemented. This all made sense of sorts in that while Congress created a one-to-one match—federal to city money for welfare—in the name of rehabilitation, it created a three-to-one federal match for money spent on social services. The upshot, reported Sar Levitan, was that it would be "a full-time job for a public assistance recipient to take advantage of all the available welfare subsidies and services." As early as 1972 a Congressional report scolded the District for mismanagement and for believing that public spending could "solve all problems."

The vast expansion of city employment and city expenses got an additional push from Jim McMillan and the members of his House District Committee, like William Natcher of Kentucky. They used the District government as a vast patronage pool for their white cronies and campaign workers. McMillan, who once had a load of watermelons dumped on the desk of de facto mayor Walter Washington, loved pork barrel spending. From 1959 to 1972, the last thirteen years of McMillan's reign over the House District Committee, the D.C. payroll roughly doubled to forty thousand workers and spending jumped fourfold. But the growth didn't stop there. Under D.C.'s first elected mayor, Walter Washington (1974–1978), city government grew by an additional 30 percent, adding almost ten thousand more public employees. In the interest of racial harmony, all of this was done by way of "adding jobs rather than replacing whites."

The bloat, waste, and corruption of D.C. government was already much in evidence in 1972, when the Nelson Commission, created to assess local governments, found the District's "personnel system significantly less efficient than those in 12 other cities surveyed." D.C. had between 1 1/2 and 3 1/2 times more personnel workers than other cities despite the fact that much of the personnel work, such as administering the civil services exams, was done by the federal government.

Commission member Senator Daniel Inouye of Hawaii discovered that the city had twenty-three officials—including the recorder of deeds and the civil defense director—driven around by chauffeurs. He also noted that the city maintained an expensive houseboat, with cooking and sleeping facilities, ostensibly to take once-a-week water samples from the Potomac. Further, the Commission found that while the District's revenues had grown dramatically, expenditures rose even more dramatically, as the mission of government and the city expanded.

In an account still apt in 1996, Senator Inouye discovered that the school system didn't know how many students it had. Assessing the rest of the government, he concluded that administrators who left millions of dollars in purchase orders "in someone's drawer" and department heads who carried hundreds of unauthorized employees on their payroll had created "a critical situation" that put "the District Government's credibility at stake." In what would become standard rhetorical procedure, an aide to "Mayor" Walter Washington attacked Inouye as a segregationist of sorts, "one of the city's masters."

Government was so large and inviting that there was scant interest in the private sector on the part of either local residents or the liberal whites drawn to D.C. during the the years when the Kennedy and Johnson presidencies promised, with some success, to rectify past racial injustice. The white liberals were part of a broad transracial consensus in liberal D.C. for remaking the city in the image of the Great Society.

The local bias against business, or at least small business, was in tune with the Galbraithian tenor of the times. Andrew Brimmer, now chair of the Financial Control Board overseeing a bankrupt D.C. and then the first black on the Federal Reserve Board, saw little promise in black capitalism "founded on the premise of self-employment." Small business and self-employment, Brimmer argued, were "a rapidly declining factor in our modern economy." It was certainly a rapidly declining factor in D.C., where government employment was the measure of all things. "Growing up in Washington," notes Dwight Cropp, now a George Washington University vice president, "you naturally aspired to a government job and we didn't much distinguish between working for the 'feds' or working for the city."

In a city where "government was the be-all and end-all, Marion Barry didn't stand out as particularly statist," says Cropp. When Barry was elected to the school board in the early 1970s, his fellow board members included a variety of leftists, among them two supporters of the radical D.C. Statehood Party who hoped to establish a socialist, if not a Marxist, commonwealth. The first race for D.C.'s nonvoting delegate to Congress in 1974 included three Marxist candidates, with the radical Statehood Party polling even with the Republicans across most of the city.

Hopes were running high when the city finally achieved home rule in 1974. Blacks may have hoped for a Black Zion, but that sentiment overlapped and included white hopes for a New Jerusalem, a light unto the other cities. Sam Smith, a local white activist whose book *Captive Capital* is the best account of those years, summed up the governing assumptions: "Washington is not only ready to govern itself; it is ready to show a good many other cities how."

These hopes were unrealized under the city's first elected mayor, Walter Washington, a familiar and uninspiring figure. Elected in 1974, Mayor Washington had already served for seven years as the city's First Commissioner or de facto mayor, having been appointed by President Johnson in 1967. A career bureaucrat in public housing—initially in the District and then in New York, working for John Lindsay before returning as First Commissioner—Walter Washington was the "walking mayor," who, says D.C. historian Sam Smith, spread the word about LBJ's Great Society to the people of the District.

After winning election in 1975, Walter Washington declared, in the language of the Great Society, "We will make this a model city." But the new mayor did little to satisfy the yearnings for a political rebirth of the District. Walter Washington was a quiet, behind-the-scenes player married to a member of the city's black elite. Congress, assuming that accommodating men like Walter Washington would continued be elected, gave the mayor's office sweeping powers. The office of the mayor had broad authority to spend as it saw fit as well as to hire and fire.

Walter Washington made little use of these powers to further his own political ends. Rather than bring in fresh faces for a fresh start, District agencies continued to be run by the same largely white bureaucracts appointed prior to home rule. Faced with a tight budget triggered by a national recession, the fiscally responsible Mayor Washington suggested a modest tax increase to balance the city's ledgers. The proposal was immediately attacked on behalf of business by Marion Barry, chair of the finance committee of the District's first elected city council.

Barry had long been a thorn in Washington's side. In part it was a clash of generations. The older, more courtly Washington had insisted that "nothing was relieved by the riots," while Barry had made himself indispensable because of the riots. The two men had danced a *pas de deux*. Time and again Barry would lead protests against police brutality and city hiring practices in front of the District offices, invoking the danger of violent outbursts, only to later slip into Walter Washington's office to quietly confer on how to cool things off.

Home rule made Walter Washington an elected mayor, but it also made Barry a member of the city's first elected city council, a perch he used to launch guerrilla forays against the mayor. Utilizing his ball-and-socket flexibility—Barry liked to brag that he was "a situationist"—the challenger attacked the mayor from the right for raising taxes to balance the budget and from the left for racist and sexist police-hiring practices. The tax increase was tiny and the District police corps was already half black with what may have been the largest percentage of female officers in the country, but, no matter, it all kept the old man off balance.

Barry, records historian Steve Diner, attacked the "bumbling inefficiency" of Walter Washington's administration, staffed, Barry exclaimed, by "hacks and retreads "from the pre–home rule era. Barry, like John Lindsay a decade earlier, exuded energy and enthusiasm. He promised to make the social service bureaucracies work for the people. He promised, in short, the true beginning of a new government, the real birth of the liberated District of Columbia.

7. Marion Builds His Machine

It was a chance meeting that opened into an emotional inferno. I was walking through Thomas Circle when, unsure of which street to take, I looked around for an intelligent face to get directions. The person I asked, an attractive African-American in her late forties, was a good pick. She was, it turned out, not only a native Washingtonian but also an architect, and she was only too happy to tell an inquiring visitor about the history of the circle. As for directions, she suggested I walk along with her for a few blocks, after which it would be easier for her to show me how to get to my destination. But after walking just a block, she stopped short, her face and manner changed. She was agitated, and her soft voice gave way to near shouting: "He's always been a thug, always been good at getting other people to take the fall."

The "he" was Marion Barry. Without my realizing it, we had just walked in front of the Vista Hotel, the site of the famous drug bust in which Barry, long a regular drug user, was caught with crack cocaine and an old flame in a sting operation that produced the now famous line "The bitch set me up." The very sight of the Vista set off wildly contradictory emotions in my guide that were clearly close to the surface. She had mistakenly assumed I realized where we were, and she, expecting a comment from me about Barry, defensively set off on a monologue. She denounced Barry for the way he had not only "ruined the city" but had left her "feeling foolish for being part of [the] place." Barry and his "thugs," she said, were an embarrassment. But then she, perhaps caught in her own internal debate, my presence only a trigger, denounced the police for treating Barry unfairly: "Why did the police have to go after him? We would have gotten rid of him."

When she realized what had happened, she winced. Embarrassed at the way she had bared her emotions, she hurried off, but not before telling me, "My friends and I once placed enormous hopes in that man and this city."

Marion Barry's brilliance was twofold. First, like Curley, like Robespierre, Barry learned how to incarnate the hopes and ideals of his followers. Second, he figured out how to use D.C. government to meld the two streams of black migration—the "peasants" and the professionals—into an electoral machine.

Barry first won the mayoralty in 1978, not as a "race man" but as the candidate of white liberals in a three-way election. He played John Lindsay, the fresh face of hope, to incumbent Walter Washington's tired, old Robert Wagner. His rivals were Washington and City Council President Sterling Tucker.

Barry depicted Mayor Washington, the candidate with the strongest support from the municipal unions, as a man of the old order, an Uncle Tom from the pre–civil rights past. Walter Washington split the bulk of the black vote with Sterling Tucker, who was backed by the black ministers and who ran the most race-conscious campaign. Tucker's key supporter, Reverend Walter Fauntroy, the District's nonvoting delegate to the House of Representatives, suggested that Barry, with his white liberal support, was a Caucasian tool, perhaps even an instrument of that supposed and feared white conspiracy known among African-Americans as "the Plan." "The Plan" was the fear by blacks, fueled by the gentrification of Georgetown that had displaced many black residents, of a plot to regain the District for white power.

Barry won white liberals in Ward Three and the *Washington Post* by promising to bring the moral energy of the civil rights crusade to the problems of urban poverty. At the time, at least to his admirers, Barry seemed to charm and elevate everything he touched—including his old marks, the "moneylord merchants" at the D.C. Board of Trade, who contributed heavily on the promise of reduced taxes. He enthralled the *Washington Post,* whose editorials swooned over his "commendable capacity for growth." Most surprising, Barry also won the support of that "army of occupation"—the police—who, along with the firefighters' and teachers' unions, were promised hefty annual raises.

With all three contenders black and the race tight, Barry, a great campaigner, narrowly won the Democratic nomination and thus the mayoralty on the basis of his white and gay support. Barry's white vote, plus the victory for Betty Ann Kane, a white, in winning an at-large council seat, set off warning flags among black nationalists. In a widely quoted column in the *African-American,* Lilian Wiggins warned that "unless there are some changes in our [black] voting pattern, four years from now we will be attending the inauguration of Washington's first white mayor." Milton Coleman's column, in the *Washington Post,* similarly suggested that Barry's white margin of victory could be "seen as an ominous sign that black political power . . . still in its infancy, is already on the wane."

Barry took the warnings to heart. He would never again be "out-demagogued" on race. The racial divide had been noticeably absent from the first two D.C. mayoral elections, in 1974 and 1978, as blacks and whites divided their voters in an almost identical pattern. But in 1982, Barry sought reelection and cruised to victory against former Department of Housing and Urban Development (HUD) secretary Patricia Robert Harris, a light-skinned African-American, on a "blacker than thou" platform; Ivanhoe Donaldson, Barry's alter ego and SNCC comrade, explained that "there has always been a black candidate in D.C. elections and Marion is that candidate."

There was a mood of exultation when Barry took over. The torch had been passed to the best and brightest of the new civil rights generation. "The optimism of the civil rights movement was their engine that first time around," said Barry adviser James Gibson. "With their hands on the levers of power for the first time, anything seemed possible."

Barry inherited both a budget deficit and a booming economy. His initial skill at handling the short-term financial crisis won him the goodwill that obscured a relentless process of machine building. Ever since he had been at PRIDE, Barry had been crafting a prototype electoral vehicle. Once in office, he had the tools to build a full-scale model. With the aim of simplifying oversight of D.C., Congress had created a powerful Office of the Mayor with sweeping authority over hiring and firing.

And hire he did. Using the city's rapidly growing tax receipts as his campaign chest, Barry was creating a base of government employment far larger than the official figures on the number of public employees. He appointed Tucker and Washington supporters to visible positions while greatly expanding the minority set-asides for city contracting. Similarly, the social programs run by the ministers, who had supported Tucker, received healthy infusions of support.

The new mayor also spread the largesse by insisting that white developers take on black partners for city projects. Finally, for the "street kids" he had a misnamed Summer Jobs Program, which usually involved neither jobs nor a program but, rather, "walking around money" for future voters.

In 1984 the city's decade of home rule was celebrated as a great success. A retrospective on the first ten years of home rule by Richard Cohen, a *Washington Post* columnist, expressed the conventional, if contorted, wisdom. "Before home rule," he acknowledged, "there were two trash pickups a week; now there is only one. Before home rule, the traffic signals worked; now they don't. . . . But the ultimate importance of home rule is not in efficiency, but in pride." The District, Cohen insisted, without a touch of irony, was "more than a city or a capital, it was an object lesson for the nation."

The success of the regime Barry had established was taken as an article of faith by liberals like Vermont's Senator Patrick Leahy, who, despite his oversight responsibilities, neither heard nor saw any evil in his haste to make the District into a showcase for progressive programs. "Whatever people say about the District of Columbia today," asserted civil rights advocate Roger Wilkins a few years later, "no matter how difficult things get, I am here to tell you that it is a lot better now for *everybody* than it was before home rule."

The trouble was that the rot had already set in. In 1984 three of Barry's closest associates, Ivanhoe Donaldson, Mary Treadwell (Barry's second wife), and Karen Johnson (Barry's girlfriend), went to jail. Almost from the start, Barry, whom a friend described as a "sociopath," had been able to sell a credulous, liberal city on an image that was wildly at odds with his actions. The D.C. workforce, already outsized, would expand even further, with one exception—the police. A first-rate, relatively corruption-free police department had its budget repeatedly cut and its personnel decisions "Barryized." Police morale and the closure rate on cases began to plummet, while crime began to rise. As early as 1980, Lowell Duckett of the African-American Police Association warned that the police were starting to lose control of the city. But that was a small price to pay, as far as Barry was concerned, for a police force that bent to his will. By the early eighties, thinking he had the police in his pocket, Mayor Marion Barry was openly buying drugs and sex.

In 1981 the first serious drug accusations were leveled against Barry, and he responded with talks of a white conspiracy to lynch successful blacks. By 1982, while crime was rising and Barry was preparing to purchase the next election with a massive buy of temporary jobs, Federal Attorney Joseph diGenova was unable to win a grand jury indictment against Barry despite the sworn testimony of some of Barry's friends. In that same year ex-wife Mary Treadwell (who drove a Jaguar, among other cars) was indicted for misappropriating PRIDE money and "skimming money from subsidized housing tenants." "Barry was never indicted," notes Jonathan Agronsky, "despite being unable to explain how Treadwell had bought him a Volvo, herself a Mercedes plus expensive art and frequent Caribbean vacations, all on her $23,000 salary."

D.C. suffered from the absence of a tabloid press. The *Washington Post,* elevated into a great national paper by its coverage of Watergate, chary of being race baited, left municipal coverage in the hands of Milton Coleman, who was part of Barry's social circle. Racially sensitive policy issues aside, Barry's night life alone would have been meat and potatoes for the *New York Post* or *Daily News.* But D.C.'s only tabloid had already folded, and the remaining papers, the *Post* and the *Star,* both quality broadsheets, weren't tempted by the sensationalism Barry's nocturnal adventures offered.

The press aside, part of the reason Barry's shenanigans went largely unremarked was that the city was booming as never before. Washington had long been well-to-do, but in the late seventies, just as Barry took office, it became fabulously wealthy. The number of D.C. households with incomes of over $100,000 grew by 60 percent between 1980 and 1986 and kept on growing. Many of the new wealthy were lawyers, whose number, growing at the rate of almost a hundred week, almost tripled during the early years of the Carter administration. But it wasn't just those at the top who were prospering. Federal pay for ordinary office workers, who need never worry about losing their job in a city where there is no business cycle, was between 13 and 20 percent higher than in the private sector.

Moreover, the lawyers, consultants, lobbyists, and policy experts needed offices and homes. That set off a building boom that enriched both the Barry administration and local developers, who were given almost carte blanche to build in return for campaign and other contributions. Caught up in a frenzy of real estate speculation, almost anyone who owned property in D.C, and that included many middle-income blacks, saw their real estate soar in value.

Barry, high on the hog during the go-go years, ran numerous fund-raising dinners on the assumption that almost anyone should be allowed to buy access. His rule was "Don't come, don't call" (i.e., if you don't come and pay for a table, then don't call at city hall). But why complain about Barry's shakedown when there was always a private solution available? It was easy enough to just ante up and get into the game.

Republicans are rightly criticized for practicing trickle-down economics, but Democrats had their own version of trickle-down. They practiced what LBJ economic adviser Arthur Okun referred to as "leaky bucket economics." The "leaky bucket" refers to government money that disappears as payoff and patronage in transit to the poor or other recipients. In the case of the District, the money that leaks out of the bucket doesn't disappear, noted journalist Tom Bethell; "it waters Washington and transforms the arid regions of federal bureaucracy into a land of milk and honey." Washington is right beneath the leaky bucket.

By the mid-1970s the Washington metro area had become the richest in the U.S. The *New Republic* noted the contrast between President Carter's populist rhetoric and life in Washington: "The vision of generations of liberals has created a prosperous and preposterous city whose population is completely isolated from the people they represent and immune from the problems they are supposed to solve."

"Blessed" with more money than it could keep track of and too few Republicans to even take notice of, the District conducted a vast experiment in social engineering under ideal conditions. "All that money," an old-line liberal friend, surveying the situation in the mid-1980s, assured me, "is bound to have done some good."

If all the money made a difference, it certainly didn't show up in public housing. Early on in his reign, Barry announced that housing was his No.1 priority. D.C. is a city without high rises—building heights are limited by law in the capital—yet it suffered from the third-highest public housing vacancy rate in the nation, with nearly one in five units boarded up or uninhabitable and a waiting list seven thousand names long. Tenants are forced to live in squalid conditions with leaky roofs, clogged drains, and crumbling buildings—this despite a repair staff twice as large as that employed by most other housing authorities. Like liberals elsewhere, Barry blamed Ronald Reagan for D.C.'s public housing problems. But between 1982 and 1992, while the number of public housing units remained constant, the staff more than doubled and the budget grew from $36 million to $130 million, until D.C. spent four times the average of other major cities on housing.

The problem in part was management. Supervision was so lax that burst pipes were left unrepaired for so long that they could literally turn into waterfalls. In the early 1990s, HUD considered D.C. public housing, which had eleven directors in ten years, the worst managed in the country. It's hard to see how D.C.'s department of public housing could have been run well. Its primary purpose seemed to be creating sole-source contracting opportunities for Barry administration insiders, because, as the city auditor put it, that was "the way the mayor and his cronies [liked] it." One ex-director of the department described it as "riddled with people who [were] not capable of doing their jobs."

If the particular problem was a management that demanded little from itself or its employees, the larger problem was the Barry administration's self-defeating subversion of standards. Partly this was a product of Washington's buck-passing bureaucratic culture. In a town where there is no private sector, where there is no economic competition to speak of, federal work, where employees are headless nails and virtually impossible to replace no matter how dysfunctional, sets the norm. In that sense, the city government is the federal government writ small; no one can be fired for failing to perform.

Administration whistle-blowers like Joseph Gutierrez, who complained about Barry steering contracts to cronies, and Alvin Forst, a cash management analyst who pointed to widespread incompetence and criminality, were fired. "People who are poor managers," Barry explained, "don't come into work saying, 'I'm going to be a poor manager today.' They are either over their head technically in the job or they just don't have good judgment." To some, that kind of reasoning might suggest that poor managers should be fired, demoted, or retrained, but not in D.C. City employment had become an entitlement. The government doesn't try to discipline incompetent managers, Barry explained, because some of them "live in the community." Firing them would mean "getting rid of people you know, and who try hard." Carolyn Johns Gray of Anacostia, a native Washingtonian and activist, sums up the changes Barry and his clique wrought. To Barry's claims that he brought black people into city government, she says, "Nonsense." By the 1960s there was heavy black hiring in local government. "The change was that Barry brought unqualified black people into government and all the rest of us are the worse for it."

If the collapse of public housing points to Barry's influence, the collapse of the public schools suggests broader currents of causation. The mayor has no direct control over the District's board of education, which usually consumes a fifth of the city budget and employs a quarter of the city workforce. The elected board, the highest-paid in the nation, is wildly overstaffed even by big city standards. The schools follow the citywide pattern of a growing number of public employees serving a declining number of Washingtonians. In 1970 the District had roughly 757,000 people and 40,000 city employees. By 1995 it was down to 586,000 people but up to between 48,000 and 56,000 city employees. Similarly, the school system lost about 33,000 pupils between 1979 and 1992 while it added 516 administrators. A 1995 *Washington Post* editorial described part of the make-work structure:

> 15 years ago when there were 150,000 students instead of the current 80,000, the superintendent of schools drove himself to work, had one lawyer and dealt with the public and the press through two aides. . . . Today the superintendent has a chauffeur-driven car, a legal staff of 9 lawyers at the cost of $559,000, plus a speech writer, 2 executive assistants, one special assistant, a legislative counsel, one administrative assistant, a communications director, an assistant press secretary; all that in addition to the vice-superintendent, 2 deputy superintendents and the group of associate superintendents and directors who command a small army of executive and administrative assistants of their own.

The public schools had become an adjunct of the race industry; that is, the primary purpose of the system was to provide protected employment for the black middle class. "When enough people are employed to solve a problem," wrote Fred Reed in *Harper's*, "means become ends." In the District this produced a system of well-paid teachers and of relatively few students per teacher, but the buildings and, more importantly, the intellectual infrastructure were in total disrepair. The one thing the teachers, who were politically plugged into the Barry administration, insisted on above all was that they be treated like other city workers, that is, that neither they nor their work be evaluated by outsiders or by objective (or, as they derisively defined them, "white") standards.

In a process that began in the 1960s, the race industry administrators running the schools, who were adept, noted Reed, "at aligning their principles with their pocketbooks," had redefined in cultural and not academic terms what counts as a good education. Intellectual excellence was defined as white and elitist; as one board member explained recently, "If you want a purely academic experience for your kids, go to a nice little house in the suburbs."

The tragedy is that this travesty of schooling has been defined as quintessentially black when in fact it is the product of an interracial struggle. In the 1950s, when the once sterling and largely black school system was overwhelmed by the arrival of poorly prepared students from segregated rural schools, the board of education and the integrated teaching staff rose to the challenge. As a group, the teachers who made the D.C. schools of the 1950s into a nationally emulated model were pre-1968 integrationist liberals. Surveys found that the teaching staff, almost 80 percent black, strongly approved of the Peace Corps, volunteers, college professors, Jews, and Negroes while they were hostile to John Birchers, Communists, the KKK, and black nationalists.

The children of the black middle class generally received a first-rate education from the system, which was heavily tracked (i.e., students were grouped according to their ability). Some of the high schools, like famed Dunbar, which attracted the kind of talented black faculty who were still denied university appointments, developed a national reputation for academic achievement.

For new arrivals from the South, the curriculum was organized along principles that would have been familiar to turn-of-the-century white ethnic immigrants to the cities. There was an emphasis on self-discipline and the "habits of orderliness." The aim was to acculturate the new arrivals from backward areas, to give them a "compensatory education, which included replacing black with standard English."

A critic of acculturation, William Simmons, complained that the D.C. high school faculty went forth into the classroom "to teach good citizenship and proper work habits." "The teachers," Simmons concluded disdainfully, "believed in the American dream." The problem as he saw it was that these black liberals were agents of white colonialism who were trying to "get the children to act like white people" and thus deny their blackness.

Federal Judge Skelly Wright, a jurist cut out of the Earl Warren mold, agreed with Simmons. "The Washington school system," he opined in a 1967 decision, "is a monument to the cynicism of the power structure which governs the voteless Capital." In response to a lawsuit brought by a local left-wing black activist, Julius Hobson, Wright ordered an end to tracking in the already 91 percent black system. Tracking, argued Michael Tigar, the plaintiff's lawyer, was biased in favor of whites and "consigns the poor and black to an inferior education"; it mislabeled children because, insisted Tigar, anticipating mulitculturalism, it was based on "an irrational ethnocentric value system." Then in an assertion analogous to the argument that higher welfare grants encourage a middle-class lifestyle and hence work, Tigar argued that it was tracking itself, by labeling some kids as slower, that created the backwardness it supposedly reflected. Treat all students the same, he said, and they will all do well academically. "A lot that was done in the name of the civil rights movement," says Anacostia activist Carolyn Johns Gray, summing it up, "undermined the city."

In the name of civil rights, Gray explains, Barry and others undermined the standards people need to live by. In the late sixties, Sterling Tucker wanted to create a new type of cop, the community service officer who "need not meet the standard educational requirements of the force" and in fact might even have a minor criminal record. "It is possible," Tucker asserted, "to actually lower standards, academic and otherwise, without impairing the quality of service to be rendered." Tucker got his way. Nowhere was collapse of standards more apparent than on the D.C. police force. The lowered physical, social, and mental qualifications for joining invited a flood of criminals onto the force. D.C isn't unique in that regard. New Orleans suffers from an even greater share of rogue cops.

The District, however, is doubly unique when it comes to crime. It has far and away the most police per capita of any city (without even counting the Park, Metro, Capitol, Executive Protective, and other federal forces in the city), and it is almost the only major city where crime continued to rise in the 1990s. All in all, in addition to the roughly four-thousand-member Metropolitan Police Force, there are twenty-four law enforcement agencies in the District with an additional seven thousand officers. The seven-thousand force alone is, as David Boldt of the *Philadelphia Inquirer* has noted, about the same size as the U.S. force set ashore in Haiti. The federal officers excluded, D.C. spends twice as much per capita on policing as Philadelphia, and yet it has an even higher crime rate. In fact, in D.C. (a perennial candidate for murder capital of the nation) the violent crime rate is comparable to the rate in jobless cities like Camden, New Jersey, and Gary, Indiana, where the state police had to be called out to restore order.

D.C. suffers from all the problems of the other major cities. As with Atlanta, it's strained by a social and family breakdown so severe that not even the economic boom both cities experienced in the 1980s could stem a rising crime rate and an accompanying suburban exodus by the black middle class. While intact black families have moved to Prince George's County, Maryland, the percentage of D.C. black families headed by a single parent tripled over the past quarter century from 25 percent to almost 75 percent. And, like most major cities, D.C. was hard hit by the crack epidemic that began in the mid-1980s and is only now slowing down.

Teen violence grew so rapidly in the late 1980s that panicked Washingtonians called for drastic measures. In the wake of two late night car crashes involving the mayor's limo and reports of almost epidemic drug use among city employees, columnist William Raspberry wanted to call on federal troops; others wanted to call out the National Guard. Senator Warren Rudman, speaking of "blood running on the streets like some Third World capital," was one of many in Congress who wanted to end home rule where police matters were concerned.

In 1989, as Barry's drug problem became a national story and Washington was acclaimed the murder capital of the country, Raspberry asked, "What do we do about our embarrassment of a mayor?" The answer, thanks to the federal attorneys, was to entrap Barry into using cocaine in front of a camera.

As with the Simpson trial, it looked like an open-and-shut case. But Barry's lawyer Keith Mundy had considerable experience winning acquittals for public officials before D.C. juries. Two of his earlier clients walked, namely, Sterling Tucker, who had been accused of being on the Howard University payroll at the same time he was on the city council, and the president of the misnamed University of the District of Columbia (it's largely a remedial institution where most freshman read at a ninth-grade level or less), who was accused of diverting school funds to his own use.

In the Barry case, Mundy launched a two-prong defense. First, he argued that Barry had been set up, entrapped by the white power structure. Second, he launched what he called his "Kunta Kinte defense," named after the protagonist from *Roots.* In order to even the score for past racial abuses, for what had been done to Kunta Kinte, Mundy called on the overwhelmingly black jury to acquit even if the evidence pointed to guilt. The jury went almost all the way in nullifying the evidence and convicted Barry of the least of the charges, one misdemeanor count. Presiding U.S. District Judge Thomas Penfield Jackson blasted the jury nullification. He said he had "never seen a stronger government case." "The ultimate irony," wrote Juan Williams of the *Washington Post,* "is that if this guy were white, black people would be on their hind legs screaming."

The trial further polarized a city already divided by Barry's escapades. Black radio host Cathy Hughes, known for her diatribes against Hispanics and Asians, simultaneously mocked the anger of whites and calumniated many African-Americans by insisting that "whether or not he [Barry] does drugs is not of importance to the black community." At a time when many in the middle class already felt they were fleeing a combat zone, columnist James Strong of the black newspaper *Capitol Spotlight* called for a civil war to settle the issue: "So far as I am concerned, Washingtonians need to engage in a good old-fashioned, blood-soaking race war."

In no other city, not even Coleman Young's Detroit, where the mayor was oft investigated but never indicted, has there been a mayor whose relationship to law has been so ambivalent and whose relationship to the police so politically compromised. In the name of a higher moral law, the civil rights movement challenged racist rules and regulations. In Atlanta, after the struggle for formal rights was achieved, the movement leaders—for example, Andrew Young and John Lewis, who went on to run the city—reasserted the primacy of our common legal system. In D.C., however, the higher-law argument metastasized into an above-the-law politics. As columnist Mary McGrory summed it up: "Do whatever you can get away with. If you're caught, cry racism."

The liberal businessmen who financed the Barry campaigns probably never fully understood the bargain they were getting into. They probably thought that the protection they won from violence or the opportunity they gained to win favorable contracts with the city were only their due for supporting civil rights. Maybe they told themselves that, at worst, the protection money, the shakedown, would probably only be temporary, until the liberal measures needed to end poverty could take hold. But in buying into Barry, they also brought the demimonde he had leveraged against them into the inner sanctums of the law.

At the same time in 1995 that police officers couldn't file search warrants because they had run out of the proper forms, that two-thirds of the patrol cars were laid up in repair, and that one out of seven cops was resigning from a demoralized force after a pay cut, Barry, newly reelected for a fourth term, was putting convicted murderer and "community activist" Rhozier "Roach" Brown on the payroll as his liaison to ex-offenders. Brown, credited with a major role in Barry's 1994 mayoral election, had galvanized the growing population of ex-offenders—one in eight male residents is in prison, on probation, or on parole—with promises of more "gate money" and conjugal visits.

In a sense, Barry had helped create his own constituency. The open secret of his drug-driven night life, carried out with an entourage of police protection, had helped "define deviancy down." As mayor, Barry had systematically subverted the sense of élan essential to any police force. He used the extraordinary power of the D.C. mayor to name compliant cops to positions above the rank of captain; plum assignments, like guarding the mayor, went to cops who were willing to ignore his own criminal activity. While Barry was leading the high life, the medical examiners' office remained vacant for most of the 1980s and the police struggled with antiquated lab equipment and had computer systems that were never connected. The upshot has been a department whose deep decline has been matched by a rise in crime. According to a study conducted by consultants Booz, Allen & Hamilton for the Financial Control Board, from 1985 through 1996, murders increased by 169 percent, robberies by 50 percent, assaults by 39 percent, and auto theft by an incredible 490 percent.

Worse yet was the atmosphere of thuggery and intimidation. Barry, from his days at PRIDE on, was adept at radiating menace when the situation called for it. It was on Barry's orders that his housekeeper was given the third degree by cops; they were not probing Barry's use of illegal campaign funds but why she had squealed about them. When the housekeeper's son died from apparently unrelated causes, it only fueled the fear. Off the record, numerous political figures in D.C. admit to being threatened directly or indirectly.

The same Marion Barry who has called congressmen "motherfuckers" to their face has, says a distinguished Howard University professor, created a mafia-like atmosphere in D.C. A sobered Richard Cohen wrote that for years many Washingtonians "have longed for statehood without realizing the city's gone one better. It's become a republic, a banana one at that."

8. D.C. Denouement

It looked like the public policy equivalent of the movie *High Noon.* In June of 1996, Congress created the Financial Responsibility and Management Assistance Authority, or the Financial Control Board (FCB) for short, to rescue the District from both bankruptcy and the breakdown of public services. The FCB, chaired by economist Andrew Brimmer, a former member of the Federal Reserve Board, and "mayor for life" Marion Barry quickly faced off. The FCB, given sweeping powers by Congress, fired Vernon Hawkins, a Barry loyalist and bureaucratic overseer of the city's vast social services empire, for incompetence and worse. Barry, vowing defiance now and forever, compared the board to "German totalitarians" and declared "war."

Hawkins, whose fingerprints were all over the failed programs of the past quarter century, was both a symbol of what had gone wrong and an example of how Barry loyalists had been rewarded. An undistinguished career bureaucrat, Hawkins was given control of the vast Department of Human Services, which spends $1.6 billion a year, a third of the city's budget, and employs six thousand people, more than the entire government of neighboring Prince George's County, which has about 250,000 more residents.

This seemed to be exactly like the kind of confrontation Barry needed to reclaim the authority that had been seized by the FCB. "This is," asserted Hawkins, who had organized a bus caravan to welcome Barry back from prison in 1992, "about what kind of city we want to live in, and who we want to control our fate—elected officials or a congressionally appointed board."

On paper the FCB had the stronger position. The federal government's authority to rule D.C. is solidly grounded in Article 1, Section 8, of the

Constitution, which gives Congress the right "to exercise exclusive legislation in all cases whatsoever" involving the capital district. The FCB was created by Congress in the wake of "mayor in passing" Sharon Pratt Kelly's disastrous administration. Elected while Barry was in jail, Kelly won election as a reformer who quoted from "reinventing government" guru David Osborne and promised to make a "clean sweep" of the city's corruption-ridden bureaucracy.

Congress, Democrats included, was initially so delighted to be rid of Barry that they couldn't do enough to help Kelly, a vice president for public relations at the local power and light utility. They gave her an additional $100 million outright, a $300 million loan and permission to override civil service rules to reshape the government.

Kelly, the daughter of a D.C. judge and part of the old mulatto aristocracy, made a hash of it all. In the course of alienating nearly everyone, she doubled the deficit and lost the city's beloved football team, the Redskins, to the suburbs. When she discovered how many middle managers were politically connected to Barry (Vernon Hawkins among them), she gave up on trying to remove them.

Robert Mallet, her former city administrator, says whites were disappointed by how slowly Kelly reduced city government, but for blacks any reduction at all seemed a betrayal. Faced with contradictory pressures, Kelly put her time and energy into building a second city hall. Unhappy with her offices in an old beaux arts building crawling with rats and roaches, she built a new city hall for $150 million—with bulletproof windows for her eleventh-floor office; $140,000 worth of oak and cherry wood cabinetry; and a $50,000 fireplace of polished granite—as the city was going broke.

As her administration fell apart and insolvency loomed, as the city fell further and further behind in paying its bills, Kelly estranged whites with her conspiratorial accusations of white racism and failed to overcome the hostility of poor blacks (Barry backers), who looked on her light skin with suspicion. When Barry returned to government by winning a city council seat from impoverished Anacostia in 1992, her weak hold on the government eroded even further. Back in government, Barry reunited with his "street buddy" from PRIDE days, Rufus "Catfish" Mayfield, and with the Reverend Willie Wilson in leading protests against Mayor Kelly's very limited job cut proposals. By the last year of her term, Kelly spent her time marching for statehood while Congress, feeling betrayed, watched as the city's operating deficit ballooned to 22 percent of its budget, almost four times the gap that New York had faced in the mid-1970s.

In April of 1995, with Barry back as mayor after winning the 1994 election, the District faced its worst fiscal crisis since 1873. With the unanimous support of the Congressional Black Caucus, Congress created the Financial Control Board and gave it wide-ranging powers over the District's budget and management.

In other cities where there had been financial control boards, city officials had cooperated in successful efforts to quickly restore their cities to solvency. (This was true of Ed Koch and Abe Beame in New York in the mid-1970s and of Mayor Rendell in Philadelphia in the early 1990s.) The District was different. Marion Barry alternatively accepted and excoriated the board's attempt to reduce the size, cost, and inefficiency of D.C. government. In a return to what one wag dubbed "the original Barry," the mayor reverted to his old double game of both encouraging street protests, this time on the part of students and public employees, and offering to mediate between the protesters and the powers that be.

Even before the FCB was created, Barry had watched the courts cart away important areas of his jurisdiction, like public housing and foster care. But he was not entirely helpless. Barry retained enormous appeal in the black community, where cutting government was wildly unpopular. In May 1966, a year and a half after Barry returned to the mayoralty, a *Washington Post* poll found that two out of three blacks approved of the job Barry had done and that fewer than one in four thought the city would be better off without him, but 59 percent of blacks and 68 percent of all voters said that Barry should not seek reelection. Of all voters, 52 percent gave Barry a rating of good or excellent, and 70 percent said he was trying to deal realistically with the city's problems. Concluded a despairing Carl Rowan, Jr., "Barry is not just a politician in this city; for many people, he's more like a cult leader. He is to Washington what David Koresh was to his followers at Waco. It doesn't matter what gets reported about him."

A month after the poll was taken, Barry and the FCB squared off. At first glance, the Hawkins firing seemed like an odd place for Barry to make his stand. A *Washington Post* editorial summarized Hawkins's career:

> Neglected children in foster care in 1980s? He was there. Disgracefully poor services for troubled juveniles? He was there. Continuous overspending, a foul and disgusting morgue, a Receiving Home for Children judged by the court to be "appalling and unfit to house animals of a lower level," overnight shelters that turn mothers with frail, cold and sick infants into the streets, questionable contracting and financial dealings at Human Services? Vernon Hawkins has been there.

Ever since Hawkins led the welcome back reception after Barry's return from prison, he had become an important figure for the mayor, the withering

Post indictment notwithstanding. If Hawkins could be taken down, then none of Barry's beneficiaries could be safe.

Barry's chief ally in the fight to save Vernon Hawkins was his "spiritual advisor," the Reverend Willie Wilson of the Union Temple Baptist Church of Anacostia. Wilson, with the help of his parishioners Marion Barry and Vernon Hawkins, had built his own city-subsidized social service empire with government funds. More black nationalist than Baptist preacher, Wilson mixed Garveyism, Christianity, and Farrakhan's Black Muslim teachings into a political cocktail to build a once insignificant congregation into a church with more than three thousand members.

Wilson had first come into public view a decade earlier. In 1987 a black boycott of Chan's, a Chinese fast-food restaurant in Anacostia, was set off by a dispute over whether a partially eaten chicken had to be paid for. When, according to an eyewitness, the patron, an older woman, threatened to have her son blow Mr. Chan's head off, Chan pulled a gun. The patron fled.

Reverend Willie Wilson of the nearby Union Temple Baptist Church took up the cause of the patron, Sarah Carter, comparing her to Rosa Parks, famed for her courageous role in desegregating bus service in Montgomery, Alabama, in the mid-1950s. Reverend Wilson, who, like the young Barry, was in the dispossessed persons business, funded by the city and the federal government, organized a boycott. Addressing a crowd of supporters, some of them yelling, "Fuck the Chinks," he compared himself to Jesus, Martin Luther King, and Gandhi. Mixing the by then empty rhetoric of nonviolence with threats, Reverend Wilson then told reporters that he wanted Chan out of Anacostia, with no discussion, although he added that he was a forgiving man. "We forgave Mr. Chan," he explained. "If we didn't forgive him, we would have cut his head off and rolled it down the street."

Reverend Wilson went on to outline his economic vision, a vision to combat what he called the "psychospiritual AIDS" brought on by pursuing integration:

> Just as Dr. King, when he went to Montgomery with the Rosa Parks situation, began to focus on the larger issue(s) . . . I look at this situation not just as a dispute between Asians and African-Americans, but as a symbol of a new time. It is a time for hope instead of hopelessness, a time for economic parity, a time, in short, for joint ventures. We are talking about partnerships. . . . Don't give me one job and then think you're doing me a favor. Give me stock! Give me shares! Give me economic parity!

The boycott sputtered out, thanks in part to the support the proprietor received from neighborhood black organizations like the Frederick Douglass

Neighborhood Association. Wilson went on to become a major figure in the city. He pursued an alliance with Louis Farrakhan and denounced those city council members who had failed to endorse a resolution praising the Nation of Islam leader.

When Republicans took control of Congress, Wilson railed against the Financial Control Board as just another version of "the Plan," that is, the attempt to restore white control of Washington. He was adept at giving his followers the sense that they were being cheated out of something they were entitled to, namely, control of the city, just as they had been cheated out of control of local businesses.

Wilson had made his mark on the city, demonstrating in a small way what Barry had achieved citywide through the riot ideology. For what finally stood behind Barry's power, despite the formal authority of the Financial Control Board, was the fear, as Barry himself put it, of "blood in the streets."

While Barry promised a church audience that he would never back down from the FCB, that he would never accept a Control Board takeover, his ally, Councilman Frank Smith, warned that social services cuts could lead to civil unrest. In a letter handed out at the church services, Smith spoke of "demonstrators outside city hall making it impossible for people to come and go," and noted, "There are rumors of possible riots."

Marion Barry's fourth wife, Cora McMasters Barry—the couple was married at Reverend Wilson's church—played it more directly. For years, as a professor at the University of the District of Columbia, Cora Barry had cultivated the racial animosities of her students, which, in true Barry fashion, she would also warn about. "Nobody knew it would be Rodney King that would send L.A. overboard. I mean, you never know," she threatened, "what one thing is going to set the people off." The warning got the attention of Gingrich's staff. "The levels of anger and paranoia we're dealing with are truly terrifying. You can't imagine," exclaimed a Gingrich aide, "how volatile this city is!"

Lady McBarry, as Cora was dubbed by *City Paper* columnist Loose Lips, did a good job of inspiring fear. A former city boxing commissioner, forced out in a scandal, she worked for Rock Newman, manager of former heavyweight champ Riddick Bowe and a close associate of Louis Farrakhan. Newman, who ran the 1994 Barry transition, was always surrounded by a phalanx of toughs renowned for setting off brawls, the most famous of which produced a full-scale racial riot in Madison Square Garden in 1996 following a Bowe fight.

Cora Barry, surrounded as she was by men from Newman's entourage, made a credible case for the dangers of an upheaval. At a meeting between the *Washington Post* and the mayor, she spoke of the pain imposed by budget cuts. "What happens," she asked publisher Donald Graham, "if you inflict all this pain now? If you cut recreation, if you cut summer jobs, if you cut all these support systems. . . . You'll have the budget you want . . . and a lot more blood rolling in the streets."

For those who expected an explosion, Reverend Wilson's demonstrations at city hall and at the houses of FCB members were thought to be the lighting of the fuse, if not the detonator. Wilson and his supporters denounced FCB chair Andrew Brimmer as a "handkerchief-head[ed] Uncle Tom" and as "the foolish Negro at the top" "doing the white folks' bidding. Wilson described the Republican leadership on district issues, Gingrich and Representatives James Walsh and Tom Davis, as "Ku, Klux and Klan" and warned reporters, "If you take notes, we will break your pencils. If you record anything we will cut your tape"—this to the cheers of nearly a thousand parishioners.

But the members of the FCB, led by its executive director, John Hill, a mild-mannered CPA, did something astounding for D.C. They didn't fold. They called Barry's bluff. Wilson's demonstrations fizzled as Hill, who had earlier rejected a sewage contract for a Rock Newman shell company, went on an offensive of sorts. Speaking to congregations and civic groups across the city, Hill, a 42-year-old native of the District, drew rousing applause when he explained that Hawkins's removal was designed to protect the city's poorest residents. He described Hawkins's supervision of social service contracts as "abysmal." "It is absolutely incredible," he explained, "that the focus is on [Hawkins] versus the focus being on getting the services to the people. In all this I haven't heard anyone talk about the people who might suffer because of the services not being provided." It was a bull's-eye. Barry backed down, declaring that his "war on the Financial Control Board was over." Wilson vowed to fight on, but something had fundamentally changed in the political chemistry of a sick city.

Hill, a former Government Accounting Office official, had broken through the iron chain of logic that held the city in thrall. It was said that if you criticized Barry, you criticized home rule; that if you criticized home rule, you criticized the civil rights movement; and if you criticized the civil rights movement, you were a racist. This meant that any criticism of Barry could unravel the black ownership of the city and lead to "the Plan," the reconquest by whites.

Herbert Reid, a professor of Constitutional law at Howard University and the mayor's legal counsel through the 1980s, when an assortment of Barry officials, including two deputy mayors, were carted off to jail, placed the iron chain of logic in a historical perspective. Speaking before a receptive Congressional Black Caucus, Reid argued that after the Civil War whites "used the indiscretions and excess of blacks to successfully disenfranchise blacks and take them out of office." A black mayor has to be protected no matter what, said Reid, because he represents the next phase of the civil rights movement. In other words, breaking with Barry would mean repudiating the civil rights movement and a repeat of the white takeover in the post-Reconstruction era.

In a city without political traditions but with a history of past failure, Marion Barry *was* government to his loyal followers. His travails were theirs, and they shared in his struggle for redemption. Barry in this sense was seen as the Rousseauistic incarnation of the general black will. Criticism of Barry was nothing less than treason.

In a city where so many had committed so much of their lives to the achievement of a Black Zion, a city governed on its own terms and independent of white standards, for blacks to break the logic was a treason committed against their own past, a repudiation of the deeply held convictions that had shaped tens of thousands of lives. Jim Gibson, long involved in D.C. government, captured the psychological significance of breaking with Barry when he asked, "If you have been a conquered people, what is your psychology about assimilation, about joining the enemy?" Explained Gibson, "There is a deep maintenance of boundaries. To fully collaborate or assimilate, to some extent, has connotations of capitulation to the conqueror." By 1996, for some at least, what Gibson called "capitulation" looked like an opportunity to lift the city from its knees.

When in 1996 Representative James Walsh, chair of the House Appropriations Subcommittee on D.C., said of John Hill, "I see him as the city manager," he was describing the future of D.C. that was already beginning to take shape. Slowly and steadily, Hill and another accountant, Anthony Williams, the chief financial officer imposed by the FCB, were day by day taking over vast areas of the city's administrative apparatus. Barry apparatchiks made life difficult for them and for Michael Rogers, the city administrator. In every department there were Barry people, ranging from the uncooperative to the downright hostile, who threw up roadblocks to reform. Williams has used his board-mandated powers to have all agency directors and finance employees in the city government report directly to him. "In each agency we'll have a mini Tony Williams," said a school finance official, anonymously. "Tell me that doesn't take the pep out of the mayor's stride."

In November of 1996, following an election that returned the Republicans to control of Congress, the FCB knocked the school board off stride as well. An FCB report found that the school system was long on violence and short on learning—and at a pretty price. The school superintendent's office in D.C. cost $5.9 million a year, as much as two nearby large suburban counties and the city of Baltimore combined. In the wake of the report, a unanimous FCB removed superintendent Frank Smith and replaced him with retired U.S. Army General Julius Becton. Like Mayor Daley of Chicago, who was given extraordinary powers by the state legislature to clean up the schools, Becton and the board of trustees appointed to replace the elected school board were freed from the union rules and bureaucratic regulations governing hiring, firing, and purchasing.

Six years earlier, when the prior superintendent, Andrew Jenkins, had been replaced, a mini *intifada,* complete with boycotts and vandalism, burst out. This time—aside from Hilda Mason of the Statehood Party and Eleanor Holmes Norton, the District's current representative, railing about disenfranchisement—the protests were largely muted. For many, particularly in the white and black middle class, city government had become increasingly irrelevant. When it snowed and the city didn't plow, neighbors banded together to hire minitractors from the suburbs to clear the streets; when the local fire house ran out of equipment, neighborhoods took up a collection; when the schools ran out of basic supplies, parents chipped in.

The FCB might not have been elected, but it seemed to represent the city's best interests, more than could be said for the city's duly elected leaders. At the meeting where the FCB announced the changes, the hecklers, wrote journalist David Vise, were drowned out by the applause.

When the FCB announced the appointment of General Becton to run the schools, Marion Barry was off in Seoul lunching on caviar and chateaubriand on a trade mission for a city without much trade. Returning from Asia, Barry insisted that he was still relevant and, to prove it, announced that because of his efforts a roast duck restaurant owned by the Chinese government would be opening a branch in the District.

Barry might well have made himself mayor for life in a city that lives off income transfers from the rest of the country. In a small city like D.C. with as many as fifty-seven thousand city workers out of a population only ten times larger, public employees and their relatives can elect their own boss. If the number of D.C. voters on welfare and Medicare are added in, those dependent on the public sector have a preemptive claim to the mayor's office. But this would henceforth be a city where the mayor would reign without ruling.

The "green eyeshade" brigade, part of a post-1960s cadre of black professionals, showed that, symbolic appeal aside, the power of both Barry and the school board over the budget (and, hence, patronage) could be pulled out from under them. The promise was to reclaim government for professional competence in the short run and perhaps undermine Barry and the old system over time.

Some Republicans, like Representative Henry Bonilla of Texas, wanted to formally impose the city manager form of government on the District. Barry had bet that Congress would bail him out with new money rather than "wade into the administrative mire of running the city." But others, most notably Speaker Gingrich and vice presidential nominee Jack Kemp, had sought, for their own mixed reasons, to in effect give Barry a financial rescue.

When Barry won the Democratic primary in September of 1994, three months before Gingrich became Speaker, the Georgian called Barry's de facto reelection "a tragic moment for this country." He said it was "a sad commentary" that D.C. had chosen to "vote for a convicted felon." But then Gingrich and Kemp began to talk—shades of the sixties—about making Washington into a model for urban America. Desperate D.C. could be used as a testing ground for Republican tax policy.

I have no doubt that both Gingrich and Kemp, two men with long and honorable records on civil rights, were sincere when they spoke of using D.C. to "redeem" the Republicans for their past failures to support civil rights and aid the inner city. But their attempt to make D.C. into the Republican version of a model city required a breathtaking reversal of reasoning about Barry that defied all the available evidence. Gingrich began to speak of Barry as "the only person who can . . . create a bridge of trust between the poorest black neighborhoods and the outsiders who sincerely want to help."

Like the liberals before him, Gingrich wanted Barry to broker the federal relationship with the "brothers." Gingrich reached out to the mayor, speaking before public meetings largely attended by black Washingtonians. For his part, Barry took to referring to Gingrich, who seemed to offer him shelter from the toughest of Walsh's proposals for cutting the D.C. fat, as a "soul mate." Carried away, Gingrich began to sound like Eldridge Cleaver circa 1965. "No whites, whether they are congressmen from Georgia or reporters from New York," he effused, "understand Anacostia."

There is something about Washington that makes men's minds go soft.

Last summer I heard the Reverend Walter Fauntroy, the District of Columbia's former nonvoting congressman, give a rip-roaring speech on how the Capital City's collapse was due to the way manufacturing had deserted D.C. for the suburbs and south China. Fauntroy's presentation of D.C. as a city victimized by impersonal economic forces was greeted with huzzahs from the audience and high praise from Eleanor Holmes Norton. So thoroughly had Fauntroy expressed the conventional wisdom about the decline of American cities that no one thought to note that the District had never had any industry other than printing.

Fauntroy wasn't alone in his confusion. In a classic case of mistaken identity, both Newt Gingrich and Jack Kemp talked of turning the District into an American Hong Kong, a high-tech commercial and industrial entrepôt. Supported by Eleanor Holmes Norton, they wanted to turn D.C. into an example of what supply-side tax cuts can do. They insisted that if D.C. adopted a Hong Kong–style flat tax, it too could grow at 5 percent a year. They believed that the elixir they were recommending was so powerful that it would overcome not only the District's lack of a commercial tradition but its famously inept delivery of basic services as well. "One of the mistakes in the past," argued Gingrich, "has been focusing too much on . . . efforts to make the bureaucracy work."

Kemp is right to say that Washington taxes are too high. They are among the highest of all the big cities, and the top marginal tax rate kicks in at an incredibly low $20,000. But Kemp is like the guy who has only a hammer and to whom every problem looks like a nail. Higher salaries will do little to reform an Emergency Medical Service that regularly shows up late and at the wrong address.

The D.C. paradigm is deadly services at deadly prices. Fiscal shortcomings aren't what produced a D.C. nursing home with a staff of three hundred for twenty-eight patients, seven of whom required amputations from bed sores that festered and spread because patients were left unattended. The nursing home receives $87,000 per resident per year in D.C. Medicaid money, one of the highest rates in the country. Federal Medicaid statistics show that the District's daily nursing home costs are 160 percent higher than Virginia's, 111 percent higher than Maryland's, 82 percent higher than California's, and even 30 percent higher than New York State's, reports Vernon Loeb of the *Washington Post.* But when a move was made to save $2.4 million a year by privatizing the nursing home, it was scuttled in 1992 by then city council member Marion Barry, always eagle-eyed when it came to maintaining city jobs.

The city council is another obstacle for the local economy. The council was led by a white guy, Dave Clarke, who wears his antibusiness 1960s identity on his lapel the way ex–football players wear their faded letter jackets—long after the glory has passed. Through strict zoning laws and a tangle of regulatory minutiae in addition to the tax rates, the council helped reduce the number of small businesses in the District by more than 25 percent during the 1980s. Council members did so at a profit for themselves: most double as rainmakers for their law firms; so after having created the regulatory maze, they then get to live off it.

Leave aside the fact that the effect of a flat tax would be to give a tax break to well-to-do Washingtonians and local lobbyists. Forget that other cities will resentfully ask, "Why not us?" Ignore the fact that the surrounding jurisdiction to which the black middle class has been fleeing, Prince George's County, has taxes every bit as high as D.C.'s. The proposal is in effect a Republican re-creation of the very policies—federal resources without local accountability—that drove D.C. down in the first place. It is another version of the shakedown/entitlement mentality that led successive D.C. governments to ask for and receive more and more federal subsidies till the District became the most heavily subsidized sixty-one civilian square miles in North America.

Its privileged position notwithstanding, the District luxuriates in the fantasy of its victimization. A few of the District's claims (for example, the complaints about its lack of representation) do have a limited currency. Along with a city manager form of government suitable to its status as a federal district, D.C. should be given voting representation in the House. The original Home Rule Charter, Barry complains, unfairly saddled the district with the bloated pension costs rolled up by Representative McMillan's Dixiecrat patronage machine of the 1960s. True, but this was a manageable problem that could have been easily put to rest during the boom years of the 1980s when the District had more money than it knew how to spend.

Other complaints are just that. Yes, the District is by Congressional restriction denied a commuter tax, but if the examples of Philadelphia and New York are typical, the commuter tax serves to drive business away. Yes, D.C. has no state government, but, again, Philadelphia and New York are hardly well treated by their state governments (some estimates indicate that New York City annually sends almost a billion dollars more to Albany than it gets back in services). Finally, there is the argument that the city has been undermined by the exodus of the black middle class to the suburbs. True, but to some extent this confuses cause and effect. The massive out-migration of the last decade has been driven as much by the collapse of the police and schools as by the lure of the suburbs.

Part of the District's continuing identity crisis is talk from both blacks and whites about how the District has become a Third World city. When Barry took office in 1979, the Third World was, as with Barry's many African trips, a powerfully positive association. But with the seemingly endless slaughter in Africa, the Third World designation has lost its positive aura, so much so that outside the fevered precincts of Garveyites and Farrakhanites, there has been in recent years an ongoing competition to suggest the most horrifying possible Third World analog for D.C. The winner may have been submitted by the Egyptian ambassador, who, struck by the increasingly squalid nature of the city, the breakdown of the water supply, and the piles of garbage, recently said, "Every day reminds me more and more of Cairo." It's a misleading comparison. With reasonable governance, an impossibility as long as Barry is in power, D.C., which is part of the wealthiest metropolitan region in the U.S., could in a few years begin to right itself. There is some support for retroceding part of the District back to Maryland while an expanded federal presence would be established in the remainder, but there's little chance that Maryland would accede.

In other cities former civil rights leaders, such as Mayors Dennis Archer and Michael White of Detroit and Cleveland respectively, have been called on by voters to reform city government. But in D.C., where, as in the Deep South, a competitive political system was never established, reform will have to come from outside the political system. It will have to come from professionals, like John Hill. They are the hope for the District's future.

Not even the integrity and professionalism of the John Hills of the world, however, will be able to redeem the District if it isn't freed from the stranglehold of racialist thinking. In an ironic re-creation of the very segregationists they once fought, Marion Barry and his allies and admirers have created in the District a "volkish" democracy, a Dixie-like political culture based on the organized cultivation of racial resentments. If in the segregationist South "white made right," in the Crow Jimism of the District "white must be wrong." Let me close the discussion of the District with an account of a brief incident that illustrates the difficulties ahead.

In many cites, including Los Angeles and Minneapolis, charter schools—small, self-governing, but tax-funded schools freed from the rigid rules of centralized bureaucracies—have been touted as the antidote to the maladies of public education. Charter schools are in many ways a revival of the ideas that animated the mid-1960s move to "debureaucratize" and decentralize New York City's schools. In New York, decentralization ran aground on the shoals of black nationalism. The District may follow in its path.

In the District, Republicans rightly impressed by the performance of charter schools to date wanted charter schools in the worst way, and that's how they got them in the period before the FCB took over the District's board of education. The first school to be created by the board of education, the overtly Afrocentric Marcus Garvey School, shows that what works elsewhere may fail in the District.

According to the accounts in the *Washington Post,* Susan Ferrechio, a reporter for rival *Washington Times,* went to the Marcus Garvey School to do a report on its progress. While waiting to speak with Mary Anigbo, the principal, Ferrechio briefly took notes on a conversation with a student. When Ferrechio was asked to show her notes to the school secretary, she refused. A struggle followed between the reporter, who was told to get her "white ass out of this school," and seven or eight students, who were led by their principal. Pushed, smacked, and kicked, Ferrechio, minus her notebook, was removed bodily from the premises. When she later returned with two cops and two other journalists, a second round of scuffling and racial insults followed, this time involving the security guard, who was Anigbo's nephew. Anigbo had been charged with assault with a knife in 1986 but was never convicted; the nephew had been convicted of assault with a deadly weapon, armed robbery, car theft, and cocaine possession.

Anigbo, who later accused the reporter of pulling a knife on the students, quickly drew the support of the Reverend Willie Wilson. Later she told a radio interviewer that if she and ten students had attacked the petite Ferrechio, the reporter would have been carried out on a stretcher. Then, in a mirror image of how racial incidents were handled during the Freedom Rides of the 1950s, reported Washingtonian Gary Imhoff, a veteran of the civil rights movement, the school and its supporters first denied the incident ever happened and then insisted that if it did, the uppity outsider had asked for it. Finally, when it became clear that Anigbo's actions were indefensible, Eleanor Holmes Norton, playing the role of the good Southern moderate, came forth to insist that we can never really know what happened and that it was therefore probably best to just forget the whole thing.

The white segregationist South and its cities couldn't revive until, pushed by the civil rights movement and federal law, they at least partially freed themselves of their racist ideology. The same holds true for the District.

LOS ANGELES

9. The Capitalist Dynamo

No city is more easily misunderstood than Los Angeles. Almost impossible to envision when standing on the banks of the Hudson or the Potomac, Los Angeles, alternatively depicted as utopia or dystopia, has repeatedly confounded the assumptions of its detractors. By New York or Washington standards, L.A. doesn't have a downtown—but it does have eighteen edge cities. Then again by East Coast standards, it doesn't have a chief executive; the mayor's authority is so limited that he practically needs city council permission to attend street naming ceremonies. Power is dispersed among not only the fifteen council members but numerous commissions and the five Los Angeles County supervisors. Government is the business of Washington, finance the business of New York, but L.A. has not only entertainment, shipping, aerospace, and high-tech multimedia products but also all the old manufacturing functions, from food processing to plastics, that never were in Washington and have long since fled New York.

Nothing better describes the way L.A. has been misunderstood than the way the South Central district has become a symbol for urban decay and despair. Once a center of heavy industry, now famed as the locus of the massive 1992 riots and a multitude of gangs, South Central has displaced the South Bronx as the country's favorite symbol of urban failure.

Supposedly reduced to an economy of minimalls, check cashing, and nail parlors, South Central served as the justification for a variety of new federal programs. It became the site for the Bush administration's short-lived "Weed and Seed" program, designed to coordinate anticrime and antipoverty efforts and the longer-lasting although equally ineffectual drive to create urban enterprise zones. HUD Secretary Jack Kemp and a variety of Democrats used the rioting of 1992 to revive the idea of urban enterprise zones. Renamed empowerment zones by the Democrats, these selected inner-city areas were freed from federal taxes and some local and federal regulations and received federal matching money for local economic development projects.

Local efforts to rebuild South Central after the 1992 riot included Cal-Start, an attempt at industrial policy aimed, with the help of Southern California Edison, at producing pollution-free electric cars. The major effort was Rebuild L.A. (R.L.A.), an ambitious attempt, initially headed by Peter Ueberroth, the wunderkind behind the successful 1984 Los Angeles Olympics, to bring a substantial infusion of corporate capital into South Central through a series of public–private partnerships.

Like all the reconstruction efforts after major riots—from Detroit, Washington, and Cleveland in the 1960s, to New York's Bushwick in the 1970s, to Miami's Liberty City efforts in the 1980s—R.L.A. has largely been a failure. The post-riot efforts in Detroit generated a vast infusion of both federal and corporate funds; the latter were eventually withdrawn in response to endless race-baiting. R.L.A. quickly descended into a multicultural parody of the Detroit squabbles, as each group demanded that the world be viewed through its own tribal lens. In L.A. neither the corporate nor the government money ever materialized, yet today Detroit is still a wasteland and L.A., casualty of the deadliest urban violence since the New York City draft riots of 1863, is on the upswing. Why?

The public face of South Central has been presented by riots, rappers, and racial politicians (like African-American Congresswoman Maxine Waters). But after two decades of heavy immigration, the majority of the population, although not voters, are now Latino. South Central has more than its share of inner-city problems, including conflicts between blacks and the emerging Latino majority, but also has between 315,000 and 360,000 jobs, the second largest concentration of work in Los Angeles County. Ninety-five thousand people commute *into* jobs there. The Alameda Corridor, twenty-one miles of factories and food processing plants running along the eastern edge of South Central connecting downtown to the port, is part of a manufacturing cluster with a net worth of more than $50 billion.

"People think that because these neighborhoods are low income, there's nothing there," says Linda Griego of Rebuild L.A. To carry Griego's point further, there are different ways to be poor. While the overall L.A. poverty rate is 19 percent, compared to Detroit's 33 percent, many of the Latinos, though under the poverty line, are working poor with a shot at a better life. Some, like Central American immigrants Estella and José Otero and their children, Ashley and Jason, live on a quiet street of well-kept homes only a few blocks from the riot's epicenter at Florence and Normandie. She works as an office clerk, he as a punch press operator. Immigrant energy from workers and entrepreneurs has given the area an economic vitality unseen in the older Eastern cities. "You have to go into the trenches," says Griego. "There you'll find a vast new working class—and a growing middle class—which represent the hope of Los Angeles."

In the midst of the booming 1980s, Mayor Tom Bradley spoke for the city when he promised that "just as New York, London and Paris stood as symbols of past centuries, Los Angeles will be the city of the new century." Bradley's predecessor, Sam Yorty, was indifferent to developing a downtown worthy of a world-class city; his was a city of neighborhoods linked largely by freeways, if at all. But Bradley, in the tradition of the conservative elites who had created L.A., sought to build a Manhattan West. With the help of city-financed tax breaks and the recycling of Japanese trade surpluses into American real estate investments, Bradley gave Los Angeles a skyline.

The culmination of the 1980s building boom came in 1989 with the opening of the 1,017-foot First Interstate World Center, the tallest building in the West. It was preceded by the opening of the Los Angeles Museum of Contemporary Art and of California Plaza, which was designed to anchor downtown shopping. Bradley also supported the building of a subway linking downtown to outlying areas. Like the Chandlers (owners of the *Los Angeles Times* and an L.A. leading family for more than half a century), Bradley hoped to give downtown the gravitational pull necessary to hold the geographically vast city together.

Assuming the country's economic future was in Asia, Bradley saw Los Angeles positioned "to lead the state and the nation into the future." When in the mid-1980s Mayor Bradley spoke of the city as the capital of an emerging Pacific Rim economy, Los Angeles was receiving more than $21 billion a year in federal contracts, largely for military and aerospace spending. A few years later, in 1989, as the end of the cold war coincided with a national recession, federal spending in L.A. dropped by $6 billion, eliminating three hundred thousand jobs. At the same time, Japan's financial bubble, which had financed the overbuilding of downtown L.A., went bust, thus ending the real estate boom. While there was a mild national recession, L.A. fell into its worst economic slump since the Great Depression. Wages dropped a stomach-wrenching 14.5 percent between 1990 and 1993. To make matters worse, the L.A. riot, the great Northridge earthquake, and a series of vast fires and mud slides left the city reeling under plagues of almost biblical proportions.

The Washington Post described Los Angeles as "economically shattered." The newsweeklies spoke of THE ENDANGERED DREAM, THE DEATH OF A COUNTY, THE END OF AN ILLUSION, CALIFORNIA CRUMBLING, and so on. Where once L.A. pessimists had spoken of the film noir tradition of rootless malevolence in the anonymous city, the new picture of hell came from the movie *Blade Runner,* which depicted a starkly divided, permanently depressed city wilting under a steady drizzle of what seemed to be acid rain. Los Angeles, said the *San Francisco Chronicle,* was "the reigning symbol of America's urban decay."

Fate seemed to conspire against the city. Wrote the *L.A. Weekly's* Harold Meyerson, "The loss of professional football, the inability to complete the city's premier concert hall, and the near total failure of post-riot reconstruction" seemed to guarantee a swift and continuous decline. "Clearly," wrote Paul Theroux, in his 1994 profile of the city, "L.A. had become, for many people, just another New York, a large-scale experiment that was going badly wrong, someplace to desert and talk about behind its back."

One of those people who were talking was Wilfred Godbold, Jr., CEO of Zero Corporation, a major manufacturer of air cargo crates. Driven out, he says, by smothering regulations, he closed his Burbank plant and moved its four hundred jobs to Utah. L.A. companies have to navigate through as many as seventy-two city, county, regional, state, and federal agencies, including the South Coast Air Quality Management district, and have some of the highest workers' disability costs in the country. Godbold's was one of many companies lured by recruiters from thirty-four other states who were working the California wreckage. In the late eighties and early nineties, L.A., which had once drawn talent from the rest of America, was losing it to the Pacific Northwest and the Mountain States.

Downtown, for many years the focus of Bradley's economic development efforts, remains in a deep slump. Property values, according to the *Los Angeles Times,* has dropped by two-thirds and a quarter of all office space remains vacant. Downtown L.A. has the dubious distinction of being the only major real estate market where owners of prime office space lose money on their rents. To make matters worse, in early 1996 Wells Fargo (based in San Francisco) succeeded in a hostile takeover of First Interstate Bank Corporation, the largest and last of the big L.A.-based banks. It cost the downtown thousands of jobs and further depressed real estate values. City hall itself is a testament to downtown's vulnerability. Since the 1994 Northridge earthquake, it has been covered with a black shroud to protect pedestrians from the badly damaged upper eighteen floors. The building will now have to be evacuated for several years so that repairs can be made.

Yet by the mid-1990s L.A. was showing signs of revitalization. Los Angeles has remade itself. A geographically vast city (464 square miles), L.A. has moved from a big company economy, aerospace manufacturers, and banks toward a highly dispersed economy driven by electronics and entertainment entrepreneurs. Los Angeles lost its branch plant economy in auto and steel, but those giants were replaced by new firms, "gazelles," often run with Asian entrepreneurship and Latino labor. These gazelles were small, nimble companies, low on cost and high on innovation, with the flexibility to quickly respond to changing markets.

Unlike the Chicago Loop or Manhattan, downtown L.A., with all of 3 percent of regional retail sales and 5 percent of the office space, just isn't that important to the economy. Downtowns are traditionally the site for corporate headquarters, but the L.A. economy isn't driven by large Fortune 500 companies. With more self-employed people than any other city, L.A. leads in both the number of people who work out of their home offices and in telecommuting, which reduces the demand for office space. Most major metro areas have twenty square feet of office space per employee; L.A. has fifteen while New York, home of the "organization man," has twenty-eight.

Between telecommuting and the movie industry's appetite for computer-generated graphics, the average Angeleno has an interest in computers unimaginable in New York or Washington. In addition to the now-ubiquitous urban weeklies listing apartments and/or people eager to meet others, there are three computer weeklies, free and widely available. In a city with more engineers than any other, talk radio, the staple of a city where so many are on the road, has hosts who not only talk about O.J. and immigration but also offer computer tips, not to mention discussions of how to start your own information-age business.

In the last few years L.A., including L.A. county—the lines between the two are often blurry—has created more new jobs than all of New York State, which has considerably more than twice the population. The difference, explains Joel Kotkin, one of the very few people who saw all along that L.A.'s extraordinary entrepreneurial engine hadn't run out of steam, is that the L.A. area is home to scores of new companies; it is these small-to-medium-sized businesses (the so-called gazelles) that have created most of the new jobs. Many of these companies sit on the increasingly fuzzy border between high-tech digital imaging and traditional filmmaking.

"The old California energy is back in the air," says David Hensley of New York's Salomon Brothers. Asian investment is back as well, although this time it's from the overseas Chinese rather than the Japanese. For the first time since the 1930s, California's economy is staging a comeback without a boom in either military spending or housing. "There's the old churning and dreaming and business adventurism," says Hensley. The most important example of that adventurism is Dreamworks, the first new movie studio in fifty years. Founded by Steven Spielberg, Jeffrey Katzenberg, and David Geffen and capitalized at $2.5 billion, its state-of-the-art computer graphics and fiber-optics plant, though off to a slow start, is expected to attract other high-tech multimedia firms.

Long Island tried to fill a mammoth Grumman Aircraft facility, now effectively abandoned, with a Hollywood sound stage, but it found no takers. It was different in Los Angeles. Many of the new companies in polycentric L.A. are located in the county's other cities—places like Burbank, where the facilities once used by Lockheed are now the new home of Disney animation. Driven by an intense and international demand for its entertainment product, L.A. County, with its heavy concentration of engineers, graphic artists, and animators, is also the center (along with Silicon Valley) of the booming business in CD-ROMs and other multimedia offerings.

Asian entrepreneurs have created a booming toy and plastics industry, while Mexican and Mexican-American entrepreneurs are the force behind the miles upon miles of food processing plants that line the Alameda Corridor. In New York City, Brooklyn, suffering an endless loss of manufacturing jobs, can't become more competitive by reducing taxes and eliminating redundant regulations; it's caught up in rules made by a Manhattan-driven economy. But in the dispersed L.A. County, with its numerous municipalities, independent cities like Burbank, Glendale, and Pasadena are able to respond quickly to new business conditions. They moved to streamline and update business and environmental regulations and forced the city of L.A. to follow suit.

Skeptics reluctantly note the revival of the L.A. economy and then, pointing to the many sweatshops whose conditions have became a national scandal, complain that L.A. reinvented itself as the capital of low-wage labor. True, but only partially. The new entertainment cluster in Burbank also has the virtue of creating high-paying jobs with average salaries of $47,000 a year, almost as much as the old aerospace work.

The rise of Los Angeles has long been treated as a morality tale. It has been seen, wrote economist Ann Markusen, as "a vindication of economic freedom over the East's sclerotic, ossified liberal sociopolitical order with its welfare bureaucracies, unions and interest groups." This is the history of L.A. as seen by the old pre-1960s *Los Angeles Times,* the then-boosterist newspaper that did so much to shepherd L.A.'s rise. The story is true, but incomplete. This story of individual freedom triumphing is contradicted at its core.

According to historian Steve Erie, Los Angeles has reinvented itself four times. In the late nineteenth century it changed from a sleepy town to a center for the railroad and real estate buccaneers. Then in the 1920s this improbable site for a great city—it lacks a harbor, coal, iron, and fresh water—began to industrialize on the basis of a branch plant economy. In the 1940s the rise of the defense and aerospace industry transformed the economy. Finally, in the last decade Los Angeles, fueled by Mexican labor and Asian capital, has become a global entrepôt.

It was the federal government—first with the administration of Teddy Roosevelt and then later with Franklin Roosevelt's Reconstruction Finance Corporation—that paid for building the giant water projects, including the Hoover Dam, that brought water to the city's arid lands. It was the city government, effectively directed by the *Los Angeles Times* and its "free harbor" campaign, that used federal and state money to build at San Pedro, adjoining Long Beach, the largest man-made harbor in the world.

The water from the dammed Colorado River arrived just in time to make the World War II defense boom possible. The war in the Pacific turned L.A. into a vast military staging area. "In 1940 the federal government spent $728 million in California but by war's end the $35 billion the federal government pumped into California gave birth to the modern city of Los Angeles," notes Markusen. The Japanese attack on Pearl Harbor and the federal decision to disperse military production as a precaution against similar attacks put the aerospace industry in Los Angeles, but innovative academics kept it there. Local research institutions like Robert Millikan's California Institute of Technology, as much as a climate perfect for test flights, helped make the area attractive for airplane manufacturing.

Modern aviation emerged not in the West Coast but in Detroit, Dayton, and Buffalo, cities of the industrial Midwest. The problem was that these cities' mass production industries, organized around auto manufacture, were a bad fit for a defense industry that resisted routinization. Accustomed to the long runs of standardized products, Midwestern companies like Ford balked at the need for the high performance and continual innovation demanded by the military.

In California, by contrast, the engineering and research institutions that burgeoned along with the military economy harnessed themselves to the problems of innovative military technology. "Nowhere else in the country," writes Mike Davis, a historian of Los Angeles, "did there develop such a seamless continuum between the corporation, laboratory and classroom as in Los Angeles." The Jet Propulsion Lab worked hand in glove with Hughes Aircraft, TRW, and other emerging military manufacturers, and the Douglas,

Lockheed, North American, Northrop and Conveyer aircraft companies located their main plants in California. In 1946 Douglas Aircraft established the RAND (an acronym for Research and Development) Corporation in Santa Monica. RAND went on to become the Pentagon's think tank. Here was the so-called military-industrial complex or, more accurately, L.A.'s local, university-driven version of an industrial policy.

Angelenos may not have been rugged individualists, but they made far better use of their federal monies than did New Yorkers and Washingtonians, who took their federal booty largely in the form of subsidies for social services and spendthrift city governments. By contrast, the city budget of L.A. goes to support infrastructure—the harbor, the Los Angeles Water and Power Authority, and the airport. This has been strong but limited government with an economic payoff.

10. Police Politics

In L.A. the relentless entrepreneurial energy of a Wild West capitalism largely freed from the fetters of institutional constraints, whether in the form of strong political parties, trade unions, or churches, produced a violently combustible city and a police force to match.

L.A.'s Progressive Era city charter produced an unusual political system with a weak mayor, a strong city council, and a police chief stronger still. The police remain the great paradox of L.A. politics. From 1973 to 1993 a liberal coalition of blacks and Jews led by Mayor Tom Bradley dominated the city's politics. Yet this coalition was never able to reform a decidedly illiberal police department. Any visitor from New York who comes to the offices of the L.A. government stumbles almost immediately on part of the reason. The sheer inactivity of the mayor's office is stunning. I've never been given so much help and so much attention so quickly by so many press officers with so little to do. Unlike New York's mayor, who makes headlines almost daily, the L.A. mayor, currently Richard Riordan, can go unsighted for weeks. On many issues the action is often across the street from city hall, at the Parker Center, the police headquarters named after William Parker, the man behind the 1937 police "reform." At times, the Parker Center overshadows city hall as the locus for L.A. politics.

In the wake of the 1965 Watts riots, Senators Abraham Ribicoff and Robert Kennedy held hearings in Los Angeles to try to make sense of the turmoil. Stunned by the testimony of Mayor Sam Yorty, Ribicoff summarized what he had heard.

Ribicoff: As I listened to your testimony, Mayor Yorty . . . you have really waived authority and responsibility in schools, welfare, transportation, employment, health and housing, which leaves you as the head of the city, basically with a ceremonial function.

Yorty: That is right, and fire . . . and sewers.

Ribicoff: In other words, basically you lack jurisdiction, authority, responsibility for what makes the city move?

Yorty: That is exactly it.

Recounts political analyst Xandra Kayden, Senator Kennedy then asked Yorty to stay and listen to the rest of the hearing, adding, "Because, as I understand your testimony, you have nothing to get back to."

The absence of responsibility perfectly suited Yorty, a 1930s leftist turned sixties populist who was far more interested in campaigning than governing. A perpetual candidate, Yorty, who first tried to run for mayor in 1945, ran in seven separate elections between 1961 and 1972. A Reagan Democrat *avant la lettre,* Yorty was much loved by lower-middle-class whites who had made it through the hardscrabble of the 1930s and feared that blacks were destroying what they had achieved. Yorty played to their fears, his talents perfectly suited to a job that demanded only that he further embellish his penchant for demagogic speechifying and mudslinging.

The one constant in Yorty's career was his sallies on behalf of the "little man." In the depression era he attacked fat cats and plutocrats, and in the 1960s he went after the *Los Angeles Times* and its "downtown machine." It all came naturally to a man whose father had been a close friend of William Jennings Bryan, the famed populist and perpetual presidential candidate. Yorty's Bryanesque rhetoric was a perfect fit for a city with so many middle-Americans, people jokingly called it Double Dubuque, a town where there was no greater political epithet than to accuse someone of "Eastern machine" politics.

Elected by the nonpartisan political process, Yorty was at one with the Progressives, who established the L.A. city charter in 1925. Drawn up by Midwesterners who saw L.A. as "the most American city in the nation," the city charter was designed to block the creation of an immigrant political machine by placing real power in the hands of high-minded professionals.

"Anyone who has read beyond the second paragraph of the city charter," Yorty explained, with considerable self-knowledge, "would be out of his mind to run for mayor." The charter, which runs to more than six hundred pages and has been amended more than four hundred times, designates the fifteen-member city council, and not the mayor, as the primary political body. The fifteen councilmanic "mayors," explains Xandra Kayden, are supreme in their own districts. "The best-paid council members in the country with perhaps the largest staffs, they originate policy, and then rule on the specifics of every project that comes into their district."

Armed with only a handful of patronage appointments, the mayor was often confined to a ceremonial role. Most personnel decisions were put in the hands of an independent civil service commission. Day-to-day responsibility for the city's essential functions, like roads, sewers, police, and fire, was allocated to thirty-two departments. In a further dilution of already diffuse power, direct management of these departments was placed in the hands of neither the council nor the mayor but, rather, well-paid professional managers protected by civil service rules. These managers, including the police chief, were overseen by commissions reporting to both the mayor and the council. The commissions are composed of the "best people," disinterested part-time citizen officials. Under the city charter almost any mayoral action, from drafting a budget to naming any of the city's more than 240 commissioners, requires council approval.

The commission members set policy for their agencies, keeping the mayor and city council at arm's length. The weakness of the system is that even in cases of incompetence and insubordination, the charter makes it almost impossible for the mayor to discipline, let alone fire, department managers. The strength is that competent professional managers are allowed to do their job with a minimum of political interference. In practice this has meant that basic services, like road maintenance and fire protection, and infrastructure investments for the water supply and the port have been managed fairly well.

Social services, including welfare and hospitals, are administered not by the city but by the county of Los Angeles. The county, with a budget and population three times that of the city, is run by five supervisors, elected from geographic districts, who serve both as legislators and as a collective executive. In other words, the social service sector, which in New York lent itself to the creation of an alternative economy, is largely in the hands of a suburban majority sensitive to taxes.

The charter's critics have described it as "a legal spider web" and "the worst city charter" in the United States. And when it comes to the police, they have a point.

In the mid-1930s, despite the reformed charter, city government was so corrupt that, in Raymond Chandler's words, "it could be bought by the hour." This was the Los Angeles of Mayor Frank Shaw, as preserved in Chandler's detective novels. As always, police were at the center of the city's politics. The city's buccaneering elites—the Downtown Business Association, the Merchants and Manufacturers Association, and the powerful *Los Angeles Times*—were willing to live with considerable corruption so long as the police could be used for union busting and the mayor balanced the budget.

James Davis, the five-foot-seven-inch, pistol-packing police chief, was described by the then-right-wing *Los Angeles Times* as a "burly, dictatorial, somewhat sadistic, bitterly anti-labor man who saw Communist influence behind every telephone pole." Davis was credited with creating the "dragnet," a police sweep through a neighborhood, often black or Mexican, that dragged in the innocent along with the guilty.

The police department's "red squad" kept unionists in line. What brought down both Mayor Shaw and Chief Davis was the police Special Intelligence Squad, a unit dedicated to silencing the non-Communist critics of both. Harry Raymond, an ex-cop turned private eye who may have been one of the inspirations for Chandler's Marlowe, discovered that the mayor was tied into big-time gamblers. In a scenario serving as the model for movies to come, the head of the Special Intelligence Squad had Raymond's car blown up as the detective was driving to court to present the evidence. The squad unwittingly demolished the careers of both Shaw and Davis, since the "hard-boiled dick" lived to tell his tale.

In 1938 Shaw became the first mayor ever to be removed by a recall campaign. Recall, along with the ballot initiative, the short ballot, and nonpartisan elections (where candidates ran without party labels), had been among the key Progressive reforms. While both the mayor and the police chief were "dirty" in antipolitical L.A. it was assumed that it was the pols who had corrupted the cops. In an ironic outcome that would have enormous consequences for L.A., a campaign for police reform, intended to insulate patrolmen from the pressures of their superiors, instead further shielded the department from supervision and accountability. The patrolmen were insulated from their superiors on the force. The police chief was given more autonomy, and his job was made a substantial property right so that he could be fired only on the basis of a process so labyrinthine that he was effectively given tenure. In a city whose government was organized on an elaborate structure of checks and balances, the police were thus given an autonomy unknown not only to any other department in Los Angeles but to any other major city in the United States. Freed from political interference, the Los Angeles Police Department would eventually go into politics for itself.

It took one more scandal, a 1949 disgrace involving prostitution and the police chief, to create the paramilitary L.A.P.D. made famous by a host of movies and TV shows. William Parker, the man most responsible for the 1937 "reforms," came to power as police chief. He remade the L.A.P.D. along the lines of the Marine Corps, creating an incorruptible but often brutal and highly politicized police squad. Parker's racism and hatred of "socialistic" public housing was in line with the department's tradition as a strike-breaking force, a department whose "red squad" was housed at the Chamber of Commerce.

Parker discouraged contact between the police and civilians on the grounds that it would feed intimacy and hence bribery. Instead, Parker's police force was organized as a ready response team operating out of patrol cars equipped with two-way radios. The new L.A.P.D. was designed along military lines as a tight command-and-control operation. Isolated from the public as they cruised through crime-ridden neighborhoods while in constant radio contact with their superiors, the police, encouraged by Chief James Parker, thought of themselves as centurions, that is, as Roman warriors riding herd on the barbarians.

The spit-and-polish style of Parker's force inspired hundreds of movies and thousands of TV episodes. Their quasi-military approach unfortunately became the envy of police departments around the country. The L.A.P.D. also resembled a classic industrial era bureaucracy. Productivity was measured not by whether the citizens felt safe but by such quantitative indices as the number of arrests or the response time to 911 emergency calls. As with education, police work was being defined by the professionals who delivered it rather than by the citizens it was supposed to serve.

By the 1953 mayoral election, the police had become the "blue knights," an autonomous force to be reckoned with. No one was beyond their reach. Norton Poulson, the candidate of the *Los Angeles Times* and the downtown establishment, described his own experience with the L.A.P.D. as follows: "I found that I was followed, 'bugged,' and checked, on the theory that I might be working with certain groups wanting to overhaul the police department and depose Chief Parker." Poulson nonetheless won and went on to an uneasy coexistence with Chief Parker.

Powerful in the years before the 1965 Watts riot, Parker became impregnable after the riot by playing on white fears of black crime and black power. The chief mocked the rioters as "monkeys in a zoo." After Watts, Parker warned that L.A. would become a majority black city by 1970 with untold consequences. Backed up by Poulson's successor, Mayor Sam Yorty, Parker threatened, "If you want any protection for your home and family . . . you're going to have to get in and support a strong police department. If you don't, come 1970, God help you."

The price of Parker's power and his paramilitary style was an intense black animus toward the police. In the wake of Watts a young man told Bayard

Rustin that "the riots will continue because I, as a Negro, am immediately considered to be a criminal by the police; if I have a pretty woman with me, she is a tramp even if she is my wife or mother."

Just as the L.A. police are unusual in their spit-and-polish Marine Corps style, so too are L.A. gangs, in a pattern of reciprocal influence, different. Los Angeles gangs have a level of organization and political pretension lacking in gangs in most of the country, with the possible exception of Chicago. L.A.'s black gangs of the early sixties turned nationalist in the mid-1960s. Members of the Slauson gang, from South Central, for instance, became local organizers for the Black Panther Party. The two major black gang federations, the Bloods and the Crips, are in turn the direct descendants of two rival Black Power groups from the 1960s, the Black Panthers and Ron Karenga's short-lived US (United Slaves).

The August 1965 riots were a turning point. Tommy Jaquette, a young nationalist leader, explains: "Before August they were gangs, now they're organizations." "Everybody," says a former gang member, "was into the Panthers. It was a protection thing to stop police harassment, to unite, to hold our ground." Pressured by the growing power of the CRIPs, whose very insignia sometimes came to denote Black Power (some said the letters stood for Continuous Revolution in Power), other gangs counterorganized into the Bloods. It was sometimes difficult to tell where gang activity stopped and political activity began. By the late sixties, the two gangs/political federations were engaged in frequent shoot-outs. In 1969, two US members shot and killed two Panthers on the UCLA campus in a fight over control of the African-American Studies Center. And even after the Panthers and US faded, the rhetoric of community control and Black Power continued to have an enduring impact.

When Tom Bradley, an African-American, ran for mayor in 1969 against Yorty, he was at one and the same time propelled politically by widespread criticism of the cops and dragged down by white fears of black gangs. Bradley, a political moderate by temperment and a former L.A.P.D. officer, had established himself as the chief critic of police excesses. He was defeated in the 1969 mayoral contest, race-baited by the incumbent Sam Yorty, who played on fears of crime and Communism. Pointing to left-wing activists in the Bradley campaign, Yorty exploited the black racist echoes of the Ocean Hill–Brownsville school debacle in New York. Yorty frightened some lower-middle-class Jewish voters away from his competitor by painting the coalition-building Bradley, who nevertheless won the majority of the Jewish vote, as a Black Panther of sorts.

During the Yorty mayoralty from 1961 to 1973, the true power of the police force's political influence was partly hidden by the close ties between Yorty and the chiefs. Both Yorty and the L.A.P.D. drew their core political support from the lower-middle-class and largely white Protestant San Fernando Valley, separated from the rest of the city by the Santa Monica Mountains. But when Bradley took office after defeating Yorty in a 1973 rematch, tension grew between the new mayor—who drew his strength largely from the wealthy Jewish West Side and heavily black South Central—and the police, with their core Valley supporters.

Daryl Gates, who rose to police chief in 1978, was widely regarded as the heir to Parker's throne, but he was also the successor to Yorty's support in the San Fernando Valley, the home of the antibusing and antitax protests behind Proposition 13. Bradley made no secret of his distaste for the force, and Gates reciprocated in kind. He mocked Bradley as "our great mayor" while the two men engaged in a running feud. Gates periodically threatened to run for mayor, but then thought the better of it. Officially nonpartisan, L.A. in fact had at the time two de facto political parties: a liberal one centered around Mayor Bradley, who was in office for five terms from 1973 to 1993, and a conservative one around Gates, chief of police from 1978 to 1993. It took the 1992 riots to break this system.

Where the police were concerned, the passions of 1960s protest politics persisted in Los Angeles all through the Bradley years. Both the cops and the gangs shared the Vietnam analogy. Some gang members and their apologists exulted in seeing themselves as an American Vietcong; a Gates aide, the head of the antidrug strike force, concurred. He described his sorties into South Central as fighting "Vietnam here." Referring to the seventy thousand gang members in L.A. County, the prosecutor also repeatedly echoed the Vietnam analogy. For his part, Gates tried to play the role of William Westmoreland, the jut-jawed commander of U.S. troops in Vietnam. In his videotaped 1986 "end-of-the-year address to the troops played at roll call," he compared the L.A.P.D. to the Marine Corps and identified the gangs as the enemy. "It's like having the Marine Corps invade an area that is still having little pockets of resistance; we can't have it, we have got to wipe them out." Those were civilians he was referring to.

There is no more overused and misused metaphor in American racial politics than to call the police an occupying army, as James Baldwin did. Whatever limited truth this metaphor once had, it has been greatly diminished over the years. However, in L.A. it was far more than a metaphor, it was a policing style, driven in part by the department's self-conception and in part by the budgetary pressures of policing a geographically vast city whose electorate was notoriously unwilling to increase taxes even for public safety.

Among the largest cities, L.A. has *both* the busiest and the smallest force, in terms of the police-to-population ratio. New York has one cop for every 195 people, L.A. one for every 400. On average, an L.A. cop handles twice as many violent incidents per year as the average New York cop. They do it by a far more aggressive style of policing. A largely motorized force remote from the people it serves, even in affluent white areas the L.A.P.D. is far more likely to send a citizen prone, to "kiss the concrete," than police elsewhere. But while the L.A.P.D. is often more effective at seizing the situation, officers often do so at the expense of the dignity not only of criminals but also of innocents caught up in their "act first, ask questions later" style of policing.

Absent the personnel to maintain control over high-crime areas, the L.A.P.D. response was Operation Hammer, a 1988 wave of mass arrests in which the guilty and the innocent alike in inner-city areas were caught up in police dragnets. Said Gates as crack was driving crime ever upward, "I think the only strategy we have is to put a lot of police officers on the street and harass people and make arrests for inconsequential kinds of things. Well, that's part of the strategy, no question about it." Though spectacular in the short run, this was an approach that proved better at generating lawsuits and long-term resentments than reducing crime.

Whenever Mayor Bradley and his liberal allies sought to rein in the police, they were faced with the difficulty of amending the charter in the face of police opposition and sheer intimidation. Like James Parker—and, for that matter, Marion Barry—Gates threatened to reduce police patrols in the neighborhood of those council members who crossed him. But that was only one of his weapons. Zev Yaroslavsky, a former councilman and now County Supervisor, was aware that the "red squad" had a file on him. He described the power of the police to intimidate politicians:

> I think a lot of people are afraid to be critical of the police department. They don't want to get into an argument with the police chief. . . . It can do a lot of damage to a person's reputation if the chief of police says you're anti-police or you're aiding and abetting criminals or that you're really pro-terrorist. You can deny it all you want, but unless you're willing to accept that criticism, and most people aren't willing, you don't get into an argument with the police department.

Thus, one of America's most liberal cities was saddled with a police force that often served powerful interests—but served its own first.

In 1983 and again in 1985, the ghost of recalled mayor Frank Shaw, the gamblers' friend, looking on, measures designed to give the mayor and the council modestly increased control over department executives were defeated after only halfhearted support from Bradley. The opposition was led in part by Gates, who, aligned with the public employee unions, attacked the reforms as "a step back into the dark age of Chicago-style patronage."

A behind-the-scenes mayor, Bradley wasn't willing or able, even when fantastically popular in the mid-1980s, to lay his prestige on the line over civilian control of the police. Instead, he reacted petulantly. He kept on cutting the police budget even after excessive pension costs had been reduced and even as crime was growing rapidly. From 1988 to 1992 the overall number of crimes reported to the L.A.P.D. jumped 16 percent, with homicides climbing by 47 percent, and robberies increasing by 52 percent. At the same time, the percentage of the budget devoted to the police dropped from 37 percent in 1977 to 29 percent in 1992. A week before the riot, Bradley made headlines with his plan for additional cuts. He had wanted to reduce the already overwhelmed 8,100-member force by 7 percent. In the face of the ongoing police budget crunch, the city council (like Bradley, ineffectually disgruntled with the L.A.P.D.) refused the money to upgrade the crime lab, the same rundown lab that became an issue at the O. J. Simpson trial.

By the time of the 1992 riots, Bradley and Gates were so thoroughly estranged that they hadn't met face-to-face for more than a year. The decentered political structure in L.A., which freed the city from the costs of an overextended government, helped produce the unaccountable police system that made Los Angeles not only the first city to experience a major postwar riot but the only city to experience two major postwar riots.

11. The Centrifugal City

Benjamin Disraeli, the great nineteenth-century British prime minister, anticipated the essence of L.A.'s segmented society in writing about Britain's class divisions. In his novel *Sybil,* he has Morely the Chartist remark, "There is no community in England; there is aggregation, but aggregation under circumstances which make it rather a dissociating than a uniting principle." In Disraeli's England, the assertions of unbridgeable differences centered on class. Today, the supposedly irreconcilable Marxist class conflict has been largely resolved only to be transmuted, often by ex-Marxists, into a new unslakable anger. This new multicultural struggle is a fight over supposedly immutable differences of racial, ethnic, and gender identity.

Multiculturalism comes naturally to a city without a civic center of gravity. Los Angeles was "decentered" long before the term was discovered by academics preaching postmodernism. The irony is that its decentering was the product of its now long-lost ethnic homogeneity.

L.A.'s monstrous and amorphous structure is usually attributed to the effects of the automobile. But, wrote historian Robert Fishman, "the automobile has been essentially a tool in the attainment of a deeper goal that predates the automobile era: the suburban ideal." And that suburban ideal, wrote historian Robert Fogelson, was in turn a reflection not so much of "chronology, geography or technology as the exceptional character of its population." While New York and Chicago were immigrant cities, the product in large part of peoples who initially had little say in the way they lived, Los Angeles was created by Midwestern Protestants, people already at home in America and already equipped with substantial resources. These were the people who wrote the L.A. charter for minimal government. These were settlers who had a choice in how they would live, and their choice was for a city built around single-family homes.

L.A. was organized around a constellation of suburban towns, modeled after the small towns of the Midwest from which so many of the new arrivals had emigrated. While there are many people who proudly identify themselves as New Yorkers or Washingtonians, there are few who describe themselves as Angelenos. "When you ask people who live within the L.A. city limits, let alone the county, where they're from," explains historian Mike Davis, "no one lives in Los Angeles." Instead, they tell you that they "live in Silver Lake, Echo Park, . . . North Hollywood, Boyle Heights, Studio City, Westwood, Encino." This attitude led to the oft-used but accurate line that "Los Angeles is sixty suburbs in search of a city."

The common, if not collectivist, dream of the people who remade New York City in the years after the the Great Depression was to harvest the full flower of the welfare state that had been sown by the left wing of the New Deal. In Southern California, utopia was a private matter. It meant building one's dream house on a setting that, though it might technically be within the city limits, was as connected to nature as a rural fastness. "For the first time in history," wrote architectural critic Delores Hayden, "a civilization created a utopian ideal based on the house rather than the city or the nation." In practice this meant that 94 percent of the city's population lived in single-family homes by 1930, by far the highest percentage of any major city. By extension, L.A. contained the most cars per person of any big city. The true center of life, the hub around which all else revolved wasn't the old downtown business district but the individual home, where household members, equipped with automobiles, lived in personally customized locales. Here was a city Frank Lloyd Wright could love.

Thirty years later, in 1960, five years before the change in the immigration laws, L.A. had the largest percentage of native-born white Protestants of any major city in the United States. Moreover, 72 percent of its residents still lived in single-family homes, compared to 28 percent in Chicago, 20 percent in New York and 15 percent in Philadelphia.

In New York, community control after Ocean Hill–Brownsville took the form of black nationalists looking to secede from a white liberal civic order. In L.A., community control took the form of suburban secession by the white home owners of the county's unincorporated municipalities. Under the terms of the 1956 Lakewood Plan, towns could buy their basic services, like police and fire protection, from Los Angeles County while retaining control of local zoning and, hence, their quality of life. In 1990 the county contained eighty-one municipalities, twelve with populations of more than one hundred thousand. Control of local land use by these "minimal cities" meant they could keep property taxes low by zoning out the low-income housing likely to increase crime and social costs.

In civic terms this meant that L.A. was a region of island communities in which, after the decline of the downtown WASP elite, there would be no attempt by the dominant ethnic group to impose, for better or worse, a common culture (political or otherwise) on newcomers. When newcomers arrived, the older residents simply moved on, exiting to newer and still relatively homogeneous islands. This continuous process of sorting and resorting meant that in L.A. people didn't rub up against each other—to remove one another's rough edges or to rub each other raw. Even with the end of racially restrictive covenants, L.A. didn't suffer from the bitter black–white clashes over territory that marked the Eastern cities. Diversity or difference—or, better yet, indifference—could flourish because one group's fate was barely tied to another's.

The absence of a strong civic ethic was relatively unimportant when L.A. was a largely homogeneous, if dispersed, "Peoria with palms." But in the years since World War II the city has been transformed by two waves of immigration: the first by blacks and Jews, the second by Asians and, especially, Hispanics. These have remade L.A. into a multiethnic mélange of sometimes mutually hostile groups.

Multiculturalism in L.A. fits an economy increasingly driven by Asian capital and Latino sweat. The positive side of this development is that, as David Rieff has written, L.A. is a "collage city in a collage world." In a "dynamic world of contingency, mobility and innovation," L.A. should do very well if it can establish even a minimal comity. But, as the Simpson trial (which rocked L.A. far more than the country as a whole) suggests, this may be beyond the region's reach. In a city famed for consciousness raising, New Age, black nationalist, environmentalist, Mexican nationalist, suburban home owner, and gay pride groups flourish. About the only form of consciousness that's out of style is civic consciousness.

The story of black L.A. can be described in terms of a trajectory that brought a historically marginal community into the center of a governing coalition during the Bradley years of 1973 to 1993 and then returned it to isolation. The same trajectory limns the rise and fall of another L.A. anomaly—a broadly appealing civic ideal.

Blacks have long been better off materially in L.A. than in the rest of the country. As early as the 1930s, Watts had the highest rate of black home ownership in the country. And blacks benefited from the World War II boom when Japanese internment and Mexican deportations created a demand for low-wage African-American labor. By 1964, the year prior to the Watts riots, an Urban League "statistical portrait" rated L.A. the best of sixty-eight cities for black employment, housing, and income. "In a Third World setting," wrote the much-traveled author Paul Theroux, "Watts would be upper middle class because its drug dealers would have been long since executed." Thirty years later the picture still holds. L.A. is America's leading city for black-owned business, and blacks in L.A. are twice as likely to be living above the poverty line as their Chicago brethren.

In the wake of the violent sixties, a coalition of two Los Angeles outgroups—blacks and Jews—whose economic success far exceeded their political clout, established a new political regime. This alliance, which produced record electoral turnout, elected an African-American, Tom Bradley, mayor in 1973 with 46 percent of the white vote. Bradley's election gave Jews the political recognition they lacked under the old white Protestant political regime, which had been run by a group of city fathers known as the Committee of 25. It also promised to integrate blacks into the economic life of L.A. through affirmative action contracting and the vigorous pursuit of federal antipoverty money.

The coalition was built on a mix of what seemed to be black self-interest and a blend of fear and concern on the part of moderate and liberal whites, whose desire to "help" was matched by their need to propitiate black anger. For a time, the coalition, in the best spirit of Dr. King, gave the city a public ethos that partially transcended ethnic affiliations.

In some ways the Bradley mayoralty was a success. Less than a fifth of the population, blacks gained considerable political ground. "The most striking fact," noted Rafael Sonenshein, the historian of the black–Jewish alliance, "is that since 1973 every citywide candidate backed in the black community won election." Sonenshein also noted that "when on occasion white liberals and the blacks clashed over candidates, the blacks won." One consequence was a sharp rise in black public employment; blacks came to be overrepresented on local government payrolls.

From 1973 to 1985 the liberal coalition behind Bradley dominated Los Angeles politics. The coalition had important limitations. It was unable to incorporate the middle-class homeowners of the San Fernando Valley and Latinos into political life or blacks into the booming private sector economy. At its best the coalition, in the person of Bradley, embodied a trans-tribal ethic. This was no small feat in a city where other institutions capable of cross-ethnic alliances—such as strong business associations, and political parties—were largely absent.

In return for racial and ethnic inclusion, the Bradley coalition promised social peace, but on terms very different from those of New York. L.A. liberalism was unlike its East Coast cousin on local matters. The Roosevelt Revolution came late to California so that the New Deal's solidaristic social democratic tendencies never took hold there. Unlike New York's, L.A.'s liberalism strongly supported economic growth. It was never heavily redistributive. Its social programs were for the most part paid for with federal and state antipoverty funds, which tripled under Bradley, rather than local tax levies. John Lindsay staked his run for the presidency on his ability, albeit in concert with the efforts of the mayors of other major cities, to solve the problem of urban poverty. Bradley was far more cautious. "Poverty," said Bradley, almost as if he were answering Lindsay, "cannot be corrected by a mayor or all of the city halls put together." Bradley insisted that there was little local government could do about the problems of South Central. Bradley always tried to keep expectations in check, a tendency due partly to his behind-the-scenes style. This, plus his ability to duck even high-profile issues like school busing for racial integration, meant that as long as the fear of violence was contained, the coalition, which came to include downtown real estate developers, would hold.

Bradley, referring to the largely symbolic power of the Los Angeles mayoralty, said, "The influence you have, the ability to get things done, is not so much a matter of law as a matter of being able to persuade people to join with you to do something you set out as a goal." Bradley's talent was in convincing both blacks and liberal whites that he represented what they wanted. While whites, explained Sonenshein, "saw Bradley as a symbol of racial harmony, Blacks saw him as a symbol of racial assertion." Put differently, while liberal whites saw the 1965 riots as an unfortunate but unavoidable cry for social justice that need never be repeated, many blacks, including part of the political leadership, saw it in a far more positive light as a model for future success. African-Americans, while generally aware that the vast majority of whites and Latinos disapproved of the Watts riot, nonetheless looked upon it as the gateway to increased power and attention. The tension between these perspectives never came to the surface during Bradley's first three terms, from 1973 to 1985.

But after his smashing 1985 landslide reelection, a new set of problems weakened the alliances Bradley had built. Late in his mayoralty, Bradley was undermined by charges of personal corruption. Yet far more important were two issues—offshore oil exploration and crime—that split his coalition and Jewish base. When Armand Hammer's Occidental Petroleum Corporation found its proposals for offshore drilling opposed by upper-middle-class environmentalists from the large Jewish Westside, his company mounted a partly successful public relations campaign to depict the opposition as elitist and even racist. More generally, in the booming 1980s the liberal coalition in L.A. was divided between those who argued that the rapid economic growth was undermining the quality of life and those who felt they had yet to benefit from the growth.

The rising toll of violence in the late 1980s, often gang related, weakened the social peace and Bradley's coalition with it. The mid-eighties crack epidemic metastasized the black gang problem. Drive-by shooting, once confined to South Central, came to the Valley and other formerly secure sections. Westwood, home to UCLA, suffered shootings and even a small riot around the showing of the black "gangsta" movie *New Jack City.* At the same time, African-American and Latino leaders representing the neighborhoods that were bearing the brunt of the crime wave began to talk about too little policing rather than too much. Police brutality began to pale before gang brutality. Councilman Richard Alatorre summed it up in 1988: "This is the era of the police. If I were chief, I'd ask for as many as I could."

Conditions seemed ripe for a cross-racial assault on crime. Surely the black working class of South Central and the conservative and moderate San Fernando Valley homeowners who looked up to Daryl Gates could agree on the need for more money to aid a police force that was seriously understaffed. It was the blacks of South Central, so often caught in the cross fire between crime and police misconduct, who repeatedly and massively supported referenda to increase the police budget through dedicated taxes. The same taxes were rejected by the largely white Valley, the mainstay of the drive for Proposition 13 (the drive rolling back real estate assessments), where antitax sentiment trumped anticrime sentiment. Cynicism and more than a touch of racism tainted the suggestion by Valley voters that anticrime money would simply be wasted in South Central. Such was the psychic distance between the two areas that the Valley (joined by antipolice liberals) voted against a proposal to allow South Central to tax itself for more police protection, on the slim grounds that such a tax increase might set a citywide precedent.

While city voters were rejecting a tax increase to fund more police, in an act of multicultural separatism county voters—the county, with a population of ten million, has almost three times as many people as the city—rejected a proposal to create an elected county executive. No one person, it was said, could represent the different groups. Los Angeles after Bradley, warned historian

Kevin Starr, could be like Yugoslavia after Tito, "disestablishing itself into a murderous mosaic of warring parts." In 1992, as Bradley's power faded, the United States experienced its first multicultural riot.

The trigger for the riots was the acquittal of the cops caught on videotape beating runaway motorist Rodney King. A strong majority of whites in L.A. thought the Simi Valley verdict a miscarriage of justice. On the defensive, police chief Daryl Gates admitted to being sick to his stomach when he first saw the videotape of the Rodney King beating, but he, true to the department's tradition, never offered an apology. When the riot erupted at the corner of Florence and Normandy, home to a group of Eight-Trey Gangster Crips, Gates was in white, well-to-do Brentwood. Speaking at a fund-raiser to defeat an upcoming referendum designed to extend civilian control over the police, Gates warned that if his power were curbed, L.A. would be no better policed than New York.

But no matter, the die was cast. South Central gangsters would see to that. In the mid-eighties Louis Farrakhan predicted that gangs would play "a very important role" in the coming race war in the United States. They were, he said, "born to settle the score." They might not have been successful in L.A. if the L.A.P.D., helpless in the absence of their supreme leader, hadn't withdrawn in panic once the violence began.

There was more than one pattern to the riot, to the desire to "settle the score" set off by the unwarranted Simi Valley verdict. An ex-Crip boasted, "We didn't burn our community, just *their* stores." Not quite. As journalist Harold Meyerson pointed out, "the riot of '92 was at once more targeted and more nihilistic" than that of 1965. It was targeted at those areas patrolled by the L.A.P.D. Rioting didn't spread to Compton and Inglewood, two independent heavily black cities intertwined with L.A. but patrolled by their own police forces. At the same time, the rioters, Meyerson noted, burned down the oldest black-owned bookstore in southern California, the district offices of gang apologist Congresswoman Maxine Waters, two public libraries, and the headquarters of the Watts Labor Community Action Council, one of the organizations that had tried to rebuild Watts after the 1965 riots.

While most of the violence was committed by young black men, the looting was integrated. Of those arrested more than half were Latino. Many of them were recent Mexican or Central American immigrants. Forty percent of those arrested already had criminal records.

There was a good deal of violence directed against Jewish grocery store owners in the 1965 Watts riot; Jews at the time were accused of exploitation because they hired blacks at the low-wage jobs created by their mom-and-pop stores. A quarter-century later, Korean grocers were accused of exploiting the black community because generally they didn't hire black help.

The already considerable resentment against Korean success preceding the 1992 riot was intensified by an ugly incident that year in which a Korean store owner killed a black teenage girl in a shoplifting dispute. The store's videotape, according to the judge in the case, showed "a five-foot-six-inch, 156-pound adolescent severely beating a fifty-year-old woman who is literally half her size, knocking that woman to the ground twice, and shows the Korean woman reaching for a gun at a time the beating was in progress." Still, the young black woman, Latisha Harlins, was killed, shot in the back as she was leaving. The Korean storekeeper received a suspended sentence, a verdict that provoked understandable outrage. But the high ground was quickly lost as a song, "Black Korea," by the rapper Ice Cube jumped to the top of the record charts with lyrics like this: "*Pay respect to the black fist or we'll burn your house down to a crisp.*"

It wasn't surprising then that young black toughs interviewed during and after the rioting described the attack on Korean stores in terms associated with the "ethnic cleansing" of Bosnia. In August following the April 1992 riots, three Korean stores were firebombed, retarding the already slow rate of rebuilding in the riot zone.

L.A. Times surveys, conducted before the Rodney King verdict and after the riots, found that the upheaval, damaging though it was, had very little effect on civic attitudes. Whites were still unwilling to spend more on the police; more fearful than ever of blacks, they instead armed themselves heavily. For all the soul searching in the media, much of it a rehash of what had been said twenty-five years before, local politics barely stirred, even though 58 percent of blacks and 76 percent of Latinos surveyed thought the rioting totally unjustified. Neither the L.A. City Council nor the powerful Los Angeles County Board of Supervisors had much to say. The congressional delegation was slow even to meet, while the state legislature was reluctant to spend a dime on reconstruction.

What moved many liberal whites beyond a dazed resignation and on to dismay and even disdain was the romanticization of the rioters by multiculturalists in the media and would-be black radicals. The psychological distance between blacks and whites, which had narrowed for a time after the Simi Valley verdict, reopened wider than ever. Some African-Americans, frustrated by the mistaken assumption that government could of itself lift and liberate them and unable or at times unwilling to take advantages of the L.A. economy, retreated into "barbershop history," that is, conspiracy theories to explain their plight. Whites, largely inured to intimidation and keenly aware of the success of the new immigrants, discovered that the attempts by African-Americans to separate themselves had succeeded with ironic effects.

Reginald Denny's truck rode through that hole in perceptions. Denny, a white trucker innocently passing through the heart of the riot area, was brutally beaten by bricks to the head from four attackers, including Damian Williams, a member of the Eight-Trey Gangster Crips. Denny's skull was crushed, "his jaw so badly smashed that it pushed up through his sinuses." Fifty others, most of them Hispanic and Asian immigrants, the secondary targets of black rage, were attacked at the corner of Florence and Normandy. Takai Hirata, another of Williams's victims, lost half his hearing and was partly paralyzed from a bottle Williams smashed across his face. Williams then attacked Jorge Lopez, who had tried to rescue Hirata. Nearby, Fidel Lopez was robbed of a $2,000 down payment on a construction job and beaten. The damage done required 250 stitches. After the attack, as he lay unconscious, Fidel Lopez's testicles were spray-painted black.

The attack on Denny was, like the Rodney King beating, caught on videotape. But radical retreads from the sixties, like former SDSer Clark Kissinger, and an assortment of black conspiracy theorists dubbed Denny's attackers the L.A. Four and turned them into either heroes, modern-day Nat Turners, or "scapegoats" for a white racist criminal-justice system. For its part, the Nation of Islam announced a legal defense fund for the Crips involved in the assault on Reginald Denny.

A grandstanding Daryl Gates personally arrested Damian Willams, the man most responsible for Denny's injuries. Williams alternately defended himself as a victim (he said he wouldn't have become a violent man if his father hadn't abandoned him) and as a political role model (he talked about the need for the renewal of radical politics under the aegis of a former Black Panther). The ostensible defense argued that Williams was a victim of a white racist structure of oppression and was therefore not responsible for his actions (particularly in the fury of the riots) and that the very idea of individual guilt is a tool of the white establishment. A more subtle message was supported by the Urban League's John Mack, who called the trial fishy and warned the city to watch out if there were convictions. Never subtle, Congresswoman Maxine Waters threatened, "If we don't get justice, we're going to have a civil war."

While billboards went up in South Central that read, sixties-style, FREE THE L.A. 4, the jury deliberated with a well-justified fear of setting off another riot. During the trial, while the L.A. Four Defense Committee was selling buttons and T-shirts, a rally held for the defendants at Florence and Normandy turned into a mini-riot by L.A. standards.

Accused of attempted manslaughter and more, Williams won something close to an acquittal. A riot averted, the city felt relief. This was mixed, for many, with dismay: jury nullification had come to liberal L.A.

John Mack declared that "the large majority of African-Americans in L.A. all feel that the verdicts are just." What's most disturbing, wrote John Taylor, covering the trial for *New York Magazine,* was the sense that "Williams [had] been made into a black hero not because he [was] falsely accused but because he in fact did do what he [was] accused of," namely, smashing a brick into a white man's head.

Congresswoman Maxine Waters, a cochair of the Clinton Presidential campaign in 1992, became a leading supporter of the L.A. Four. Though her own offices were burned down in 1992, she was a longtime practitioner of the riot ideology. As a legislator in Sacramento, Waters freely accused people who disagreed with her of racism. "Maxine," explained a colleague, "has come to see a merit in intimidation." After the 1992 riot, Waters made the case for defending the gang members, if not for violence directly, by arguing that they drew attention to the victimization of blacks by white society. The pictures of Waters dancing with gang members to celebrate a truce is well remembered by many Angelenos. More recently, Waters has been barnstorming for her favorite new conspiracy theory; she insists, without evidence, that crack was intentionally introduced into South Central by the CIA through Nicaraguan contras. This version of "barbershop history" neatly ties together her old foes in one package while proving once again that her constituents are blameless victims. Waters's rantings led an Asian-American businessman to ask, "Why would I want to hire people who threatened me?"

For most workaday business people, the gangster aura holds little charm. But L.A. is a partial exception in this regard. Each city is both a beneficiary of and bedeviled by its core industry. In New York, the financial services sector, which profits from issuing new bonds, is usually little concerned with the Big Apple's crushing debt. In Washington, where government is the be-all and end-all, there are no competitive standards for job performance. In Los Angeles, the selling of the black outlaw image has been big box office for the entertainment industry.

L.A. music impresario Peter Sellars thought himself bold and original when he exclaimed, "The breakdown of morals in America is a pretty exciting thing. " A self-satisfied Sellars no doubt thought himself an advanced thinker, but his statement has a long pedigree. Centuries earlier, the Enlightenment giant Denis Diderot, the first to conceive of victimless crime, compared great crimes to great works of art because "noble and sublime deeds share with great crimes the same quality of energy." It was an idea advanced by the Marquis de Sade and mined in the twentieth century by many, including Graham Greene, whose contribution was to contrast the grandeur of crime with the pettiness of middle-class life. Greene's English Catholics could be murderers and yet superior by being more real than "the great middle law-abiding class that believes in right and wrong." This theme of lawlessness conferring an elevating grace was taken up after World War II by Jean Genet in France and Norman Mailer in the United States, writers for whom the morally privileged transgressors were black teenagers rather than English Catholics. Hollywood and the record industry added little except to mass-market these addled assumptions.

The most influential of the "gangsta rap" groups, NWA (Niggas with Attitude), laid out their credo in a song, "Gangsta, Gangsta," recorded before the 1992 riots:

Here's a little something 'bout a nigga like me
Never shoulda been let out of the penitentiary . . .

Monster Kody seems to have stepped right out of the song. Monster earned his moniker as a thirteen-year-old, when he so severely stomped on the face of one of his robbery victims that the police gave him a *nom de guerre.* In the wake of the riots Leonce Bing, one of the scriptwriters for the black gangsta movie *New Jack City,* led the way in marketing Monster Kody. Bing, an ex-model who lives on a tony island off the coast of Seattle, is convinced that gangs hold out the promise of black redemption.

Like his big brother, Li'l Monster also became an object of adulation. Li'l Monster, also a murderer, became the subject of a documentary film. After being lionized on *Nightline,* he moved on to the college lecture circuit. For his part, big brother Monster Kody wrote a book about his exploits that was compared to Eldridge Cleaver's *Soul on Ice* by the *New York Times* and described by a *Los Angeles Times* reviewer as an "altruistic" effort for "the betterment of most of humanity" and a "triumph of the human spirit." The reviewers differed on just what level of greatness Monster's work had achieved, but both were convinced by his book that for most people in the inner city there are no choices. Monster, they were certain, had been forced into a life of crime by a callous society.

The reviewers, the TV shows, the magazine articles in *Esquire* and the *Los Angeles Times Magazine,* and the two young men themselves depicted their violence as a mere efflux of the poverty and deprivation they had experienced in South Central. Li'l Monster came on *Nightline* to explain that his father had to be a criminal because he couldn't feed his family and that now he, Li'l Monster, was similarly forced to be a criminal, something he would pass down to his children. In a 1989 *Harper's* Roundtable, Monster Kody, his life framed as a product of "society's indifference," said that dope dealing was the only way he could "grab" the "American dream." Morgan Entrekin of Grove Press agreed. One of the many publishers interested in the book, Entrekin described Monster as a "primary voice of the black experience." Similarly chilling was the comment of a British publisher who explained interest in the book, which was to be made into a movie, on the grounds that "getting that close to evil is very interesting." Blacks here, by dint of liberal racism, had been reduced to little more than primitives playing the scripted role of entertainers for the moral adventurers determined to find amusement, if not purpose, from inner-city anger.

It's only fitting that as a subject of *faux* feelings, Monster is something of a fraud. The book *Monster: The Autobiography of an L.A. Gang Member,* notes journalist Mark Horowitz, has as its core contention that Kody Scot had no choice but to be a gang member, a premise the reviewers and TV interviewers accepted. But the great singer and songwriter Ray Charles was Kody's godfather, his biological father was a pro football player, and he grew up in a two-parent home; when his mother's husband left, he lived in a house big enough for a recreation room with a ping-pong table. His younger brother Li'l Monster followed in his path, but three of the brothers, one of whom found a surrogate father, went straight. One is an actor, another is in the Air Force. Their mother, Birdie Canada, says Kody and Kershaun (Li'l Monster) joined gangs because "it was something they wanted to do. Because they didn't have to." She's right. Kody had jobs but he didn't like them because, as he explains in his autobiography, "working was considered weak." But robbery and mayhem were fun. "I enjoyed being Monster Kody. I lived for the power surge of playing God, having the power of life and death in my hands."

"Destroying," noted the historian of French fascism Eugene Weber, "is not a pleasure to be despised." Some gang members may operate out of low self-esteem or the absence of opportunities, but others are drawn to the images of glamour and power legitimated on the big screen and by credulous liberals, who, having been fooled once by Eldridge Cleaver, are determined to be fooled forever more. Striking a gangster pose in a movie-defined city means that young men get to play big roles in an ongoing street theater. Being a gangster means that almost everyone else has to make way. It's no small delight for a group of fourteen-year-old boys walking down the street side by side to force all adults, particularly whites, to stand aside and scatter.

And scatter they have. In a prophetic passage in *The Fire Next Time,* James Baldwin warned, "The Negroes of this country may never be able to rise to power, but they are very well placed to precipitate chaos and bring down the curtain on the American dream." Not really, as the example of upwardly mobile Latinos suggests. But politicized black violence is capable of bringing down the curtain on any hopes for inner-city blacks. Isolated by a black middle-class out-migration, the young black kids who are struggling to make it have to succeed in the face of the gang culture legitimated by political leaders, parts of the press, and popular culture.

One of L.A.'s star female rappers, Lichelle Laws, "the Boss," known for her "Born Gangstaz" recording, is the product of Baldwin Hills, known as the black Beverly Hills. The beneficiary of ballet and piano lessons, Lichelle sings about how she's "trying to get to Watts, but I'm stuck in Baldwin Hills." When upper-middle-class white kids play at being "gangstas," they themselves may get caught in a downward spiral, but there are rarely collective consequences for the community at large. For blacks, however, the marketing of ghetto pathology is a danger not only to individuals but to the community at large.

In the 1993 mayoral election, whenever Democrat Richard Katz, one of the fifty candidates for mayor, asked audiences, "How many of you have thought about leaving Los Angeles?" he usually saw a thick show of hands. No wonder. A post-riot *Los Angeles Times* poll found that 45 percent of L.A. would have liked to leave, given the chance. The post-riot demographics of L.A. have been framed by two dueling trajectories: the path of lower-middle-class whites and blacks desperate to leave and that of Latino immigrants, often illegal, desperate to arrive.

12. *Reconquista?*

Los Angeles has been made and remade by repeated waves of migrations: midwesterners at the turn of the century, Oakies in the 1920s and 1930s, blacks in the 1940s and 1950s, and Latinos over the past two decades. Just as the arrival of the earlier groups later reshaped politics—Yorty was the product of the Oakie migration, Bradley of the black migration—the Latino migration is sure to reshape L.A. and its politics.

No city in recent years, with the exception of now largely Cuban Miami, has gone through the same kind of near-total demographic transition. In twenty-five extraordinary years, L.A. has gone from the whitest and most Protestant of America's big cities to a majority Latino and Catholic city. Only 9 percent of its population was foreign-born in 1960, but by 1980 that figure had jumped to 27 percent; by 1990 it was an overwhelming 40 percent. More than 750,000 of L.A.'s 3.5 million residents entered the United States between 1980 and 1990. Meanwhile, L.A.'s black population declined from 505,000 in 1980 to 487,000 in 1990 while the Latino and Asian populations doubled to 1,400,000 and 341,000, respectively. Referring to California's Mexican past, Michael Meyers of *Time* magazine wrote, "The question is not whether *reconquista* will take place, but how and with what consequences."

Will Hispanics, now 44 percent of the population of Los Angeles County, follow the typical ethnic model of private sector mobility, asks sociologist Peter Skerry, or will they choose the black and Irish models of state-sponsored mobility? To put it somewhat differently, will Latinos follow a nationalist/separatist path, or will they try to set the tone for all of L.A.? There are those, like Assemblyman Louis Caldera, a West Point graduate and Harvard

M.B.A., and Gregory Rodriguez, a professor at Pepperdine University, who see Latinos as the new common ground in L.A., the one group that can talk to everyone else. In the words of an editorial from a Mexican-American newspaper, the hope is to "do what the blacks had failed to do; incorporate all into the human race and exclude no one."

Caldera, whose mother only recently became a citizen after thirty-five years in America, is a pro-business Democrat and a supporter of charter schools and English immersion classes who sees a middle-class future for Mexican-Americans. For his part, Rodriguez is so sure of the Hispanic prospects as a classic immigrant group rising primarily through the private sector that he argues that Hispanics, in order to lead, will have to break with affirmative action. By getting rid of group racial policies, he says, "Republicans might be doing us a favor." Ending them will reduce tensions and, besides, he says, "It's time to throw away the training wheels; we want to go for the gold."

Many are going for the gold. A fifth of all Latinos have left the Catholic Church to join Protestant denominations, which they associate with upward mobility and becoming American, while 30 percent of native-born Mexican-Americans in Los Angeles County marry non-Latinos. Almost half of the Latinos in suburban Ventura County to the north, where they are a fifth of the population, have a college degree. All in all, this suggests the possibility of a prosperous mestizo future.

On the other hand, there are those right- and left-wing tribalists, like Xavier Hermosillo, a businessman, and Rudolph Acuna, an academic, who, like sixties Chicano militants, echo the Black Power approach. The sixties Chicano militants declared, "The call of our blood is our power . . . our inevitable destiny." They spoke of the "sun people" reclaiming the lost land of Atzlan stolen by the Anglos.

Irredentism was still popular among student militants at a 1993 UCLA "strike" demanding a Chicano studies program. The "strikers"—complete with posters of Cesar Chavez, Pancho Villa, and the Ayatollah Khomeini—won a partial victory for their new program even as UCLA, caught in the state fiscal crisis, was phasing out the schools of nursing and architecture as well as the gymnastics and swim teams. One week after the strike ended, Richard Riordan was elected mayor with unprecedented Latino support.

Hermosillo, a small business man who is aware of Latino numbers, insists, Black Power–style, to both African-Americans and Anglos, "We will not overcome you, we will overwhelm you." From this perspective, Latinos need what *Los Angeles Times* columnist George Ramos calls a "brown version of Johnny Cochran." Some of the nationalists are, like Hermosillo, pro-business; others, like neo-Marxist Rudolph Acuna, are still stuck in the 1960s, romanticizing Latin gangsters, the *Cholos,* as the agent of liberation from Anglo colonialism. They both talk, in the language of the "riot ideology," about the new immigrants as "a quiescent mass that's ready to explode." Still others, activists who support MALDEF, the Ford Foundation-funded Mexican-American Legal, Defense and Education Fund, are legalitarian liberals intent on creating group rights for Latinos. What they all have in common is a belief in ineluctable separateness, a sense that Latinos are of birth and necessity a people apart.

In practical politics, the lines between these two roughly defined camps—the integrationists and the separatists—are often blurred. Most Latino pols in L.A. are classic ethnic operatives—with a twist. What's different is that most represent "rotten boroughs," districts where, because of recent immigration and the youth of the average Latino, the percentage of voters to the total population is tiny. This means that the real voting base is that small fraction of the population already eligible to vote and sometimes directly dependent on government employment and programs. In practice this means that Latino-elected officials, like County Commissioner Gloria Molina and City Councilman Richard Alarcon, support the failed bilingual education programs for the same patronage reasons they oppose charter school reform. Their support is based on their getting their group's cut of the local government and social service jobs. As more Latinos become naturalized and vote, they're likely to elect officials with a wider range of views, if only because the vast majority of Latinos, native and immigrant alike, work in the private sector.

There are a great many poor Latino immigrants whose poverty derives from low wages. Although there are four times as many poor Latinos as blacks, 80 percent of the Latino males in South Central are in the workforce, compared to 57 percent for blacks. The visible effects of their strong work ethic and strong families can be seen in Lynwood, an area adjoining Watts. Statistically, it's even poorer than Watts, but there is a vibrant street life and an abundance of shops. But it's when you leave the city proper and move east into the county and the town of Huntington Park, a step up from Lynwood, that you feel the full force of a lower middle class emerging among Mexican immigrants.

In 1960 Huntington Park, population twenty-nine thousand, was a largely Mormon town and a typical L.A. suburb. The town's claim to fame was its main street, Pacific Boulevard, a superb shopping strip that drew customers from across the county. But then the Watts riot, a mile away in L.A. proper, brought white flight, which left the town with a 40 to 50 percent vacancy rate for commercial properties. A ghost town by 1970, Huntington Park was revived by the Mexican immigration. Today the town, now 96 percent Latino, has a population of seventy-five thousand. It is not nearly as prosperous as nearby Monterey Park, famed site of a giant Asian shopping center and home to a rising Asian middle and upper middle class. Nevertheless, Huntington Park, located adjacent to the Alameda Corridor, with its many low-wage Latino employees, has become a magnet for the upwardly mobile. Through rotating credit arrangements—families cosigning loans for each other—Huntington Park is the place where extended immigrant families moving out of South Central have a chance to buy a modest two-bedroom California bungalow for about $130,000.

Huntington Park's revived main street, Pacific Boulevard, now has six hundred stores, stretches for miles, and again attracts shoppers from all over the county. The boulevard pulsates to the beat of *banda* and *ranchera* music as peddlers sell cucumber spears and coconut slices on the sidewalk. There are two Latino nightclubs, more than a dozen bridal shops selling communion and baptismal dresses, and a host of bilingual medical clinics. Other shops specialize in *banda*-style Western outfits and cowboy gear. With retail sales of $87 million annually, Pacific Boulevard rivals the Latin shopping district along Broadway in downtown L.A. and is the place where Latino businesses, which have expanded in the county at three times the rate of the Latino population growth, get a start.

The strength of their conventional values gives the Mexicans another advantage. For all the *Viva Zapata!* imagery some Latino college students are drawn to, "these people," as a TV producer once complained, "just aren't hip." With the exception of the Ford Foundation, the same organization that underwrote Ocean Hill–Brownsville and is now promoting bilingualism and Latino group rights, no group is likely to take the people of Huntington Park as the cat's-paw for some emerging movement. Or, as a member of former mayor Bradley's inner circle put it, "The problem with Mexican-Americans is that they aren't a cause the way blacks are."

The strivers of Huntington Park are never going to be hip and are unlikely to be taken up as pop icons by the L.A. media—and that's all to the good. My experience of walking the bustling streets of Huntington Park, which were filled with families, and of going into the shops and talking to merchants and their customers reminded me of Flushing, Queens, a lower-middle-class launching pad, in the 1950s. I felt the texture of a closely woven society, so that despite the area's problems I walked away with a sense of optimism.

Familiar though it seems, Huntington Park represents something new in the history of American immigration. The sheer number and continuous flow of Mexican arrivals here means that the dynamics of acculturation into American life are unique and unprecedented. When forty-three-year-old Jaime Sanchez, who came to Huntington Park to work as a dishwasher twenty-six years ago, says "Living here feels just like I am in Mexico," it's more than a simile. With fewer than 15 percent of the area's Latinos being third-generation or older, the new arrivals are so numerous that they have quickly recreated much of the world they came from, minus its stifling political and economic controls. The older Latino community is forced to adjust to the newcomers almost as much as the newcomers are forced to adapt to America.

The new arrivals fleeing from the desperate poverty of southern Mexico bring a powerful work ethic and a strong sense of kinship. They represent a traditionalist family-centered alternative to what only thirty years ago looked like a Latino future defined by both the romanticization of gangsters and political claims to victimization. It's no longer necessary to be an outlaw to be authentically Mexican-American. With their *banda* music, peasant food, and family values, the new immigrants are re-Mexicanizing many of the almost assimilated Latinos. Speaking Spanish in public, which marked someone as an outsider just a decade ago, is now an asset in an increasingly bilingual economy.

But there are clouds on the horizon. Some are political, while others, perhaps more threatening, are economic. Re-Mexicanization has brought both cultural strengths and a set of contradictory currents to the issue of Mexican-American identity. The pressures of adaptation produce counterassertions of ethnic authenticity, as reflected in terms like *coconut* (meaning "brown on the outside but white on the inside"). The new arrivals from Mexico, often fierce cultural nationalists, live in far closer proximity to their homeland than has any previous immigrant group. They have been far and away the slowest group to naturalize and vote. Some of that changed after California Proposition 187, an anti–illegal immigration ballot initiative supported by Republican Governor Pete Wilson, passed overwhelmingly in 1995. The already large majority for Proposition 187 was only augmented when rallies against the proposition featured Mexican flags, a sensitive subject in a state where some of the school textbooks for bilingual classes are supplied by the Mexican government and some of the history texts feature maps that show the southwestern United States as part of Mexico (other texts show it as the mythical Aztec homeland of Aztlan). While these territorial claims may seem absurd to some, they have a resonance in a city whose neighborhoods are marked by Spanish names and whose major street, Pico Boulevard, is named after the last Mexican governor to rule before the California Republic was created.

The vote to pass Proposition 187, which, if implemented, would have denied all social benefits and schooling to the children of illegal immigrants, produced a backlash among Latinos. Many saw the initiative as an attack on all immigrants. The fight over Proposition 187 was a defining political moment for the Latino community.

The average Mexican immigrant is little interested in politics. After living under Mexico's "kleptocratic" regime, the newcomers, like Sicilians of yore, bring a well-bred cynicism toward politics and all matters official. For many who had become citizens, the vote against Proposition 187 was the first they had ever cast. The referendum's aftermath produced a doubling of naturalization rates and a groundswell of interest in political participation.

As with so many things Mexican-American, the fight over Proposition 187 generated a set of crosscurrents. It bred both a bitter resentment of the largely Anglo anti-immigration movement and a heightened sense of America's appeal. In its wake a South Central man, speaking for his family, exclaimed, "However bad 187 is, it's not as bad as a day in Michoacan." One angry Latina applying for citizenship exclaimed, "Now I can vote to get rid of that Pete Wilson." But the ambiguity of the situation does not end there; as another new voter put it, "Wilson has no right to tell us what to do; we Mexicans were here first."

Mexico and southern California, once Mexican territory, are so closely intertwined that some fear that L.A. will "melt into Mexico." A 1993 L.A. mayoral candidate and a number of academics have proposed, in recognition of a cross-border identity, that noncitizens be allowed to vote in local elections. For its part, Mexico has decided to allow its citizens living in California to vote in Mexican elections. The realistic possibility that a close Mexican election could be decided by California voters has produced an unprecedented level of Mexican government and political party activity in southern California. The reigning Institutional Revolutionary Party and its left- and right-wing rivals have become far more visible as they take stands on California issues to influence potential voters in Mexican elections.

The concept of dual citizenship, now endorsed in principle by all parties in Mexico, would allow Mexicans in America to retain their property rights and *Mexicanidad,* Mexican nationality, even as they become U.S. citizens. José Angel Pescador Osuna, the Mexican consul general in Los Angeles, explains: "It is important that they [Mexican immigrants] are becoming citizens of this country, but that they keep their Mexican cultural roots. People were afraid of being ashamed in Mexico because they changed their nationality. Now they will not change their nationality."

Dual citizenship is not unknown. The creation of a European parliament in Strasbourg, France, represents an experiment in a kind of dual citizenship. Closer to home, in Canada the combination of Quebecois nationalism and strong provincial governments represents a de facto version of dual citizenship. In Quebec, as in Los Angeles, an old Anglo conquest is still resented by people who often feel separated by language and religion. Canada is, of course, continually on the verge of breaking apart. It remains to be seen just how deeply the concept takes hold, but the separation of nationality and citizenship, particularly on a mass scale, represents in the United States an unprecedented experiment in multiculturalism.

The immigration issue has been fought out along a number of fronts: crime, costs to local taxpayers, the displacement of low-income blacks and whites. Illegal aliens do impose enormous welfare, medical, and academic burdens in a state where false papers are easy to come by. Low-skilled native workers are displaced, although the cities that have not received immigrants, like Detroit and Cleveland, have far higher black poverty rates than Los Angeles. Immigrants create new jobs and sometimes even new industries, as well as displace old workers. These issues are important but secondary to the crucial issue of how well the immigrants who have already arrived will be incorporated into American life.

There is a tension between rising Mexican-American family incomes and declining individual wages. Mexican-American mobility has been family mobility. It has come as unskilled and often uneducated family members, cousins, and in-laws have pooled their incomes to buy a home together. Their precarious foothold on lower-middle-class status is in continual danger of being washed away by the onrushing tide of newer arrivals, who threaten to further erode the already low wage levels.

Skilled Asians, who often arrive with a higher education and sometimes with capital, are making it into the middle class faster than any previous group. Asians attend college at a higher rate than whites, with native-born Asians far ahead of whites on this count. There are high levels of intra-Asian separation. Residentially, Asians from any particular group are more likely to interact and intermarry with whites than with other Asians (Koreans and Japanese, for instance, bear historic animosities). But the picture of Mexican and other Latino arrivals is far more mixed.

According to UCLA sociologist Roger Waldinger, "L.A. is not so much a dual as a plural city, in which the myriad of new ethnic groups has created a segmented system, where each group largely lives and works in its own distinctive social world." Different ethnic groups not only largely live apart when they arrive, but also work apart in distinct economic niches. Koreans, for instance, are heavily overrepresented in small business, blacks in government. Mexicans and Central Americans are in gardening, hotel and restaurant work, and manufacturing; heavy Mexican representation in these areas guarantees a continuous flow of friends and relatives into the same jobs. The arrival of low-paid, hardworking individuals has, with the help of Asian and Anglo entrepreneurs, reshaped L.A. into the most important manufacturing city in the United States. But it has also made Los Angeles the capital of low-wage labor.

So long as the emigrants helped create more jobs than the number of people arriving, pooled wages were generally sustained at levels sufficient to offer the promise of upward mobility. The problem is that Mexican immigrants are now beginning to pay the price for the post–World War II Mexican policies that tried to assure national greatness through population growth. Mexico's population growth so far exceeds its job creation capacities that California has become a giant safety valve. The danger is that the relentless Mexican population pressure will tend to bring wages north of the border into a low-level equilibrium with those to the south. The sheer size of the immigration, legal and illegal, particularly of the unskilled, has created not only hellhole sweatshops but also mobility traps as downward pressure on wages from immigrants crowding into the same niches leaves little hope of advancement.

Even with the economic recovery, wages continue to fall in a range of industries, including garment and plastic manufacturing, recycling, and food processing. At the same time that rail spurs are reducing the demand for truckers, in the last ten years the number of drivers at the competing and adjacent ports of Long Beach and San Pedro has more than doubled. The upshot, says Robert Millman, a lawyer for trucking companies, is that "these days shipping companies pay what they want to pay." The income for truckers, once one of the occupations that gave a man a shot at a better life for his family, has fallen by half in the last few years. Similarly, a General Accounting Office study of janitorial pay in downtown L.A. office buildings shows that by 1983 unionized workers had achieved a healthy $12-an-hour pay scale. However, downsizing and nonunion competition from firms hiring illegals drove compensation down to minimum-wage levels.

The problem of low-wage labor will only grow more intense. While there are nine times as many Mexican-Americans in college than in jail, Mexicans are far and away the least educated of southern California's immigrant groups. Many recent arrivals have only a sixth-grade education and speak an Indian dialect rather than Spanish. The risk is that the pressure of being trapped in low-wage work without the educational skills to eventually move to the high-wage sector will generate tremendous resentment over time. First-generation immigrants compare their situation to the one they left, but their children and their children's children will compare their situation to the rest of Los Angeles. Los Angeles has what might be called an hourglass economy; there is tremendous growth in both high-tech jobs and in unskilled jobs but relatively little in between. In the 1980s the number of households in L.A. making more than $75,000 grew at a phenomenal 459 percent; at the same time, the number of people living in poverty also grew, albeit at a far more modest 35 percent. While immigration has helped fuel the area's economic dynamism, it has also given it, the underground economy excluded, the country's poorest congressional district, poorer even than the Mississippi delta region, the traditional "winner" in that category.

Given the opportunities offered in L.A. and the energy of the immigrants, many in the barrio will move out of abject poverty. The problem comes in the succeeding steps. There is no way to make the leap across the vast chasm separating high- and low-skill employment. Howard Ezell, the former western regional commissioner of the Immigration and Naturalization Service, warned that the process of continuous large-scale immigration means that southern California "will become a Third World country with unemployment and uneducated people." The *Economist* put it differently, warning of an immigrant-driven underclass. Perhaps, but it's not likely. Even under the pressure of a sharp economic downturn, tightly textured cultures like those of the arriving immigrants are unlikely to unravel. Rather than a descent into family breakdown and growing criminality in Latino communities, Los Angeles would probably experience a sharp upsurge in ethnic animosity, expressed as hostility to both wealthy white Anglos and blacks, who are seen as beneficiaries of a disproportionate share of government largesse.

Trapped on the bottom rungs and without the hope of a quick educational boost, Mexican-Americans, like turn-of-the-century Italians, another group who rose through backbreaking physical labor, may find their best route to opportunity through trade unions. Under the North American Free Trade Agreement, unionization will drive some industries, like electronic assembly, into Mexico, but it can also replace some of the missing middle rungs on L.A.'s job ladder. If it is done right, private sector unionization might offer something of a solution to L.A.'s social and civic problems.

The new president of the AFL-CIO, Bronx-born John Sweeney, who made his mark organizing immigrant janitors in downtown L.A., looks to southern California as the seedbed for union growth. For sixty years the AFL-CIO held its annual meetings in or around Miami. In 1997, under Sweeney, the federation convention moved to a unionized downtown Los Angeles hotel. L.A., enthuses Susan Cowell of Unite, the garment workers' union, "is the labor movement's top priority." She and others note the potential for organizing the largest manufacturing labor force in the United States, almost half of it Latino and 17 percent of it organized, compared to that of New York, where 27 percent of the labor force is unionized.

Sweeney's ally in organizing L.A. will be Miguel Contreras, the first Latino leader of the politically powerful Los Angeles County Federation of Labor. Contreras, who grew up in a farm worker family, learned organizing under the tutelage of Cesar Chavez and his United Farm Workers. Contreras is married to Maria Elena Durazo, local head of the Hotel and Restaurant Workers Unions, who is best known for her innovative tactics. In the wake of the 1992 riots, she negotiated with hotel and restaurant owners through a publicity campaign that included wide distribution of a videotape that warned of the dangers of coming to L.A. Contreras has also played the riot card, warning that unless organized labor succeeds, 1992 could happen again.

Self-destructive tactics aside, the problem for the unions is that in spite of all the workers concentrated in L.A., the new dispersed small-shop economy seems impossible to organize. That led to LAMAP, the Los Angeles Manufacturing Area Project, an attempt at community-based organizing many hoped would give Sweeney a prototype for a national campaign. Structured as a multiunion and immigrant-driven attempt to organize the job-rich Alameda Corridor, LAMAP evangelizes for unions broadly among Latinos in order to then indirectly unionize individual shops.

The LAMAP strategy is in a sense a throwback to the tactics once used successfully on what was then the Jewish Lower East Side of New York. The International Ladies Garment Workers Union (ILGWU) found that the Jewish workers scattered in numerous small garment workshops were impossible to organize company by company. But then the tragic 1911 Triangle Shirtwaist Factory fire, which claimed the lives of 146 people, many of whom were trapped inside the burning building by locked safety exits, transformed the union's fortunes. The ILGWU found itself in the forefront of a widespread movement for the reform of working conditions that both boosted union membership and made Tammany Hall sit up and listen. It was as a consequence of the Triangle Fire that Tammany's Boss Murphy and his heirs, future New York Governor Al Smith and future senator Robert Wagner, author of the New Deal's most important piece of labor legislation, began the legislative reform of factory working conditions. Those reforms later served as models for New Deal labor legislation.

L.A. union organizers are hoping that the anti-immigrant Proposition 187 is, in effect, their Triangle Shirtwaist Factory fire, the galvanizing event that helps drive both unionization and reform politics. Politically, the postproposition efforts by organized labor have been a considerable success in defeating conservative Republicans and in electing liberal Latino Democrats in the L.A. area. Unionization remains a different matter.

The LAMAP campaign targeted specific industries, like food processing and garment and plastics industries, that must be close to downtown, rather than focusing on individual companies. Despite some victories, LAMAP has been a disappointment. The continuous arrival of new workers willing to work for less than the prevailing wage makes unionization almost impossible. You can't reduce poverty by continuously importing more poor people.

Both history and logic argue for the unions to support immigration restriction. American unions were strongest between 1924 and 1965, when immigration restriction limited the labor supply. Although the logic of the situation requires the unions to support a closed-border policy to tighten the local labor markets, the very alliance with Latino groups at the heart of the LAMAP campaign makes that approach impossible. The anti-immigrant sentiment behind Proposition 187 backed labor into a corner. Immigration restrictions are so strongly identified with anti-Mexican and even racist sentiments that it is impossible for labor to talk about immigration restriction without alienating the very workers they want to organize. The only thing labor can talk about is the need to unionize Mexico in general and the *maquiladora* plants along the border in particular. That's a shame, because in a burg where ninety-two languages are spoken in the schools and where even the highest public officials are virtually anonymous, a revived union movement might, at its best, offer something of a cross-cultural ethic for a city suffering from a shortage of civic capital.

Day to day, the separation of people into different occupations and housing niches limits interethnic hostilities. Multiculturalism in practice means indifference to the fate of other groups that live inside their own neighborhoods and occupational niches. But the psychic costs inherent in newcomers' attempts to adapt to a new land, on the one hand, and the sense of displacement felt by native-born people, on the other, make for a combustible combination. This mulitculturalist paradise has no shortage of potential conflicts. At the moment, the hostility between blacks and browns is the most salient because of the changing demographics of South Central L.A., where much of the black lower middle class has left while a growing Latino population, much of it from Central America, continues to arrive.

Says Steve Erie, a professor at the University of California at San Diego, "It was no accident that the flash points for the 1992 rebellion and riot were in the same neighborhoods that have undergone the greatest ethnic transition." There are relatively few African-American neighborhoods in L.A. Today only 7 percent of the city's blacks live in neighborhoods that are 90 percent or more black, compared with 71 percent in Chicago, 61 percent in Detroit, 43 percent in Atlanta, and 31 percent in New York. "No question about it," exclaims a black owner of a welding shop on Florence Avenue in South Central, "we are losing. It damn near is a Latino city." A retired black truck driver, sounding like earlier generations of whites bemoaning the arrival of blacks, says, "Mexicans like dirt fronts, they don't like lawns, they park their car in front of their houses, they raise chickens, they hang out their laundry to dry in the front yard. They don't like grass. That's why we moved out."

13. Secession?

I arrived in L.A. to visit relatives on the day that the first Simpson verdict was announced. In following the case from Brooklyn, I didn't grasp just how much more intensely the case was affecting attitudes in Los Angeles.

The first thing I did upon arriving was to go to my sister-in-law's house for my nephew's birthday party. There a heated discussion about the verdict was under way. The discussants included a well-known actress and a successful sitcom writer. The writer, who was the most articulate of the lot, was outspoken in criticizing the racism of the verdict, the intelligence of the jury, and the black celebration over the outcome. Repelled, he was vociferous in insisting that he had to get his family out of Los Angeles and away from the endless threat of riots. I asked him if he was a conservative Republican. He looked at me with astonishment and responded, "No, I'm a liberal Democrat." I then repeated some of the things he had said. He smiled, recognizing the incongruence, and replied that he was no longer sure of what he was politically but that, yes, I was probably right in suspecting that he was no longer a liberal Democrat.

It was a conversation that was to be repeated in various forms during the period that extended from the Simpson verdict to the Million Man March. Time and again I listened to self-described liberals mock not only the Simpson verdict but the coverage of the trial in the Los Angeles Times. *Though they spoke without the venom of the talk radio callers, the effect of the trial was profound in crystallizing nagging questions about the Bradley mayoralty and the* Los Angeles Times *in particular and about liberalism in general. A longtime supporter of civil rights who was both a leader in the Jewish com-*

munity and one of the very few individuals involved in the civic life of L.A. as a whole saw the trial as a threat to the rule of law, which had inspired his involvement with civil rights thirty years earlier. After Simpson's lawyer Johnny Cochran, a man closely associated with former mayor Tom Bradley, played the race card in his summation to the jury, this longtime liberal concluded that "blacks had ceased to be America's moral touchstone." He also asserted that many others would echo his belief that in its politically correct coverage of both the riot and the trial the Los Angeles Times *had lost touch with the city and was now in danger of losing its authority in the San Fernando Valley, two-fifths of the city, to the more politically moderate voice of the Valley-based* Los Angeles Daily News. *He proved prescient. Within six months the Valley was buzzing with talk of secession.*

The reaction of my relatives from a once safe section of the city was typical of those whites I spoke to. My sister-in-law went on about how gang killings had come to her neighborhood. She talked of a city "out of control and falling apart" with "no one in charge" and with "no safe neighborhoods anywhere." An acquaintance echoed her fears in describing how the arrival of an aggressive homeless population had changed the character of her Valley neighborhood. The sense of pervasive menace so common to New York was new and all the more unacceptable to those living in large parts of the city, including the Valley, the West Side, and Topanga Canyon. A Valley liberal, mourning the loss of "the small town feeling we once had," concluded, "We used to read about the drive-by shooting. It was all in Latino East L.A. or black and Latino South Central, and that ain't the case anymore."

The harshest response came from those who, adverting to the Reginald Denny verdict, argued that since the rioters in black L.A. had seceded from the rule of law, they were seceding psychologically from L.A. By that they meant that while they wouldn't pay any more in taxes for police protection, they had since the riot lost all faith in the L.A.P.D. and were going to arm themselves. I winced.

There were some striking similarities between the 1993 Los Angeles and New York mayoral elections. Both were traditionally Democratic cities that had been rocked by a recession that lingered even as the rest of the country recovered; both pitted "rainbow coalition" candidates against centrist white Catholic Republicans; and in both cities, the multicultural candidates tried to portray their opponents as the candidates of the rabidly right wing and of the fat cats while the Republicans made public order and the economy their campaign issues.

In Los Angeles the Democratic candidate Mike Woo tried to re-create the Bradley coalition. In seeking Latino support, Woo and Riordan updated the approaches taken by Bradley and Yorty in their 1973 clash. Wrote Richard Mauin, "Where Bradley said 'wait until we are all free,' Yorty said, 'you Mexicans are fine people, got all the street names in Los Angeles, and I am offering you a chance to get a little closer to the good things—jobs, suburbia, a preferred station in the local caste system without having to deal with those aggressive *mayatas* blacks.' "

Woo showed courage and cemented his black support by being the first public official to call for the resignation of police chief Daryl Gates in the wake of the riot. But Woo's "rainbow campaign" dismayed many white voters by referring to the riot as a "rebellion." Woo tried to tie Riordan to Ronald Reagan and Pat Robertson, but Riordan, playing off the aftermath of the riot, tied Woo to the Bradley era's decline of the police and public safety.

Clinton Reilly, the man who ran the Riordan campaign, saw how much of the conventional political landscape had been swept away in the riot's aftermath. Reilly, who had been the strategist behind Frank Jordan's winning 1991 campaign to unseat San Francisco Mayor Art Agnos around the homeless issue, saw that public order was the public's primary concern. Riordan, who had quietly been a Clinton supporter, rarely mentioned the recent riots but caught their resonance with a campaign mailer that featured an unflattering picture of a homeless man on the front and proposals on panhandling and graffiti within. Reilly TV ads showed a woman nervously walking down an alley clutching her purse as the voice-over cites the Hollywood crime stats: "Woo opposes the death penalty. . . . Woo allowed cuts in L.A. police force from eighty-four hundred officers to only seventy-six hundred." Riordan also pointed to the decline and disorder of Woo's Hollywood council district.

For his part, Woo played into Riordan's hands. He responded with themes first laid out on a presidential level by Adlai Stevenson in arguing that the urge for order was a disguised call for conformity. "My goal," said Woo, "is to make sure Hollywood Boulevard remains an exciting, diverse, and exotic place." He explained: "Homeowners will see kids with ghetto blasters. I don't want to drive out the eccentric and interesting people, who are no harm to anyone else. I want to encourage real street life on Hollywood Boulevard."

Richard Riordan won the mayoralty with heavy support from the white and Latino middle class of the San Fernando Valley on a platform of "safety, safety, safety." When Woo campaigned on the need for more social services as a cure for crime, disgruntled liberals in his own neighborhood started an "anyone but Woo" organization to publicize the pervasive sense of menace on the streets of Hollywood.

In an election where twice as many voters thought graffiti, rather than health care and the environment combined, should be the first priority of the new mayor, Woo, a Democrat in an overwhelmingly Democratic city, lost by seven points to Republican Riordan. Riordan captured 43 percent of the Latino and a slim majority of the Jewish vote. By and large, people prefer not to choose between the antiseptic and the antisocial. The shame of our contemporary cities is that they so often have to make such a choice.

When Riordan took office, he inherited a city in an advanced state of civic disintegration. Like liberals in New York and D.C., Bradley had pursued a public sector strategy, that is, a combination of government jobs and social services for minorities and subsidized downtown real estate development for West Side Jewish liberals. Although never as extensive as on the East Coast or as expensive as in New York, the L.A. strategy failed just as completely, albeit with less damage to the economy. Bradley insisted that there was "little local government could do about the problems of South Central." The "underlying alienation" of African-Americans, Bradley asserted, "is due to the fact that since 1980 there has been a tremendous reduction in federal funds and of interest in the cities of the nation."

Bradley was working from a mistaken map of the world, and it was a mistake that would have enormous consequences for L.A.'s future as a unified city. Had he looked at D.C. or New York, he could have seen that money for social services wasn't the issue. Had he looked at the success of the immigrant population in L.A., he might have seen a far better model of opportunity. He did neither, which in the wake of the 1992 riots raised the question of what had been accomplished by the money Bradley spent on social programs and downtown redevelopment, since neither had been able to head off the violence.

Worse yet, Bradley's ethnic politics, which started off with a strong transracial emphasis that might have helped bind the city together, mutated over time into the distribution of group entitlements, a policy that generated resentment more effectively than rewards.

Many, disheartened by the recession that began in 1989 and in response to the late 1980s crime wave and the 1992 riots, had already given up on the idea of a unified city of Los Angeles. This is partly a matter of sheer size and distance. L.A.'s 467 square miles could contain the combined areas of San Francisco, Milwaukee, Minneapolis, Pittsburgh, Boston, Cleveland, and St. Louis—with Manhattan thrown in for good measure. Disgruntled residents of the San Fernando Valley in the north and those in the port area of San Pedro in the south are sixty miles from each other, and both have to drive as much as thirty miles of crowded highway to deal with city agencies located in downtown L.A.

But more than geography was implicated in the city's civic collapse. The sheer size of the new immigration left many longtime Angelenos feeling like strangers in their own land. When Tom Bradley was first elected in 1973, the city had nearly 700,000 voters. Twenty years later, when Bradley left office, the city (illegals aside) had grown by more than 700,000, but Riordan won with an electorate that had shrunk by almost 80,000 voters. The same years saw a virtual white withdrawal from the countrywide Los Angeles Unified School District (LAUSD); the growth of widespread support for the breakup of the LAUSD; and increasing social isolation, brought about either through the creation of restricted access housing or of neighborhoods bounded by gated roads. "A city where 40 percent of all households have unlisted telephone numbers," wrote columnist George Will, "is experiencing a great withdrawal from public life."

The middle class in general, but middle-class whites in particular, had either withdrawn from the city psychologically or had hunkered down in their own sections of the city. The Simpson trial (which for many symbolized, as did the riots, the collapse of law and public order) completed the process of disengagement from public space and public life.

Candidate Riordan campaigned on "safety, safety, safety," but Mayor Riordan had a great deal of difficulty in delivering on his campaign promise of 3,000 more cops. The departure of Daryl Gates didn't end the bickering over police policy. Daryl Gates's successor, Willie Williams of Philadelphia, the department's first African-American leader, inherited an impossible situation. He was asked to revive a demoralized department while caught in the cross fire created by an unworkable charter that divides civilian responsibility for the police among the police commission, city council, and mayor.

The indefensible Rodney King beating and the testimony of Mark Fuhrman notwithstanding, Willie Williams's L.A.P.D. is no longer a whites-only paramilitary machine. It is now 15 percent black, the only police department of the fifteen largest U.S. cities that has a higher percentage of African-Americans than in its city's population. Overall, 53 percent of the L.A.P.D. is made up of women and minorities, the preferred hires of recent years. Police brutality has been on the decline, in part because of the cost of defending against expensive lawsuits, and complaints of bias have also dropped.

The problem is that as crime continues to plague the city, the number of arrests in L.A. continues to decline; arrest numbers have plunged dramatically, from 290,000 in 1991 to 189,000 in 1995. This is in large measure a matter of police demoralization. Nine hundred cops have quit the hangdog department in the last two years. This has left Riordan running just to replace cops, not add new cops (a goal that assumes the city could afford to pay for them).

Riordan's bind is that his core constituency in the Valley demanded both lower taxes and more police. Valley voters, egged on by the heirs of Howard Jarvis's Proposition 13 movement, rejected not only new taxes but even a general obligation bond issue to pay for new police stations. Police are expensive. L.A. has the second most expensive cops in the country. The three thousand cops Riordan wanted to add to the L.A.P.D. would have tacked $180 million onto the city's $2.2 billion discretionary budget.

The San Fernando Valley is separated from the rest of the city by a suburban mentality as much as by mountains. The Valley simultaneously rejected higher taxes to pay for police citywide, saying it already bears too much of the overall tax burden, and insisted on more police protection for itself. The logical outcome has been a move for secession.

Consider Los Angeles, as Harold Meyerson wrote in the *L.A. Weekly*, "as a solar system where the sun (downtown) is shrinking . . . and the gravitational pull on outlying areas grows weaker and weaker." The Valley, which was originally drawn to join L.A. by its need for water, has been rumbling over secession since the 1970s, when taxpayer and antibusing revolts animated an antidowntown activism. More recently a movement to break up the massive LAUSD, which covers 708 square miles and all or part of twenty-eight cities, has fueled the Valley drive to separate. State Senator Paula Boland, who is leading the charge to break up the school district, is also heading up the legislative effort in Sacramento to create a separate city.

As in New York before Ocean Hill–Brownsville, there's widespread support for decentralization. For many, L.A. is so large and downtown is so distant that the city government seems more like an aloof regional authority than a local government. UCLA's Eric Shockman notes that as early as 1948 Los Angeles had a mayor (Fletcher Bowman) who proposed dividing the city into five boroughs, each of which would direct all its local services, including public safety, and would have the authority to levy taxes for increased services over and above that provided on a citywide basis. But, as in New York, sentiment in L.A. for decentralization has been caught up in a cultural and racial undertow.

Liberal Angelenos sometimes refer disdainfully to the Valley (the home of the forever seventies white-bread TV family, the Brady bunch) as "twenty-nine malls in search of a city." The Valley, says Meyerson, would be the ideal centrifugal city, with "the most backyard pools and the fewest public parks." Though the Valley is now about one-third Hispanic, its critics see a strong element of racism, a flight from black L.A., as the factor driving the secession movement.

Critics claim that if the San Fernando Valley secedes, other parts of Los Angeles—the Port of San Pedro, the beachside bohemia of Venice, and the wealthy Westside—might do so as well. The Valley itself might break into a poor and more Latino eastern half and a wealthier, whiter western half, leaving the inner-city poor isolated. True, but that's just the point. For the secessionists the liberal strategy of buying off inner-city violence, a strategy begun in the wake of Watts, has failed. As a disgruntled and usually apolitical Angeleno said, "I'm tired of paying off those damn people. If they want to riot, they better not come here because I'm arming myself." Both the violence and the costs of the bribe have grossly increased. Secession, like individual outmigration, is in part a strategy to shield people from the cost and casualties created by an urban underclass.

An extensive investigation by the pro-secession *Los Angeles Daily News* found that Valley taxpayers get back as much as they give to city government, but the report did little to quell the discontent. Many Valley residents continue to be convinced that they're shortchanged by the city. As one resident of Van Nuys told me, "Under Bradley the city took our money and spent it on Bradley's downtown developer friends and black allies. What did I get out of that?" The more constrained and cerebral proponents of secession point to the one in four city dollars that goes to support the city's slow-moving bureaucrats, nine out of ten of whom work in distant downtown. Like northern Italians looking to separate themselves from southern Italy, Valley residents see the welfare state as an elaborate transfer mechanism that drains money from the productive to reward the politically well-connected.

The Valley through its enthusiastic support of Proposition 13 was, in a sense, the author of its own alienation. "Prop" 13, a state ballot initiative passed in 1979, placed a cap on property taxes. Designed by its advocates to curtail the growth of government, in the Valley it was supported as the home owners' revenge against Mayor Bradley and his allies, the public employee unions. But it backfired.

Faced with a choice of laying off unionized public employees or finding new revenue sources, Bradley and the strongly pro–public employee city council chose the latter. They began to impose a bundle of new user fees, minor business taxes, parking taxes, and sewer, utility, sanitation, and ambulance charges that infuriated Valley home owners. During the Bradley years an average of four new taxes, fees, permits, or other revenue enhancers were introduced annually with the enthusiastic support of the city council—the strongest supporter of increased city spending. But even the increased user fees couldn't keep pace with the costs imposed by the growth of union benefits and other city spending, so the city began to cut back on such basic services as street cleaning, libraries, road repair, and infrastructure maintenance.

The city budget soared from $986 million in 1977, to $2.3 billion in 1987, to $4 billion in 1997, an increase of about twice the rate of inflation but a growth rate not nearly as high as that for the city debt, which exploded from $201,000 in 1977 to $3.6 billion in 1997. The combination of rising taxes to pay for the growing budget and declining services only further infuriated the already angry Valley.

In New York during the Ocean Hill–Brownsville hostilities, the dividing line was between those who wanted a common culture and those who wanted to separate, but in "multi-culti" L.A. almost every group sees itself as an aggrieved minority of sorts. The representatives of the Valley, like Ronald Close of the Sherman Oaks Homeowners Association, are every bit as good as blacks and South Central Hispanics in playing the percentages game; they complain, often without justification, that while they are *X* percent of the city they only get *X* minus *Y* percent of city services. In L.A., absent shared beliefs, the only way to talk about politics is to complain that one group or another isn't getting its fair share of the loot.

The Valley voted two to one for Riordan with the expectation that it would have a champion at city hall. But Riordan, a resident of tony Brentwood on the Westside, has been a disappointment. The mayor, who has (with a degree of accuracy) mocked some of the San Fernando populists as rednecks, has been picketed by Republican activists as a RINO (Republican in name only). The attacks on Riordan by Woo supporters obscured the fact that Riordan was and is a moderate, a man closely connected with downtown real estate projects and public and Catholic-funded social services for South Central. Faced with the likelihood of Riordan's reelection—he faced only a weak challenge—the discontented in the Valley found secession all the more appealing.

Short of building a moat, what the Valley wants is control of neighborhood matters. The Reverend Tom Rush says that the people of Pacoima feel they're helpless over little things "like maintenance of the streetlights, sidewalks, the storm drains that overflow at times" and getting the city to "remove abandoned cars." They don't want to have to go downtown to decide whether they can gate off areas to keep criminals out or deny liquor licenses on shaky streets. They want strict enforcement of the loitering laws as part of an intense quality-of-life policy that maintains what they see as the imperiled middle-class quality of life in the Valley, and because they compare themselves not to L.A. but to their thriving low-cost neighbors, the independent cities of Glendale and Burbank, they want it without higher taxes.

The *Los Angeles Daily News,* bitter rival of the downtown *Los Angeles Times,* has been promoting the movement by arguing that something called San Fernando Valley City would be "America's richest, safest city." Home to four Fortune 500 companies, it would lack cultural institutions and a commercial hub, but that's all right for most in the Valley, whose ideal is the anticity of L.A.'s Midwestern settlers. Theirs would be a city, the supporters of secession argue, that, like the small, nimble companies that drive the L.A. economy today, would be capable of quick effective adaptation, a city bound to thrive.

Riordan says he supports the breakup of the countywide Los Angeles Unified School District but is opposed to the Valley's secession. He warns that if the Valley middle class is allowed to leave, L.A. could go downhill like New York or, worse yet, Washington, D.C. Unable to deliver on his police promises and aware of polls showing widespread support for breaking L.A. up into more manageable units, the mayor praises community groups at every opportunity. Riordan mentioned the word *neighborhood* twenty-two times in his 1996 State of the City Address and talked of how he "doubled street maintenance for the Valley."

When talking about neighborhoods didn't calm the fever, the mayor also went in the other direction. Riordan suggested that the city bureaucracy would be more responsive if the mayor had more authority over city services. Riordan has proposed for the next election a charter reform initiative designed to both give the executive more power at the expense of the city council and offer more self-government to discontented areas. "The city," says Riordan, "is run by a system of fifteen, without anyone with the power and accountability to hold responsible. It's hard to get things to happen." The city council not surprisingly has proposed its own ballot initiative on charter reform.

Symbolically, Riordan, whose close ties with the Catholic hierarchy have given him an entrée to some Latino voters, seems to have placed some of his hope for binding the city together in building a new Roman Catholic cathedral downtown to replace historic but undersized Saint Vibiana's. The new cathedral symbolizes the city's return to its Roman Catholic origins after a period of Protestant ascendancy, but it does little for the city as a whole.

When Riordan reluctantly did take a stand on the 1996 California Civil Rights Initiative (CCRI), designed to eliminate racial quotas, he incoherently announced that he was against both quotas and the initiative (the initiative simply restates the language of the 1964 Civil Rights Act, by barring any discrimination based on race). "I oppose it," Riordan explained, "because it is divisive. It takes one of our greatest assets, our diversity, and tries to turn it into a liability." But diversity without a counterbalancing core of common values is not necessarily a virtue. As the comedian Cheech Marin pointed out, "The best thing about being Latino in L.A. is that everywhere you look, and everything you see and touch and feel, tells you that you belong here. The worst thing is that everyone else feels the same way, and it's turning L.A. into a battle zone."

Evoking the fear of riots, the left-leaning city council overwhelmingly denounced CCRI. Council member Richard Alarcon compared it to *Mein Kampf*, and council member Ruth Galanter warned that the initiative's passage could produce another round of race riots, a theme echoed by the UCLA chancellor, as well as by corporate executives and former California governor George Deukmajian, a Republican. "All you have to do is evoke the specter of riots," noted University of California regent Ward Connerly, the African-American leader of the pro-CCRI campaign. "If there's one thing people in L.A. are afraid of it's another riot. It's like threatening to yell 'Fire!' in a crowded theater."

The threat of new riots, and concerts by Billy Joel, Tupac Shakur, and Snoop Doggy Dog to rally support against CCRI notwithstanding, there was broad approval in L.A. for the antiquotas ballot initiative at the time Riordan took his position: the *Los Angeles Times* poll of city voters showed 69 percent approval, with 60 percent support from Hispanics and 56 percent from blacks. Support for CCRI was particularly strong in the secessionist Valley. Claims Valley secession leader Bob Scott, "Racialism is tearing L.A. apart, and that's why many Valley people want out."

A consummate backroom deal maker, Riordan seemed not to sense the opportunity that had been handed to him. Given the chance to break with the riot ideology and enunciate a larger civic vision for his city, Riordan, who had no strong challenger on the horizon for the 1997 election, balked. By failing to support CCRI, which eventually passed statewide 54 to 46 percent, with 53 percent support in the Valley but only 39 percent in the city as a whole, Riordan missed an enormous opportunity to establish a transtribal ethic for his fractious metropolis. In a homogeneous city the folkways of the tribe can serve as a substitute for shared principles; in a city like L.A., where the citizenry lack a shared story, they need a principle of procedural fairness to at least loosely bind them together.

BACK TO THE FUTURE

14. The Moral Deregulation of Public Space

Sometime in the 1980s we came to the end of our national romance with cities and the public spaces that define them. *Urban* once suggested *urbanity,* a cosmopolitan sophistication that represented the best of bourgeois America. The cities we celebrated had been engines of innovation, their streets settings for the creative disorder that has inspired our arts as much as our economy. For many, the public character of their private self was revealed in the pleasure they took in being described as streetwise. But the streets—they were the very depiction of democracy—that once inspired our largely urban common culture now too often induced fear, as even the most innocent of experiences became fraught with potential danger. It was surely a milestone of decline when some cities gave up their long-standing campaign to teach children to "cross at the green, not in between," because the corners were dominated by drug dealers.

What unnerved most city dwellers, however, was not crime per se but, rather, the sense of menace and disorder that pervaded day-to-day life. It was the gang of toughs exacting their daily tribute in the coin of humiliation. It was the "street tax" paid to drunk and drug-ridden panhandlers. It was the "squeegee men" shaking down the motorist waiting for a light. It was the threats and hostile gestures of the mentally ill making their homes in the parks. It was the provocation of pushers and prostitutes plying their trade with impunity. It was the "trash storms," the swirling masses of garbage left by peddlers and panhandlers, and the open-air drug bazaars on city streets. These were the visible signs of cities out of control; cities, regardless of their economic health, that couldn't protect either their space or their citizens.

"When you take your child to a public playground and find a mental patient has been using the sandbox as a toilet," wrote liberal columnist Lars Erik Nelson, "it's normal to say, 'Enough, I'm leaving.'"

Nelson was by no means alone. In the early 1990s, polls found that 43 percent of Bostonians, 48 percent of Angelenos, and 60 percent of New Yorkers wanted to leave. The 1989 Gallup poll found that only 19 percent of the country's people wanted to live in cities. Many who left, generally the better off, sorted themselves into the suburbs, leaving the poor, who are most in need of public space, to suffer the consequences. The ex-urbanites were determined to never again be left at the mercy of public authorities.

Many former city dwellers moved into areas organized by homeowners' associations, private governments that stand beyond the reach of the city and its experiments in civil liberties. In the suburbs one of eight Americans, thirty million people, belongs to a community association; four-fifths of the 150,000 such associations administer territory as well as buildings. In return for erecting a bastion against the pathologies left to fester in the metropolis, citizens of these private towns agreed to a covenanted conformity that dictated everything from the size of their mailboxes to the type and number of visitors permitted. These shadow cities generally established "one dollar, one vote" governments that re-created the preindustrial world of power for the property holders.

But even many of those who stayed in the city underwent an internal migration that kept them at a more or less comfortable distance from the problems they associate with disordered public space. In all three cities discussed in this book, the design of public space has been driven by the fear of crime, panhandlers, and graffiti. Architect Oscar Newsman's "defensible space" principles, what urbanist William H. White has decried as "the fortressing of America," are so fundamental to design that they have at times been written into zoning regulations.

Cities that revitalized their downtowns created building-enclosed spaces that are climate and crowd controlled, like Battery Park City in lower Manhattan, and are deliberately kept separate from the street. Similarly, in a tribute to a lost urbanism, MCA built City Walk, a two-block shopping and entertainment center (covering an area of 100 million square feet) in the ethnically mixed but middle-class San Fernando Valley, a section of Los Angeles that talks about seceding from the larger city. Billed as "an exact replica of Venice Beach and Sunset Boulevard" (minus the menace, graffiti, and homelessness), the mall tried to re-create the variety and unexpected pleasure of what street life was once like.

From Los Angeles in the West, to Chicago in the upper Midwest, to southernmost Miami, neighborhoods reacted similarly—closing off once fully public streets to impede the flow of drug traffickers. They tried to achieve in some small measure the kind of security that was once taken for granted even in many poor neighborhoods and that now comes only with private police and "covenanted communities." Those who can't or won't leave increasingly turned public space into a potent political issue.

In the early 1990s, elections in Los Angeles, New York, Rochester, Seattle, and San Francisco revolved around public space and public safety. In 1992 tolerant San Francisco approved Proposition J, a ballot initiative prohibiting "harassing or hounding acts in connection with soliciting money or any other valuable thing." The proposition argues that "aggressive solicitation undermines the public's basic right to be in and enjoy public places without fear" and "[jeopardizes] the City's economy by discouraging visitors."

On the East Coast, Ed Rendell made his early mark as mayor of "Filthadelphia" by literally scrubbing city hall, while quality-of-life issues shaped not only the 1993 mayoral races in Boston and New York but many local elections. New York has in recent years been preoccupied with public space issues, ranging from the Billie Boggs affair (in which the ACLU helped a homeless schizophrenic literally fight for her right to live and defecate on the streets) to the Tompkins Square Park riot (where police fought a pitched battle to retake the park from squatters and self-styled anarchists who had set up living quarters there). In the early 1990s in Manhattan, "the Wildman of 96th Street" became a symbol of government's inability to perform its most basic functions; for years authorities were unable to either jail or institutionalize a crack-addicted vet who pushed people in front of cars, stalked women, and generally terrorized parts of Manhattan's Upper West Side.

In 1968 a thousand Boston home owners were polled on what they thought was the city's biggest problem. For both blacks and whites, reported political scientist James Q. Wilson, "The issue which concerned more respondents than any other was variously stated—crime, violence, rebellious youth, racial tension, public immorality, delinquency. However stated, the common theme seemed to concern improper behavior in public places." Almost three decades later that concern has only intensified.

How can we explain the unparalleled social breakdown of public life during a period of both peace and prosperity? Poverty per se is not a good answer. New York was a far poorer but far more tranquil city fifty years ago. The breakdown has proceeded regardless of the phase of the business cycle. Nor is it primarily a matter of Reagan–Bush policies. New York, for instance, boomed in the eighties, and minority income grew even as the breakdown continued unabated. In "Defining Deviance Down," his justly acclaimed article for the *American Scholar,* Senator Moynihan describes the mechanisms of accommodation to growing levels of violence and pathology. We can as a society, he argues, accept only so much deviance. The excess gets defined away until the pathological is routinely accepted as unavoidable—at least for those who can't or don't flee. But except for a reference to family disintegration, important as that is, he doesn't explain the source of the breakdown in public conduct.

Would it have been possible, prior to the utopian/libertarian fervor of the 1960s and its accompanying moral deregulation, for officials to define the case of either Billie Boggs or "the Wildman" narrowly in terms of their legal rights? Over the past quarter century we have carried out a great experiment in what the left-wing Freudian Herbert Marcuse understood as "radical desublimation." In that experiment zealous reformers of various stripes tried to eliminate the tension between individual desire and communal conscience solely in favor of desire, on the grounds that the release of tension would move us "beyond all known standards . . . to a species with a new name, that shall not dare define itself as man." In that new and higher state there would be no need for either self-control or social coordination, since, in much the same manner as the free market for goods and services, the free market in morals was to produce growth, albeit of the personal and self-expressive kind.

But since there is no such thing as a self-regulating market in morals, instead of an equilibrium we have a downward spiral. An unparalleled set of utopian policies produced the dystopia of day-to-day city life. Particularly damaging were those policies concerning the concept of victimless crime, the deinstitutionalization of the mentally ill, and the decriminalization of public drinking.

Jane Jacobs, whose 1961 book *The Death and Life of Great American Cities* set the terms of how public space has been discussed ever since, argued that "lowly, unpurposeful and random as they may appear, sidewalk contacts are the small change from which a city's wealth of public life may grow." According to Jacobs, "The tolerance, the room for great differences among neighbors, . . . are possible and normal only when the streets of great cities have built-in equipment allowing strangers to dwell in peace together on civilized but essentially dignified and reserved terms."

In the late 1960s and early 1970s, some of the "built-in equipment" was systematically dismantled. The movement to decriminalize what were known as victimless crimes (crimes in which none of the consenting adults directly involved has either cause or desire to press for legal action) was caught up in a new Vietnam-era version of the old argument that you can't legislate morality. The moral authority of American institutions and the force of conventional norms were shattered by the cultural conflicts that broke out over Vietnam and racial injustice. Traditional authority and conventional morality were equated with authoritarianism or worse.

The need for a modicum of order, for instance, became entangled with both the need to redress racial wrongs and a romantic individualism. In *Coates v. Cincinnati,* for instance, the Supreme Court struck down a loitering statute of long-standing provenance, one typical of other cities' statutes. The court argued that it was unconstitutional to outlaw loiterers who by congregating might "annoy" others, because enforcement "may entirely depend on whether or not a policeman is annoyed." The statute, they concluded, was an "invitation to [racially] discriminatory enforcement."

In another loitering case, the 1966 *Papachristou v. City of Jacksonville* decision, Supreme Court Justice William O. Douglas dismissed the connection between crime and disorder. Douglas insisted that "the implicit presumption in these generalized vagrancy standards," which allow the police to move people on so that "crime is nipped in the bud," is "too extravagant to deserve extended treatment." Douglas went on to speak colorfully of the rights of "rogues and vagabonds" to roam the countryside as "loafers or litterers." Citing Walt Whitman's "Song of the Open Road," and Vachel Lindsay's "I Want to Go Wandering," he struck down loitering laws on the grounds that they forced "poor people, nonconformists, dissenters, [and] idlers" to adhere to middle-class "lifestyles."

Like the deinstitutionalization movement, the *Papachristou* decision embraced an ideal of personal liberty freed from the fetters of both reason and responsibility. The problem, wrote Joseph Featherstone, was that "the protest against uniformity and cultural oppression, which was valid, turned into denial that we need common ideals, which was not so."

Edwin Schur, the leading proponent of decriminalizing "victimless crimes," hailed the *Papachristou* decision. Schur spoke for many of his fellow sociologists, then at the peak of their since shattered self-confidence, when he argued that social science research demanded reform. He insisted that past support for laws against victimless crimes rested on hypocritical moralizing, misinformation, and "unsubstantiated assertions of the 'horrible consequences' likely to follow from decriminalization."

In an argument parallel to that of the anti-anti-Communists, Schur turned the tables on the proponents of "traditional morality" by arguing that the cure was worse than the disease. "Proscribed behaviors [don't] necessarily constitute social problems," he argued. "It is the proposed 'solution' that is the gist of the problem." According to Schur, "Social problems are simply conditions about which influential segments of the society"—read the uptight white middle class—believe "something ought to be done."

The problem, it seemed, was less in the inherent actions deemed criminal than in the constricted morality of those who attempted to impose their values on others through police action by complaining about the harm being done. In an influential 1972 report done for the National Institute of Mental Health, sociologist Gilbert Geis said that "it may be argued that such harm, at times, is a function of an unreasonable sensitivity [or insensitivity] on the part of the sufferer . . . upset by a newspaper photograph of a marijuana orgy at a rock festival." Earlier, Geis had acknowledged the risk of decriminalization. But he went on to argue that "under certain conditions, certain societies [like certain people] are better off dead, at least if we maintain that there are values whose preservation is more important than the survival of people or societies." Geis acknowledged that the decriminalization experiment might fail catastrophically, but he took it philosophically, arguing that while it was possible that the point of no return would be passed long before its existence was noticed, it was worth the gamble. Here was a liberalism people would flee from.

The intellectual bullets forged by the sociologists were fired by the police chiefs and legal reformers. Policing vice, they argued with considerable evidence, was inherently corrupting while maintaining civility by arresting drunks and crazies was derided as social work, as opposed to "real police work." But the most important claim made again and again by the mésalliance of police chiefs and liberal law professors was that by decriminalizing vice and other minor offenses to civility the police would be freed up to concentrate on major crime.

The 1967 Task Force Report of the President's Commission on Law Enforcement and Administration of Justice captures what shortly became the conventional wisdom of numerous books, articles, and reports: "Only when the load of law enforcement has been lightened by stripping away those responsibilities for which it is not suited, will we begin to make the criminal law a more effective instrument of social protection." What followed, however, was both the slide into day-to-day disorder and steadily rising major crime.

What went wrong? First off, the reformers, straining to be hip, often trivialized the collateral consequences of the behavior they wanted decriminalized. "That prostitution tends to encourage derivative kinds of criminal activity can hardly be denied," wrote Geis, "any more than it can be denied that kissing may lead to illegitimate births." In the reformers' ideological calculations there were only individual rights and state power; the informal networks of society, like neighborhoods, were never mentioned, let alone considered. It was as if an economist had written about chemical production without considering externalities like pollution.

Held hostage to a utopian vision, liberal decriminalizers like Geis were willing to sacrifice individuals and neighborhoods in the name of a great experiment. American society, Geis acknowledged, "has much in it worth protection—but that protection may only be had under strict circumstances which involve permitting the free sway of Epicurean behavior unless or until such a time that such behavior clearly threatens the existence of others or of the society." As for the possibility of the point of no return passing unnoticed, Geis argued that "no one doubted that the uses of democratic principles is a highly dangerous way to run a government."

In New York City, where decriminalization was carried the furthest, not even running a red light carried criminal consequences. In that city, where 3 percent of the people hit by cars in the 1980s were already lying in the road, traffic tickets were "defined downward" in an effort to unclog the courts. Even serious traffic violations like reckless driving became merely civil offenses, so no warrants were issued.

In the early 1990s, when then New York Governor Mario Cuomo was asked about the problems of violent mental patients on the streets of Gotham, his answer, according to Lars Erik Nelson, was that it was not true that there were such problems or if it was true, it was not his fault because he was powerless. Cuomo said, "The Constitution says you cannot lock up a person just because he's a nuisance, urinating in the street." When asked about changing the law, Cuomo replied that it couldn't be done. He explained, "Suppose you had a law you could lock up anyone who is endangering his health. I could come to you and say, 'You're drinking, you're smoking, I've got to lock you up.'" The slippery slope, it seems, slid in only one direction, and for Cuomo, at least, no notches were permitted. In legal terms Cuomo was arguing that the patient's liberty interest must be paramount, so that, as the ACLU put it, someone like Billie Boggs should not be subject to the strictures of social conformity, which might affect his or her "fiercely independent lifestyle."

Cuomo's argument was drawn from the writing of the influential sociologist Erving Goffman, who claimed in his 1961 book *Asylums* that mental hospitals were responsible for most of the symptoms of their patients. Goffman argued further that he knew of no supposedly psychotic misconduct that could not be precisely matched in everyday life by the conduct of persons who are not psychologically ill.

The American Civil Liberties Union similarly played the Goffman game to defend Billie Boggs. Did she urinate on the sidewalk? So did cabdrivers. Did she tear up or burn the money she had begged? This was a symbolic gesture similar to the burning of draft cards during Vietnam. And on it went. The woman who called herself Billie Boggs (her real name was Joyce Brown) was described by her New York Civil Liberties Union attorneys as a "political prisoner," a victim of social indifference and of Reagan's housing policies—this despite a loving family and Social Security checks she never bothered to collect. Far from insane, she sounded, said her attorney Robert Levy, "like a member of the board of the Civil Liberties Union."

Freed from the clutches of New York City hospitals and wined, dined, and reclothed at Bloomingdale's, Billie Boggs was hustled onto talk shows and the Ivy League lecture circuit and exploited to score legal and public relations points. But when the spotlight faded, she was back on the streets within weeks, screaming and defecating; eventually she was arrested for fighting, harassing passersby, and using drugs. As former civil rights hero Charles Morgan put it, the ACLUers had become "ideologues frozen in time."

When the fight for deinstitutionalization began, it was aimed at freeing men and women who had been made passive by many years of often unjust and unnecessary incarceration and who by and large posed little threat to society. The story from there is usually told in terms of the failure to provide calming psychotropic drugs and other types of assistance through community care, so that many mentally ill people moved from the back wards to the back alleys (and eventually to the main streets).

Paul Friedman, an early director of the NYCLU Mental Health Law Project, was critical of community care. He worried that "because the deprivation of liberty is less in community-based treatment than in total institutionalization, . . . the resistance against state intrusion will be less and the lives of many more persons may be ultimately interfered with." The project's founder, Bruce Ennis, was even more blunt. Ennis was willing to see the mentally ill "go to the wall." "I'm simply a civil libertarian," he explained, "and in my view you don't lock people up because they've got a problem." He went on, "It's never been very important to me if there is or is not mental illness. My response would be the same." Summing up, Ennis said, "Lawyers are doing what they think is right in terms of civil rights, whether it's good for the patients or not." This mix of principled ignorance and militant nonconsequentalism had one meaning when attached to the first deinstitutionalized populations; it had another when mental patients cut off from care and those never institutionalized in the first place came increasingly under the sway of alcohol and drugs.

For the militant libertarians driving judicial policy, individual freedom no longer depended on the rational capacity of the individuals involved. What was important was that no outside agency—not the state, not society, not the community acting through the state—could be allowed to restrict the liberty of an individual. And even for most violent crime, the ACLU opposed prison, preferring community rehabilitation. The judge who presided over the Billie Boggs case argued, sixties-style, that society, not Joyce Brown, was sick. "The sight of her," Judge Lippman argued, "may improve us. By being an offense to the aesthetic senses, she may spur the community to action." But this was a one-way social contract in which the community, invoked rhetorically by Lippman, was required to aid dysfunctional individuals solely on their terms. Here was yet another version of dependent individualism.

Judges like Lippman and lawyers like Levy led psychiatrist E. Fuller Torrey to quip, "If mentally ill patients persevered in their behavior as lawyers do, with so little attention to the consequences of their behavior, we would cite it as evidence that they were in need of further treatment."

The full meaning of the militantly anticonsequentialist perspective was made manifest in the Larry Hogue case. In and out of mental institutions, generously provided for with a $3,000 monthly VA check, Larry Hogue began in the mid-eighties to terrorize parts of Manhattan's liberal Upper West Side. As Robert Spoor of the New York State Office of Mental Health noted, "the charges against Hogue [had] always been misdemeanors." Arrested more than forty times, Hogue had never been convicted of a felony. He had, however, chased people down the street with a club, threatening to murder them; set numerous fires, including fires under cars; repeatedly strewn garbage all over sidewalks; defecated in the back seat of a car after first threatening to kill its owner and then breaking into the auto by smashing part of a marble bench into the auto's window; masturbated in front of children; and lunged at terrified women with a knife.

Local community groups made a concerted effort to see Hogue incarcerated or institutionalized. But under then-current mental health law, individuals like Hogue could be institutionalized only so long as they presented an immediate threat to themselves and others. The staff at Manhattan State Hospital told community leaders, "Hogue is more violent than you think," but they were unable to hold him "because of his rights." The official story about Hogue was that while it was true that he behaved wildly when he was on the crack he bought with his VA check, he was perfectly fine when off drugs; thus, the mental health authorities had no recourse but to release him. In fact, part of the reason he was so quickly released was that mental health authorities couldn't control him either and wanted to get rid of him as quickly as possible. According to Dr. Michael Pawel, a psychiatrist who treated Hogue, no one wanted to deal with an unruly patient who wasn't going to get better, a prognosis typical of dual-diagnosis patients, that is, those afflicted by a combination of mental illness, drugs, and drink.

In 1974, at the peak of public support for the decriminalization of victimless crimes, historian David Rothman tried to explain the movement's success. "We are witnessing," he wrote, "the dissolution of the Progressive version of community as a viable concept, indeed, the breakdown of normality as a viable concept." He went on, approvingly, "There no longer seems to be a common weal that can be defined or appealed to as a norm for action." In fact, he concluded, "No consensus allows for a clear and uncontroversial division between sane and insane behavior, no unity exists around the once self-evident proposition that it is better to be sane rather than insane."

Faced not with the feigned apocalypse of the 1960s but with the all too tangible evidence of social breakdown, it is far harder in the 1990s to stick to the ideologues' "though the heavens may fall" perspective. Even for the preternaturally liberal Upper West Side of New York, the Larry Hogues of the world make it clear that there can in such cases be clear division between sanity and insanity.

15. The Politics of Public Order

It was John Lindsay's boast that New York averted a major riot under his leadership. But that was small consolation for those who suffered from both rising racial tensions and rapidly rising crime rates. Every few years since the Ocean Hill–Brownsville battle, the city has been convulsed by a major racial incident. In 1974 it was an ugly fight over low-income housing in a middle-class Jewish neighborhood in Forest Hills, Queens. In July 1977 a temporary power blackout unleashed massive looting in the Bushwick section of Brooklyn; three thousand of the looters, many employed, were arrested. For those who remembered that a similar blackout in 1965 was marked by massive restraint, the looting in 1977 was an indication, coming on top of the mid-seventies fiscal crisis, of the city's vulnerability and civic decline.

In 1984 Bernhard Goetz, the so-called subway vigilante, shot four black teens, would-be attackers, in Manhattan. The assailants, armed with pointed screwdrivers, looked on the nerdy-looking Goetz as an easy target, and Goetz, high on drugs and fear, responded with force in excess of what was needed to protect himself. Then, in the closing years of the Koch administration, the pace quickened. In 1986 a black man was hit and killed by an oncoming car when white teens in largely Italian Howard Beach, Queens, chased him and two other black men (all, it later turned out, had criminal records) out of their neighborhood. A year later the Tawana Brawley hoax emerged, making the Reverend Al Sharpton into one of the nation's best-known racial racketeers; Brawley, who lived in fear of her stepfather (he had been convicted of murdering his first wife), concocted a story of being raped by white men to escape punishment for her own late night absence. In 1989 a white woman jogging in Central Park was raped and nearly beaten to death by a gang of black teens. That same year Yusuf Hawkins was killed in an unprovoked attack by a gang of white teens; the crime was magnified by the silence of those who had witnessed the murder.

In a city exhausted by racial incidents, David Dinkins was elected mayor as a racial healer in 1989. He succeeded Ed Koch, the tart-tongued, incumbent three-term mayor, who had been undermined by the scandals and racist incidents that had roiled his last term.

The message of the Dinkins campaign was double-edged. "Reject New York's first serious black candidate for mayor, a man universally admired" as a healer, warned Dinkins's supporter Ken Auletta, "and risk producing more black haters like Sonny Carson" (of Ocean Hill fame).

Dinkins's metaphor for the city was the "gorgeous mosaic," an unfortunate choice since Canada, which describes itself as a mosaic, is always on the verge of breaking apart. Early on, Dinkins had an easy opportunity to show that the metaphor of the mosaic suggested something other than separate laws for separate groups. In the very first month of his term, a boycott began of a Korean grocery located on Church Avenue in Brooklyn (an area, incidentally, only a few blocks from my house). The boycott, set off by a dispute over how much a black customer owed the Red Apple Market, was led by Sonny Carson, a convicted extortionist. It was an ugly scene. From what I could tell by talking to local merchants, the boycotters, who threatened store employees and intimidated would-be customers, had probably been involved in attempts to shake down other neighborhood stores. I listened as Sonny Carson's Afro-fascist goons shouted about how the Koreans were "slant-eyed monkies." "In a manner reminiscent of Sufi-Abdul Hamed, 'Harlem's Hitler' of the 1930s, Carson demanded that the offending store be transferred to black ownership, charging that Koreans were out to 'destroy' the community's culture and economy," wrote columnist Jim Sleeper. This was not the bargain the city had expected.

Carson's involvement in the boycott—he had been kicked out of the Dinkins campaign for antiwhite remarks—was a ready-made chance for Dinkins to assert his moral authority. Instead, Dinkins dithered, seemingly afraid to offend Carson. When a court injunction limited the picketing, the Dinkins police department, run by Police Commissioner Lee "out of town" Brown, failed to enforce it. Eight months into the boycott, Dinkins was still unable to unequivocally condemn the tactics on the part of Carson, who proudly told the press (in response to other charges) that he wasn't anti-Semitic, just antiwhite. Dinkins never fully recovered from the debacle, the first of a number of incidents in which he surrendered the sovereignty of the city to the mob.

Two years later, rioting was set off in the center of the city's drug trade, heavily Dominican Washington Heights, after "beeper boys," young drug runners, falsely accused the cops of killing Kiki Garcia, an innocent civilian. Dinkins rushed to apologize for the police atrocity. Never once, in either begging the rioters (many of them themselves beeper-toting teen drug dealers) for peace or in explaining that he understood their anger, did the mayor ask his audiences, which surely included hardworking Dominican victims of gang intimidation, to consider the possibility that Garcia's death might be drug related.

Garcia, the supposedly innocent victim, was an illegal immigrant heavily involved in the drug trade; an inquiry demonstrated conclusively that he had pulled a gun on the cop. A videotape made by neighbors shows Garcia tossing bags of cocaine in the air while an unseen narrator refers to the cocaine as "food" and brags, "It's legal here on these blocks, it's *Liberated*."

For many of those who still had faith in Dinkins's judgment, the Crown Heights pogrom was the final blow. It was set off when a young black boy, Gavin Cato, was killed by an Hasidic Jew in a traffic accident. The stabbing death of a twenty-nine-year-old Jewish scholar, Yankel Rosenbaum, and four days of raw anti-Semitic rioting followed. The police failed to react for forty-eight hours as a mob rampaged through the Jewish section of the mixed (black and Jewish) neighborhood. The slow response produced furious criticism. The anger was only intensified when a largely black jury acquitted teenager Lemrick Nelson of Rosenbaum's murder. Arrested with a knife and three dollar bills all bearing Rosenbaum's blood, Nelson initially confessed. But Nelson, later convicted in other stabbing incidents and on civil rights changes in the Rosenbaum case, was acquitted of criminal charges after his lawyer put on a racial defense. To further racialize the case, after the acquittal the jury attended a victory party for Nelson.

Sued by victims of the rioting in civil court, the Dinkins administration insisted on its impotence. The mayor's lawyers argued that "the plaintifs simply had no constitutional or federal right to have the police respond to their calls for assistance, or to receive police protection against potential harm caused by private parties." The Reverend Al Sharpton, who stirred the crowd at Gavin Cato's funeral with his thinly veiled anti-Semitic assault on "diamond merchants," insisted that it could have been worse. "Had we had another type of mayor, who ordered the cops to go in and whip heads, the death count in Crown Heights would have been much higher, the property damage much higher." Well after the fact, Dinkins acknowledged that there had been "errors" and, under pressure, described Rosenbaum's death as a "lynching," but the memory of the Crown Heights situation would dog Dinkins into the next mayoral campaign and help elect Rudolph Giuliani mayor in 1993.

For the vast majority of New Yorkers, unaffected by the three major incidents of the Dinkins administration, there was another, more pervasive, problem—the growing number of mentally ill people on the streets of New York. The patience of even the most tolerant New Yorkers was beginning to wear thin when it came to dealing with "street people."

The long-term homeless are in many ways the underside of the underclass. Ralph Nunez, CEO of Homes for the Homeless, an organization that runs group homes for homeless mothers and their children, says that the title of his nonprofit agency is a misnomer, that the problem is not housing per se. He notes that half of all the homeless families in New York are back in the shelters in a year after being given permanent housing. The problem is "disaffiliated, dysfunctional people." My friend the late Michael Harrington grasped this situation when in his 1984 book *The New American Poverty* he insisted that the so-called homeless could be best described as "the uprooted." What distinguishes the long-term homeless from very poor but more stable individuals and one-parent families is "their more severe level of personal distress." This distress, usually a product of physical and sexual abuse intertwined with drugs and alcohol, destroys family and other social ties.

The term *homelessness* was promoted as a political counter to the term *underclass,* popularized in Ken Auletta's late 1970s book of the same name. In New York it was the city's sweep of panhandlers and "box people" to prepare for the 1980 Democratic Convention that activated organizations like the Coalition for the Homeless to redefine the issue as a matter of our "sick society's" failure to provide "housing, housing, and housing." The term *homeless* was, from the start, something of an intentional fraud. Dinkins's first director of homeless services, Nancy Wackstein, admitted as much when she acknowledged that she, "like every advocate in town . . . had hewed to the party line that the solution to homelessness is housing." Explained Wackstein, "The belief was if you focused on drug problems or family breakdown . . . you'd get no public support for helping them."

The homeless, in short, were a kind of sociopolitical cat's-paw, the symbol of all that the sixty-eighters thought had gone wrong in America. The homeless, explained New York's most prominent "homeless advocate," Robert Hayes, "are indeed the most egregious symbol of a cruel economy, . . . an unresponsive government, a festering value system." According to Louisa Stark of the National Coalition for the Homeless, any discussion of addiction or the role the sixties themselves played in promoting drug dependency distracted discussion from the "structural defects of society."

Hard as it is for non–New Yorkers to believe, in the early 1980s a group of young lawyers—some of them working for Mobilization for Youth, the same group that had inspired the welfare expansion experiment of the 1960s—tried to apply the old Piven and Cloward principles to the emerging homeless problem. In a city that had just emerged from a near brush with bankruptcy, the idea was to so overload the city shelter system with self-declared homeless people that the city, though unable to afford it, would be forced to build more permanent housing—this in a city that constructed more housing than all the other large cities of the United States combined in the 1980s.

Supported by a number of judges who emerged from the city's left-wing legal services organization and led publicly by a young Catholic lawyer, Robert Hayes—who, as he later acknowledged, had overstated the number of homeless to create a sense of crisis—the neo-Pivenites argued that anti-homeless legislation inevitably involved not behavior but poverty. They insisted that although homelessness was an involuntary act whose attributes (e.g., sleeping in the parks and defecating in public) affected public life, it could not be penalized without criminalizing poverty itself.

New York was rich in legal talent, and in the 1980s some of it was devoted to imaginative argument for expanding the right to public shelter even though the city was already expending half the local public housing money in America and even though half of those who were given public housing ended up back on the streets because of drug or other personality problems. Once out on the street, the homeless received the protection of the Legal Aid Society, the ACLU, and other lawyers who insisted that only if the homeless were "in your face" and making life miserable for others would the city expend the money necessary to solve the problem.

Faced with a revolt on the part of the lower-middle-class tenants of public housing, overwhelmed by homeless families, Dinkins backed off his earlier assumption that the problem was just housing. He began to acknowledge that some of the homeless were unsocialized children who had had children or were dual-diagnosis mental patients. But while he acknowledged this, he didn't act on it, despite having added a vast number of new cops to restore public order to streets, like those on the Upper West Side and the Village, that had taken on the appearance of open-air mental institutions. While Dinkins was, as always, slow to act, the public, whose own sentiments had swung sharply against the street people, was clamoring for change.

The scenario is familiar. As an election approaches, an entrenched political establishment that is faced with failed economic policies that have impoverished its people plays on racial fears to hold on to power. The establishment tries to frighten supporters into a frenzy by accusing its opponents of adhering to an alien ideology that threatens the local folkways. This was played out to an at times not so subtle backdrop of threatened racial violence if the old order was challenged. This could be a description of New Orleans in 1900 or Atlanta in the Klan era of the 1920s, but what I am describing is not a distant memory, it is New York City during the 1993 mayoral election.

The central thread of the 1993 New York mayoral race was the partially successful attempt to demonize David Dinkins's challenger, moderate Republican Rudy Giuliani, a former U.S. attorney in the Reagan administration, as at the very least a white racist and quite possibly a crypto-fascist proponent of such outlandish ideas as cutting the size of city government and cracking down on aggressive panhandlers. Bill Lynch, the Dinkins campaign manager, said Giuliani reminded him of David Duke, while others, including ministers close to the mayor, compared him to Mussolini and Hitler. Giuliani gave an inoffensive but overheated speech at a rally of mostly white off-duty cops, who shouted, "No police, no justice." The rally got out of control and set off wild warnings. A disk jockey on WLIB, the black radio station owned by Dinkins's family and political allies, warned that under Giuliani blacks might be forced to take up arms against the imminent police state; he also suggested that journalists critical of Dinkins ought to be eliminated.

The threats and warnings of violence had their effect. Respected analysts of New York politics argued that it was better to reelect a failed Dinkins than risk the riots that might follow the defeat of the city's first black mayor. A poll by NY1, an all-news cable television station, found that a third of those sampled predicted riots were Dinkins defeated. But while the Dinkins supporters warned of riots, for many New Yorkers the Dinkins administration had been defined by riots, racial incidents, and the growth of aggressive panhandling—in short, by the collapse of public order.

President Clinton, whose endorsement of Woo in L.A. had backfired, tried to take a more subtle tack. It was hard to defend the Dinkins record. Under his mayorship the number of New Yorkers receiving public assistance had risen by 273,000 to the highest levels since the Great Depression. When the Los Angeles County health system teetered on the brink of bankruptcy, Clinton, looking ahead to the 1996 election, came to the rescue with a $346 million check, but with New York so solidly in the Democratic camp, he was unwilling to help Dinkins with a financial bailout. The president tried instead, like Governor Cuomo, to play a version of the race card. A willingness to vote against Dinkins, he said, was "not as simple as overt racism," but Dinkins, he said, was facing a tough campaign because "too many of us are unwilling to vote for people who are different than we are."

Dinkins brought in a long list of national politicians and celebrities, including two Kennedys, the senator and the congressman; the president, the vice president, Hillary Rodham Clinton, and Tipper Gore; and Barbara Streisand and Danny Glover to campaign for him. The parade of celebrities and politicians who came spoke as though they were freedom riders of sorts who had come to rescue the city from its customary mores. But for many New Yorkers, it was precisely those customary liberal mores that were responsible for the decline of their day-to-day life. That decline was strikingly evident in Greenwich Village, a neighborhood that found itself under siege from the street life it once embraced. "After decades of trying to fix the rest of the world," wrote Village denizen Michael Gross, "Villagers have been forced to recognize that now it is their world which needs help."

Far from the celebrity certainties of Hollywood campaigners, a homeless man named Jeffrey Rose grabbed a baby away from its mother on 71st Street and First Avenue and began stabbing the baby in the face with a pen. Eight years earlier, Rose had been arrested for pushing a man through a glass counter at an East Side deli. He then tried to get himself committed at Bellevue but was only observed overnight, given a prescription for the antipsychotic drug Haldol, and released. Ettie Shapiro, director of the local Neighborhood Center for the Homeless where Rose was sometimes a client, responded: "The fact is, as human beings we have very little control. And people don't want to face it." When another representative of the city's burgeoning social services industry told a community meeting in the liberal neighborhood once represented in Congress by John Lindsay that Rose had had a hard life, residents replied, "Don't give us this liberal crap."

In a similar vein, at a community meeting across town on the west side of Manhattan, an area inundated with the walking wounded, residents demanded a moratorium on new social service facilities. "Something died recently," said Joe Brown, a computer programmer and community activist. "We are today announcing the passing of brain-dead liberalism."

Dinkins seemed unable to respond to the new mood. One of the defining moments of Dinkins's defeat came when Marcia Kramer, a local TV reporter, asked the mayor on camera how he would respond to her reasons for moving to the suburbs:

> Last year I moved out of the city because I got fed up with what I couldn't stand, the fact that there was a homeless person who took up permanent residence on my street corner, begging . . . menacing.
>
> And every day when I came to work, I met two or three people who were urinating on the street. . . . These are the kinds of things that scare people (away from the cities).
>
> The question to you: Is there anything you can do about it? Or are the rights of so few who are doing this to take precedence over the rights of the rest of the people who live here?

Dinkins wouldn't engage the concerns that were driving liberalism down. "Sorry you left us," he told Kramer. "Sorrier still that we can't raise your personal [commuter] income tax."

The mythology of law enforcement, reenacted again and again by Clint Eastwood's "Dirty Harry," depicts the police as eager to "bust heads" and clear out the streets at any cost if only they weren't held back by liberals and bureaucrats. But the reality, as discovered in the seventies and eighties, is that the police (and especially the brass) have not only managed to live amicably with the civil libertarians but learned to use them for their own purposes. In 1980s New York, when the police were hit with often justified criticisms about corruption, inefficiency, and laziness, they wrapped themselves in something very new to them—high-minded principles. "We'd like to move the drug dealers off the corner," they'd say, "but the law doesn't permit us to hassle people who are loitering."

Police chiefs turned to both academia and J. Edgar Hoover of the FBI to show why they shouldn't be held responsible for rising crime rates. Hoover insisted that most homicides went on "beyond the control or the ability of the police" to influence them. New York University law professor Graham Hughes expressed a widely held belief when he said, "The failure to prevent most crime does not make the state at fault, for most crime is probably not preventable." Hughes insisted, "No very dramatic reduction in crime is likely until the psychic trauma created by social inequality and the broader neuroses-generating character of American life are significantly modified." Oblivious to the proliferation of alcohol and drug treatment facilities near NYU, Hughes insisted that the best way to prevent crime was to put more money into social services.

New York Mayor Ed Koch, wildly popular for his first two terms (1978–1986), saw that the public was more concerned with how politicians felt about crime than with any particular policy. Koch was a master at providing the illusion of change. The key to his popularity was his ability to express outrage, and Koch did it with flair and wit. Koch, a former reform Democrat—he was the man who toppled Tammany's last boss, Carmine DeSapio—discovered that he didn't have to do much about crime as long as he mocked the hated John Lindsay and the lachrymose liberals. Koch drew cheers and laughter when asked what to do about liberal wimpiness on crime; he responded, "Mug 'em—and if that doesn't help, mug 'em again." The Koch rhetoric so incensed liberals that they barely noticed that, rhetoric aside, the mayor was putting most of his money into social services and most of his effort into lowering standards at the police academy. Not only did he not add a significant number of black and Latino officers, but Koch pushed the standards for police hiring even lower than they were during the Lindsay mayoralty. In fact, when his director of personnel complained that the department was hiring functional illiterates, the mayor fired her.

The cops, led by Koch's police commissioner, Benjamin Ward, took the cue. To be on the force in the Koch years, you didn't have to know or do much. Inactivity serves some cops just fine. While there were severe sanctions against overzealous law enforcement, there were no penalties for failure or inaction. While responding to complaints from a Brooklyn residential neighborhood overwhelmed by street prostitution, a police captain explained that if his men were too forceful in removing the pushers and the prostitutes from the streets, they themselves would be subject to arrest and a possible suit for a civil rights violation. An active or perhaps overly active cop, the captain explained, could destroy his career (and, by extension, the substantial pension that went along with it).

For most cops faced with an ambiguous situation—and cops rarely live in or have a stake in the neighborhoods they patrol—the response is simple. Why risk injury, or worse? Just keep walking. The cops are safer; the ACLU is happy, because there has been no violation of the search and seizure provisions of the Fourth Amendment; and, of course, the punks and pushers are delighted to maintain what one of them described to me as their "privacy." The only loser is the neighborhood and its people.

The Reverend Donald Hanson, pastor of St. Luke's Lutheran Church on 46th Street, ran into this iron triangle when he spoke with New York Police Commissioner Benjamin Ward. Hanson, who hails from Minnesota and its Farmer–Labor Party, is a classic New Deal liberal. He turned a sleepy, largely German-American church into a multiethnic center of social welfare activity. His parishioners serve one hundred thousand meals a year to senior citizens, the homeless, and the homebound. He also runs a center for battered women and children, and ESL (English as a second language) classes for Spanish-speaking immigrants. Dismayed by the daily assaults on his parishioners, Hanson told Ward that it was "absurd to use civil rights laws to protect junkies who prey on the poor." According to Hanson, Ward responded by insisting that "criminals have rights, too." Said Ward, echoing the ACLU's rhetoric, "You can't arrest people just because they look funny or suspicious." "What?!" replied Hanson. "If I had an aversion to funny-looking people, do you think I'd spend my time feeding street people every day?" Then he asked Ward why the police couldn't be allowed to make reasonable distinctions.

Why indeed! The answer in part is that the ACLU is living in the past. The worldview of its leadership was formed during the heroic struggle for civil rights, when police discretion was synonymous with police repression. "We made it work in the South," says Norman Siegel, the effervescent director of the NYCLU who went to Mississippi as a law student in 1966. "We made the country live up to its constitutional ideals, we made the country live by the Bill of Rights. Likewise," he concludes, "we can make it work in the North."

But can they? Part of the strength of the civil rights movement was that it marched under the banner of knowledge and enlightenment. Seeking to dispel the myths of racial inferiority, it insisted that knowledge would set us free. But Siegel's ACLU policy is based on a principled blindness, a willed ignorance of the facts of underclass street life. This means that if an experienced police officer comes upon a group of known drug pushers, men with a long list of previous offenses, in an area frequented by drug traffickers, the officer, by the ACLU's canons, should say or do nothing except in the unlikely event of his observing them at the exact moment of a drug transaction. The effect of this principled blindness is to strip the law of its moral standing as the socialized conscience of the community.

For the ACLUer this is as it should be. The past, they argue, has no meaningful pattern. In the manner of hip psychotherapists, they suggest that at any given moment we are all equal in potential, regardless of our prior conduct. The memory slate must always be wiped clean, so that the pusher and the 9-to-5 workaday "chump," as they're described by the lowlifes, can be treated equally. No one can actually live by this philosophy in their personal life. You can be sure that even the most devoted civil libertarians believe the pattern of past actions has a predictive value when, for example, choosing a baby-sitter for their children.

There was no hue and cry to give the police free rein. Most New Yorkers, particularly minority people, were well aware of the potential for police abuse. And insofar as they thought about issues of due process, they were probably broadly supportive of the NYCLU's highly justified efforts to monitor police misconduct. But what they didn't understand was why efforts to rein in police misconduct have to lead to free reign for neighborhood toughs, characters they had watched go through the revolving doors of justice time and time again.

Neighborhoods were demoralized as they watched cops repeatedly walk by local pushers without reacting. A Brooklyn police lieutenant responding to a complaint about pushers plying their trade with impunity responded as follows: "You know what they are, I know what they are, and even the cop on the beat knows what they are, but that doesn't mean they [the police] can do anything about it." That was in part because the department decided, in the wake of the 1972 Knapp Commission, which uncovered widespread police corruption, to preclude beat officers from making drug arrests. The department decided to protect itself from future black eyes at the cost of leaving neighborhoods unprotected.

The situation on Manhattan's famed Restaurant Row, just west of Broadway on 46th Street, was, in the words of one longtime resident, "a living X-rated movie." On one corner, operating hand in hand with the open drug dealing, were four bordellos. In a parody of the equal protection clause, one bordello was for heterosexuals, one for homosexuals, one for transvestites, and one for those who followed that minority-among-minority lifestyles, transsexuality. The bordellos were the center of the drug trade for out-of-towners, who come into the city through the nearby Lincoln Tunnel. Thriving and bustling, the bordellos, which drew long lines for their advertised specials, sometimes serviced customers on the stoops in full view of passersby. Just a bit of bacchanalia? A carnival ground for victimless crimes and the carefree fellows celebrated by Justice Douglas when he voted to overturn the country's vagrancy laws? Not quite. The hookers and the drug traders eventually took over the streets, so that not only were restaurant customers scared away and jobs lost, but local residents were effectively imprisoned in their apartments.

Over a period of several years, local residents like Reverend Hanson and restaurateurs repeatedly petitioned virtually every city and police official who might be of help. The restaurant business is a major source of city tax revenues. Although ordinary citizens might despair of police protection, surely such an important interest would get what it needed. It didn't. More to the point, according to the police, it couldn't.

The police said that they wanted to help, and they did make a few more arrests. The problem, the police explained, was that with the complete elimination of loitering laws in *Papachristou v. City of Jacksonville* (1972), which was hailed by the ACLU as a victory for civil rights, they couldn't break up the knots of known drug dealers who congregated on the streets unless they had sufficient "probable cause." That is, they couldn't move on the dealers unless an undercover cop directly observed a drug deal being made.

On West 46th Street, the restaurants and residents turned to the Guardian Angels and their charismatic, albeit self-promoting, leader, Curtis Sliwa. "The Guardian Angels," said Howard Goldfluss, a retired New York State Supreme Court judge, in *Newsday,* "are a phenomena whose time has come." The smooth-talking Sliwa was to street safety what bombastic Paterson, New Jersey, high school principal Joe Clark was to school safety. His charisma filled the moral vacuum created when the ACLU not merely tempered but displaced the discretionary authority we once placed in teachers and police and transferred it to their own bailiwick—the purely formal logic of the courts. It is there, says famed civil libertarian Charles Rembar, who has become increasingly critical of the ACLU, that "doctrine becomes sanctified, and if the facts don't fit they are disregarded."

The residents of 46th Street say that there was "a different environment in two days." The Angels, mostly black and Puerto Rican youngsters, had no secret weapon. They simply patrolled as the police had before the onslaught of procedural purity. In a reversal of what had become the normal order of things, they saw to it that the pushers and pimps were the people who got hassled. "The majority of the community," said Reverend Hanson, "was no longer held hostage to the junkie's 'civil rights.'" The police were understandably embarrassed by the Angels' success and responded in the language of the ACLU. They spoke of how only the police had the expertise needed to apprehend wrongdoers, and they warned the Angels not to violate the rights of people they suspected of crimes. It's illegal, said Assistant Chief Thomas Walsh, to "verbally harass people, or even to ask them to leave." The mayor's office was also annoyed. The *New York Times* noted that turning to the Angels was "a bit like having to turn to Donald Trump to fix the Wollman [skating] Rink" after the city had failed repeatedly. Once more it was the private sector to the rescue while government was again hung out for ridicule. The Angels were, it turns out, a preview of what might be done in part with community policing.

Spurred in part by the crack epidemic, crime spiraled out of control in the late 1980s. Between 1988 and 1990 the city hit its historic high for murders. Car theft had become effectively decriminalized, and in the summer of 1990 a series of high-profile crimes had the city panicked. Liberal columnist Sidney Schamberg spoke of a "combat emergency" so severe that "we might have to suspend some civil liberties." The tabloid headlines screamed at the new mayor DO SOMETHING DAVE. He did. Under pressure from the public and from City Council President Peter Vallone, Dinkins went to Albany. He convinced the state legislature to pass the Safe Streets, Safe City bill, which allowed the city to impose a $500 million income tax surcharge. The money was used to add 2,800 cops to the 33,000-strong N.Y.P.D.

The new Safe Streets, Safe City officers were to be used in re-creating an updated version of the old ideal of the cop on the beat. No longer would the police serve merely as a ready reaction force isolated from the community in patrol cars; they would once again engage the problems on the street. Dinkins hired more cops, but he didn't want to make more arrests. He thought it pointless to go after the low-level local drug dealers. Arresting them, he argued, would just clog the courts. The upshot was that while Dinkins's police commissioner, Lee Brown, gave after-dinner speeches extolling the virtues of community policing, he rarely expended administrative effort to implement it. Referring to Safe Streets, Safe City, a Harlem cop who wished to remain anonymous asked, "What's the difference if you've got twenty-five thousand people sitting around doing nothing or thirty thousand?"

Crime nonetheless began to drop slightly in Dinkins's last two years, probably because of the unsung hero of the anticrime efforts, Governor Mario Cuomo, who had quietly (so as not to disturb the state's Bourbon liberals) doubled the state's prison space. But while crime began to decline, fear did not. This was because at the same time they hired more cops, the Dinkins administration continued to decriminalize even more minor offenses. A misdemeanor arrest for a quality-of-life offense—like playing an earsplitting boom box or drunken menacing—was replaced with a "desk appearance ticket" (DAT), but half the people given such a ticket never bothered to show up in court.

It was easy to game the system. Advised a professional shoplifter, "The best move is to do misdemeanor crime for felony money. Don't ever do felonies. Felonies send you to jail." This is no small matter in a city where, on average, businesses lose $4,200 a year in what is in effect a crime tax, not to mention the additional $7,300 a year spent on target hardening like roll-down metal shutters and iron bars for the windows. The regulars all know about New York State Penal Law 155.25—get caught boosting less than $1,000 a year from a store and the charge is petty larceny, a misdemeanor.

While Police Commissioner Brown speechified about community policing, the chief of the city's separate transit police, William Bratton, a native Bostonian, was carrying out an experiment in activist policing. George Kelling, Bratton's mentor, was the father of "community policing." In the now famous 1982 "Broken Windows," an article in the *Atlantic* written with James Q. Wilson, Kelling argued that the police had misunderstood their core mission.

The modern police force was organized as a rapid response force. However, the cops arrived on the scene to catch the perpetrators in only 3 percent of all cases, and crime continued to spiral out of control. In their pursuit of high-tech professionalism, the modern police force had forsaken the most important service the police could provide—maintaining order. Crime is often a by-product of disorder. To quote Kelling and Wilson:

> Where disorder problems are frequent and no one takes responsibility for unruly behavior (like broken windows) in public places, the sense of "territoriality" among residents shrinks to include only their own households; meanwhile untended property is fair game for plunder and destruction . . . [and] a concentration of supposedly "victimless" disorders can soon flood an area with serious victimizing crime.

Kelling and Wilson had explained what many an inarticulate home owner understood intuitively: the hooker in front of the house was not just a moral eyesore; she would also over time become a danger to life and limb.

Kelling's approach also spoke to the well-justified fears of African-Americans who had been roughed up by police caught up in the hot pursuit of a fleeing suspect. Kelling came to the "broken windows" thesis through his work with the Newark Police Department, which experimented in the mid-seventies with restoring foot patrols to a few neighborhoods. Kelling found in Newark, only recently the scene of a major riot, white cops working amicably and effectively in a black neighborhood by exercising the low-level discretionary authority needed to maintain order. The cops occasionally made arrests, but most of their work consisted of talking with people to establish rapport; moving miscreants on; and, most importantly, asserting through their presence the common standards of behavior essential to making people feel safe.

What Kelling had rediscovered, as he freely admits, were the original principles of policing once laid out by Sir Robert Peel. The aim of the police, Peel explained in his 1829 manifesto "Principles of Law Enforcement," is first and foremost "keeping peace by peaceful means." Arrests should be a last resort. "The test of police efficiency," wrote Peel, "is the absence of crime and disorder, not the visible evidence of police action dealing with them." These were the policing principles repeated seventy years later in the first New York City charter, which reads as follows: "It is hereby made the duty of the police department to especially preserve the public peace, . . . remove all nuisances in the public streets . . . restrain all unlawful and disorderly conduct." Looking to avoid trouble, turn-of-the-century New York cops got into what would today be derided as social work. Police stations, for instance, were built with room for migrants who needed sleeping space as they moved from city to city in search of work.

Bratton, following Kelling's conclusions, self-consciously reversed all the assumptions about decriminalization and victimless crime that had become fashionable two decades earlier. He argued that crime flourishes in the absence of order on a small scale; that a broken window left unfixed or an abandoned car left untowed suggests that an area has been liberated from the constraint of the law; that if windows are repaired, if cars are towed quickly, and if graffiti is quickly painted over, crime is unlikely to take hold.

The return to an emphasis on keeping order was bitterly resisted by the police themselves, who derided "empty holster" cops as something less than manly. They were joined, for different reasons, by liberals and civil libertarians, who made what might be described as an anti-anticrime argument. Like the anti-anti-Communists of a generation ago, they argued that the constraints imposed by the citizenry by active policing were far worse than the original problem.

There was little Bratton could to win over the ideologues at the NYCLU, but the discovery that as many as one in ten fare beaters was wanted on an outstanding felony warrant began to change the minds of the transit cops. They saw that there was a "seamless web" between controlling petty crime and restraining major crime. As one cop put it, "We got this great new chief and this great new strategy: robbery, fare beating, and disorder; you deal with one, you deal with all."

The one major public order success of the Koch years had been the campaign led by his transit chief, Robert Kiley, to eliminate graffiti on the subways. Norman Mailer predictably saw graffiti removal as yet another sign of incipient fascism, but the public loved it. In the spirit of the anti-graffiti success, Bratton and Kiley insisted on creating a sense of ownership for public spaces. "Just as every big building has a super," Bratton argued, "every subway station ought to have a manager who takes a personal interest in what happens there." That included bringing in social work help to give some of the homeless who hung out in the subways an alternative. Finally, by reestablishing older norms Bratton made it easier for the public to set its own standards. Rodney James, who wasn't homeless but did his pitch on the subways every day, much to riders' annoyance, discovered something in the new atmosphere: "People don't give anywhere like what they used to . . . "I could probably make just as much working at McDonald's."

Rodney James was right, and so was Bratton. Both subway crime and the sense of menace on the subways declined dramatically. Between 1990 and 1994, felonies on the subway declined by 75 percent, robberies by 64 percent.

Considering the issues he had raised in the election campaign against David Dinkins in 1989, there was little to foreshadow Giuliani's success with street crime. He had made his reputation as a great federal attorney who had won a number of important white collar and organized crime cases. But in 1989 Giuliani, like Dinkins, declined to endorse a Metropolitan Transit Authority proposal to keep vagrants from sleeping on the subways. His big crime initiative was using drug forfeiture money to fund drug treatment. By the early 1990s Giuliani had embraced the "broken windows" argument, and so it was only natural that he would turn to William Bratton as his police commissioner. However, before police and public order reform got under way, Giuliani faced a challenge from the racial racketeers who had threatened to make the city ungovernable if he won.

Giuliani received the support of many Democrats, including Robert Wagner, Jr., son of the former mayor and grandson of Senator Wagner, one of the architects of the New Deal, but he won only 3 percent of the African-American vote. He tried to reach out to this segment of the population—his first trip after being elected was to Harlem—but barely a week into his mayoralty he was faced with an incident involving a false report of robbery at a Nation of Islam mosque. Several police were set upon, and a female officer was slammed to the pavement by a Nation of Islam thug. Yet the Nation of Islam, backed by a chorus of racial hustlers, including Al Sharpton, demanded a police apology. By keeping cool and adopting a "let's look at the facts" approach to the incident, Giuliani began to turn the tables on his would-be tormentors. In the absence of evidence that the police had acted improperly, Giuliani refused to apologize. In a city where racial politics had rejected the incumbent Koch and had elected and then rejected Dinkins, Giuliani made it clear that he was establishing a new set of rules. "You can't let community pressure change the facts," a Giuliani aide explained. "Once you do that, you give up the single standard of the rule of law."

Having held his ground, Giuliani got off to a fast start. His police commissioner, Bratton, quickly made good on a Giuliani campaign pledge by cracking down on the "squeegee men" who were shaking down motorists stopped at certain traffic lights. A study of the "squeegees" by George Kelling found that three-quarters had homes and that the majority had criminal records for drugs, assault, robbery, or other felonies. Bratton's hard-edged advice to the city's aggressive panhandlers—"Get off drugs, get off the booze, get off your ass, and get a job"—struck a responsive chord among the working poor and middle class alike.

Before the Giuliani mayoralty an activist reverend from the East Brooklyn congregations once said, "The main characteristic of this department is not corruption or brutality but bureaucratic inertia." The new police commissioner set out to change that. William Bratton, a natural leader of men, shook up the top-heavy N.Y.P.D brass at One Police Plaza, the oversized command-and-control center designed for an earlier era. Like the corporate executives who had successfully restructured their companies, he moved to streamline at the top and decentralize at the bottom, pushing resources and responsibility down to the precinct level. He installed a management system that pinpointed the crime targets and made extensive use of specialized units to zero in on neighborhoods where crime was taking root.

Announcing that his No. 1 priority was fear reduction, Bratton took the narcotics squads off their bankers' hours of Monday through Friday, nine to five, and created round-the-clock narcotics teams (surprising some dealers in the process). Perhaps even more important, he allowed ordinary street cops to make drug arrests under the supervision of precinct commanders, who were held personally responsible (i.e., their careers could be in jeopardy) for corruption.

The numbers speak for themselves. Crime has dropped nationally and in some big cities (although not Washington, D.C.), but nowhere has the drop in crime been as sharp and as sustained as in New York City. While New York City crime was declining slightly from 1991 to 1993, between 1993 and 1995 violent and property crimes dropped 26 percent in New York City compared to 2 percent nationally. Murders by teens, which were deterred by Bratton's aggressive weapons searches, dropped 28 percent. Over the first three years of the Giuliani mayoralty, auto theft dropped 46 percent, robbery 41 percent, and murder 49 percent, so that in 1996 New York recorded the fewest murders in a year since 1968, when John Lindsay was mayor. Of the city's seventy-six police precincts, crime dropped in seventy-five during 1995; only rape seemed immune to the general decline.

There were some other elements to the city's success. The maturing of drug markets meant that the dealers weren't fighting as much. The growth of Business Improvement Districts (BIDs), where local businesses taxed themselves to augment city services with private police and sanitation, meant that the "broken windows" were being repaired more quickly in the thirty-two neighborhoods where they had been established. But the primary reason for the sharp drop in shootings was largely that police friskings for such minor violations as loud radio playing and public beer drinking discouraged people from carrying unregistered guns. The underside to the Giulliani-Bratton-Kelling achievements was that the flush of success obscured the ongoing problem of excess police force used against minorities.

Bill Clinton should have thanked his lucky stars that David Dinkins had been defeated. If his candidate had won, Clinton would have had the millstone of a sinking New York City around the presidency. Instead, as a gift to the rhetoric of President Clinton's reelection campaign, New York City, though only 3 percent of the population, made it possible for the incumbent to bask in statistics showing a national decline in reported crimes between 1993 and 1995, since the city accounted for more than one-third of that decline.

When Bratton left his post after a highly publicized clash of egos with the mayor, there were fears that the city would begin to backslide, but the city passed its first post-Bratton test with flying colors. In June 1996 a one-man crime spree by John Royster, himself the son of a murderer, left one woman dead, three severely injured, and the city in a panic. The quick resolution of the case under the new police commissioner, Howard Safir, vindicated the argument that arrests for small quality-of-life crimes often pay dividends on larger cases: Royster was captured when he was arrested for jumping a subway turnstile. A week later the police collared the long-sought-after Zodiac killer.

Unfortunately, New York's successful shift of course on public order wasn't matched by a similar shift on economic issues. There was no parallel broad-gauged willingness to rexamine the reasons for the city's economic entropy.

16. Mining for Fool's Gold

New York's Make-Work Economy

For all of his considerable success in reducing crime, Mayor Giuliani has had a far more difficult time in turning the city's economy around. A formidable job, it's a task that may be beyond even the best of mayors. Over the years, the more the city's policies drove out business, the more dependent the city became on social service jobs partially funded from Washington. As I discovered in countless conversations, the inflow of federal money had obscured, for all but the most sophisticated of New Yorkers, the fact that the city was sending Washington far more money than it received in return.

After World War II, New York had more than a million manufacturing jobs and about a quarter of a million people on welfare. Today the numbers are roughly reversed: New York has about 1.1 million people on one form of public assistance or another and fewer than three hundred thousand manufacturing jobs. As Councilman Antonio Pagan explained ruefully during the Dinkins years, "The social services sector has replaced light industry as a source of employment, and it's only going to grow." It did, but to no good end. In the world of social services, a Bronx official of the Alinskyite Industrial Areas Foundation told me, "No one is ever accountable."

The social service industry has been our equivalent of Soviet agriculture. In the social service business failure was the basis for success, since the inability to rehabilitate simply meant that even more money was needed.

In the fall of 1992, just as the presidential election was entering the home stretch, a perennial New York scandal burst into the news again. A *Daily News* article on famed Erasmus High School described how the custodian, who enjoyed a base salary of $65,467 plus numerous perks, could rarely be found at the school. It seems that he had "wheeled his private 30-foot boat onto the school's athletic field and ordered three custodians to repair it during school hours. The boat stayed there for three months." The same custodian was later filmed by *60 Minutes* sailing his repaired 30-foot yacht off Sheepshead Bay.

The custodian's scandal was made to order for Georgia Congressman (and later House Speaker) Newt Gingrich, who had long made New York's failures a metaphor for the decadence of the welfare state. "Gee, if we can win the cold war, . . . what will we do for an encore?" Gingrich asked. "Well, . . . we could bring *perestroika* to the New York School Board." The Georgian's sarcasm so angered New Yorkers, who were accustomed to mocking their benighted but no longer so poor Bible-thumping Southern cousins, that it almost obscured the issue.

The custodian scam was more than a matter of a few freeloaders living high off the hog on public money. It spoke to the very nature of the political system and government services in a city in which the means to satisfy public needs, government, had become an end in itself. In New York, as La Guardia had feared, the public had been put in the service of the municipal unions.

The physical plant of the city's schools, which had to be maintained by the custodians at great cost, was beset by leaky roofs, sagging floors, crumbling walls, and the like. At one point the school system, which operates on an $8 billion annual budget, capital expenditures excluded, spent $1.5 million on wooden windows for 174 schools, but the windows then rotted because the custodians weren't contractually obligated to keep them painted.

In fact, New York custodians are obligated to very little. They are independent contractors who can hire friends and relatives to work for them; they can even use board of education money to buy themselves jeeps. At the same time, they enjoy the protection of their civil service status. In practice that means that while they earn considerably more than teachers or cops, custodians are required to sweep the cafeteria floor only once a week, sweep classrooms on alternate days, and clean schools' windows three times a year (whether they need it or not)! By comparison, the common room at New York's Rikers Island jail is by court order required to be mopped three times a day. And while the courts insist that the same prison's libraries must be open seven days a week, any neighborhood or civic group that wants to use a school after three o'clock or on weekends has to pay the custodian directly. Even school teams [have] to pay for the use of a pool, gym, or field.

The first calls for reforming school maintenance came in 1942, and they've been coming ever since. The New York City Council president in the 1980s, Andrew Stein, took up the cause, as did the schools investigations commissioner, Ed Stancik. Neither achieved much success. That's because the custodians were extremely well connected and were also only one of the many interest groups feasting off the carcass of the dying school system. The custodians enjoyed enormous clout in New York's state legislature, where they were represented by labor lawyer Basil Patterson, a close personal ally of Mayor David Dinkins; and by Harold Ickes (son of FDR's secretary of the interior), a lawyer for a variety of mob-related unions who went on to become a key player in the first-term Clinton White House.

But it's more than just friends in high places that maintains the custodians' power. They are also protected by their allies in the public employee union "movement," who fear that reform of the custodians augurs broader school reform. School superintendents, fearing that custodial reform is the opening wedge of broader school management changes, have refused to cooperate with private companies doing custodial work. Donald Singer, president of the Council of Supervisors and Administrators, argues that "there is a movement to try to privatize public schools, not just custodial services. Are you then going to privatize health services at the schools, food services, teaching services?" Asks Singer, "Where does it stop?"

Better to ask, "How did it start?" How did New York put itself in hock to its public sector unions, and how did it set itself up for criticism not only from Gingrich but a host of other officials who represent jurisdictions that, in effect, live off the dollars Washington siphons from New York?

Gingrich, later speaking for his part of the country, the suburban South, railed on about New York's "slow motion self-destruction" and its "culture of waste." We are, he alleged, "subsidizing the Cosa Nostra when we aid New York." Referring to corruption in garbage collection and construction, he insisted that his home of Cobb County and the rest of America will no longer "bail out the habits that have made New York so extraordinarily expensive." Gingrich wasn't alone. Gordon Wysong, a Cobb County commissioner, bragged, "We're the power now. These suburbs built on white flight are only going to become more conservative and powerful. New York has been deposed and won't accept it." Todd Leithead, originally from Connecticut and former chair of the Cobb Chamber of Commerce, says the Big Apple can't match the suburban lifestyle, which has drawn RJR Nabisco, IBM, AT&T,

Home Depot, and Hewlett-Packard. Says Leithead, "New York embodies the historical way that people chose to live and work until World War Two, . . . we [Cobb County] are the solution and the evolution of the way people will live and work for the next hundred years."

There's some truth to Leithead's remarks—but also a good deal of dishonesty. The same New Deal so revered by New Yorkers was similarly revered by Georgians, although for different reasons. For New York, the activist government initiated by the New Deal subsidized the social service sector organized by public employees like the custodians and teachers. In Georgia, where the current governor, Zell Miller, issues down-home encomiums to FDR's greatness, the New Deal meant that though they had themselves become well-to-do, they were still entitled to the privileged treatment they had received ever since FDR, a Georgian at heart, declared the South to be the nation's No. 1 economic problem.

The Georgia economy was modernized not so much with Wall Street investments as with federal credit. FDR put Atlanta on the modern map when he routed regional airmail traffic through there. It was the federal government that paid for much of the subsequent airport expansion, culminating in today's Hartsfield Airport, which makes Atlanta both a travel hub and a thriving location for corporate office space. Eisenhower's interstate highway program connected the city to the surrounding counties of what is now a thriving region whose economy is propped up by heavy military spending for major military suppliers like Lockheed and an Air Force Reserve base. By the late 1960s, with the city partly freed from the fetters of racism by a civil rights movement heavily supported and bankrolled from New York, Atlanta's per capita income surpassed New York's. Atlanta was becoming wealthy, but the subsidies still kept coming, particularly to the benefit of Cobb County. Cobb is third among suburban counties in the number of federal dollars it receives—$7,491 per person, which is 57 percent above the national average and about $3,200 more than a New Yorker receives. While Cobb's critics of big government got back $1.80 for every dollar they sent to D.C., the "moochers" in New York City got back eighty-two cents.

New York City was sending Washington roughly $8 billion to $9 billion a year in taxes and fees more than it got back, and it was doing it year in and year out. While New York's liberals talk about social justice, other regions are stealing their socks. The New Deal game has been turned against them.

Gingrich—and, for that matter, much of the South—gets to have it both ways: they get to both criticize big government and live off its largesse. It's a contradiction Georgians have learned to live with comfortably and New Yorkers seem unable to turn to their own advantage. When Gingrich asked sarcastically, "Could it be that poverty, racism, crime, and violence have been solved in New York, [so that] you should share your wisdom with the rest of the country?" he drove New York liberals into a frenzy. New York pols stuck in the world of "what about Mississippi" rightly respond by reciting once again the city's contribution to Southern civil rights, but then they go on to insist that New York's underclass is yet another reflection of the city's moral superiority, its capacity for greater compassion.

Once they're finished posturing, New York's representatives in Washington should be asked why they've allowed not only Gingrich but Georgia and rubes everywhere to take New York to the cleaners. What is there in the structure of New York politics that gives New Yorkers the school custodians at home and the short end of the stick in Washington year in and year out? Why do supposedly sophisticated New York pols, who ought to understand that New York and Washington are rival centers of power, believe in Washington more than Washington believes in itself? Part of the answer to both questions lies in the way New York replaced a private sector economy over the past thirty years with a public sector economy based on selling its poverty to Washington in return for social service dollars.

February 1967 was a dreadful month for the New York City economy. "Within a ten-day period in February 1967 both American Can and Pepsi-Cola," wrote John Teaford, "announced plans to leave for the suburbs; Olin Mathieson announced it was shifting its headquarters for chemical operations to Connecticut and Bohn Office Machines announced it was looking to leave." That same February, fourteen other corporations, with 11,500 employees in Manhattan, began to plan their exits. In 1956 New York was the headquarters of 140 of the Fortune 500 companies. It was down by only one at the start of 1967 but by 1975 it had dropped to 98 headquarters and the end of the fall was nowhere in sight.

The shock of February 1967 and the huge manufacturing job losses of 1969 and 1970 that followed—the city lost 120,000 manufacturing jobs—might have been expected to produce second thoughts about the city's path. They didn't. The New York economy was in free fall, and Lindsay's primary response was to add more municipal workers to the sixty thousand he had already hired between 1966 and 1968.

The city's ability to produce wealth was taken for granted. Nothing—not even the decline of the once thriving docks, the railroad shutdowns, and subsequent manufacturing decline—could shake that certainty. The city elites backing Lindsay, little interested in either outer borough ethnics or the manufacturing economy, placed their faith in a new New York based on the Manhattan financial industry and an expansion of the social service industry in the outer boroughs.

The need for a social service industry indigenous to the black community was first fully laid out by the eminent psychologist Kenneth Clark, who wanted to build "a new culture designed to enable the ghetto to service itself." White social workers and their clients, he argued, were cut off from each other not only by different languages and by "psychological alienation" but, most importantly, by "different standards of behavior." He argued, "It may be that many lower-class persons who now refuse the role of client will accept the same therapeutic help if it is offered in a course of training as part of a position as paid or volunteer trainee."

Clark's ideas were extended and expanded in a path-breaking book—*New Careers for the Poor,* written in 1965 by social service entrepreneurs Arthur Pearl and Frank Riessman. In an earlier version of what we now call the "mismatch thesis," they started with the assumption that because of automation the poor of the sixties were "unlike the poor of the past." They believed that the contemporary poor—and here they meant mostly racial minorities—had no chance to move up the job ladder as it existed and that it was therefore necessary to create a new job ladder. They envisioned "millions of new nonprofessional jobs and careers" and argued that creating the new jobs—home assistant, home health care worker, Medicaid monitor, neighborhood coordinator, child advocate, parent education coordinator, drug treatment worker, and homemaker—would "greatly improve services for the poor by providing service by the poor."

Pearl, Riessman, and their colleagues from the New York magazine *Social Policy* developed a twofold critique of the New Deal state, which they said had mistakenly embraced both professionalism and the principle of the government as the employer of last resort. Requiring credentials prior to employment, they argued, eliminates the poor from many opportunities, as does an emphasis on "measured intelligence, aptitude, or delinquency record," since these "indices may reflect only the effect of an impoverished existence and therefore would not predict capabilities in a new context." They hoped that new context would come when policy switched from the New Deal concept of the government as employer of last resort to the more enlightened policy of government as the employer of first resort. Like George Wiley and the welfare rights advocates who assumed a guaranteed income would induce middle-class behavior, the theorists of the "new careers for the poor" assumed that giving people jobs would produce job-associated discipline and mobility. They insisted that the great virtue of these human services jobs was that they would produce "much more employment per dollar invested" than the traditional public works jobs that build infrastructure. To help pay for the social services spending, Lindsay initiated a local income tax that made New York the highest-taxed locality in the country.

The city was placing an enormous bet. Not only was it rapidly increasing taxes to pay for the growth of government, but it was also shifting the kind of government services it would provide. Between 1965 and 1975, the percentage of the budget that went to the basic city services that businesses depend on (such as police, fire, roads, and schools) fell from 46 to 30 percent of the budget while welfare spending quadrupled and social service spending, including hospital expenditures, rose from 22 to 37 percent of the budget.

Worse yet, because of the rapidly rising cost of municipal labor, owing to both salary increases and workload reductions, city expenditures for basic services tripled in cost (while declining as a percentage of the budget) but declined in quality. In effect, while municipal employees were paid more to do less and vast numbers of private sector workers were moved onto the public payroll directly or into city-subsidized social services, business and the middle class were paying much more to get less.

The rise of employment in the public sector and its decline in the private sector were more than statistical artifacts. In practice the one often produced the other—and not just in higher taxes for declining basic services. Even high-end textile manufacturers paying four times the minimum wage and medical benefits found that they couldn't compete for workers with the higher pay offered by a thirty-five-hour-a-week city job that came, as it does today, with medical insurance that required no copayment. As one textile owner explained, "I had loyal long-term employees tell me they had no choice but to go to work for the city." He moved his jobs to the South, and his eighty employees were added to the statistics for lost manufacturing jobs.

The greater the number of private jobs leaving the city, the greater the necessity for the government to become the primary employer. The spending spree that had begun with Mayor Wagner's third term in 1961 continued until 1975, when the city teetered on the edge of bankruptcy. During those years the city's budget grew in real terms from \$8.6 billion to \$21.1 billion. As noted by Charles Brecher and Ray Horton of the Citizens Budget Commission, the real per capita spending nearly tripled between 1961 and 1975, since the city's population fell by roughly one million over the same period. During that period the city government's relative size had grown from about a tenth to nearly a quarter of the city's economic output. Brecher estimated that when the federal government's activities in New York are added in, the local public sector represented 28 percent of all employment by 1975 and between 35 and 40 percent of all income. New York, complained one wag, was "Eastern Europe kept afloat by Wall Street."

Journalist Ken Auletta summed up the situation: New York's "experiment in local socialism and income distribution redistribut[ed] much of its tax base and jobs to other parts of the country."

Beginning under LaGuardia and accelerating under Wagner, New York began to pay for one year's overexpenditure by rolling the costs over into the next year; however, the vast accumulated debt eventually led the banks that had been lending money to the city to balk. The financial house of cards came down on Lindsay's successor, the hapless five-foot-two-inch Abe Beame, a man as unprepossessing as Lindsay had been glamorous. Fittingly enough, the city's brush with bankruptcy came in 1974 when the state bonds financing the city's Mitchell–Lama housing projects, a middle-class housing entitlement, went belly up and set off a panic.

Beame's response to the crisis was to follow the path pioneered by Lindsay, who had declared that both he and the city were victims. Beame, noted Auletta, "blamed in order: the banks, state Senate Republican leader Anderson, President Ford, and finally the press." At one point he called for a congressional investigation into "who started the whispering campaign against the city." At other times he blamed larger economic forces, which was partly true. But at no time did this man, an accountant and the city comptroller—that is, financial watchdog—during the Lindsay years, who had been elected as the guardian of fiscal probity in a city hungering for some post-Lindsay competence in government, ever acknowledge his own complicity. Instead, through his howls of victimization he presented the spectacle of a New York, the home of Wall Street, that was at once powerful and pitiful. It was a presentation that inspired contempt.

The whole economic and social edifice begun in the New Deal and remodeled in the 1960s came crashing down in the mid-1970s. New York had bankrupted itself in pursuit of policies that both eroded the economic base and produced a poverty rate that when adjusted for price levels approached Mississippi's. New York in the 1970s, the high point of federal transfer payments to the cities, accounted for an astonishing one-third of the increase in ghetto poverty nationally. Here was a failure of near-Soviet proportions.

Ken Auletta spoke of New York's rescue from bankruptcy as "the Left's Vietnam." Senator Moynihan warned that "the bankruptcy of New York City would be to the Northeast what Sherman's march was to the South. It would also be a seismic event in the world at large." Referring to the hostile national response to the New York City economic crisis, Moynihan asked "What if it turns out that the New Deal was a one-way street?" He then answered his own question: "I will tell you what will happen. There will be a response of bitterness and reaction that will approach in duration if not in intensity the response of the South to its defeat in what we now call the War Between the States."

And it's true there were consequences—in Los Angeles and nationally. The L.A. antitax movement, headquartered in the San Fernando Valley, seized upon big-spending New York's troubles to generate support for the ill-conceived Proposition 13, the radical tax-cutting measure that undermined California's fiscal stability. New York's combination of high taxes and near bankruptcy became Exhibit A in the growing national movement for tax cuts and smaller government.

But in New York the interests that had invested deeply in and profited heartily from failure—the bankers and brokers who profited from city debt, the public employee unions whose expansion had been financed through a siphoning off of private sector wages, the politicians who had become dependent on the votes of those who worked for government directly or indirectly, those who received welfare or middle-class entitlements like the Mitchell-Lama housing subsidies, the social activists who insisted that the city's welfare expansion had been a huge success, the vast coterie of liberal academics and intellectuals who were convinced that New York was the vanguard of civilization—generally refused to rethink their assumptions. Indeed, the bankruptcy only reinforced their hidebound sense of moral superiority since it was taken as a sign of New York's vast compassion. New York had failed, it seemed, only by being too generous, too good. Better to whine about Republican meanness than to question the whole semireligious edifice upon which so much failure had been built.

In a sense, Moynihan gave a better answer to his own question when he noted that family breakdown was extraordinary by historical standards and concluded, "Yet there is little evidence that these facts are regarded as a calamity in municipal government." That they were not was in part because breakdown supports a vast network of social workers, for whom personal pathology is a job opportunity. It was far more than just social workers, though. John McKnight of Northwestern University listed the new cadre of social service jobs. His list included but was not limited to the following:

> job trainers, street gang workers, land clearance experts, urban education specialists, environmental aides, urban environmental specialists, legal assistance lawyers, library consultants, job locators, public health physicians, parole consultants, nurses,

> public housing officials, teachers aides, civil rights watchdogs, employment counselors, prevention specialists, police trainers, urban housing specialists, rat abatement experts, vocational counselors, literacy specialists, drug counselors, defensible space architects, and the administrators, auditors, lawyers and consultants to support them all.

For the new alternative economy, the more dysfunctional the families, the better they served as Keynesian multipliers by generating immediate spending.

It was this multiplier effect that Dick Morris, later the politically ambidextrous adviser to President Clinton, then a card-carrying liberal, stumbled onto when he wrote his 1978 book *Bum Rap on the Cities,* a full-fledged attempt to defend New York from its critics. "Eighty percent of the money spent on welfare in New York City," Morris thundered, "went to middle-class providers of [social and medical] services." For instance, it took one dollar to administer every two dollars of welfare distributed, he discovered. Only San Francisco was comparable, and only Washington, D.C., spent more. Worse yet, Morris believed, was the "profiteering" in health services, where Medicaid mills "ping-ponged" their clients around their group offices and ran up huge reimbursables whether or not the treatments were needed. New York's Medicaid costs were twice that of Michigan and more than seven times that of Florida. But Morris missed the most important reason for the Medicaid costs: Medicaid had subtly been turned into a jobs program for New York and, as such, had become politically invaluable.

Between 1961 and 1971, municipal hospitals in New York City hired four thousand additional employees while serving 20 percent fewer patients. The hospitals were an enormous favor-dispensing and patronage center. Medicaid gave the city's legislative delegation gratitude and campaign contributions from providers, unions, clients, and the many workers hired to take on nonmedical work, such as personal care attendants paid for by Medicaid. Medicaid patronage helped make the city's legislators politically invincible.

Not even the fiscal crisis of the mid-seventies shook the reasoning behind New York's social welfare and Medicaid spending. New York, it was argued, was taking the federal government for all it was worth. If the feds were willing to match city and state dollars with a dollar of their own or sometimes two or three, why shouldn't New York grab for this "free" money? The trouble with pursuing this "fool's gold" was twofold: First, the "free" federal money had to be matched by local money in a city whose rising taxes and declining services were driving business away and plunging the city into near bankruptcy. Second, while New York City and the state were receiving an inflow of social services money overall, they were sending Washington far more than they received.

"New York is a liberal state," explained Senator Moynihan, "and you can't break out of the notion that anything you get from the federal government is sort of free. But all the formulas are the other way around." Moynihan was right, and it only got worse. In 1984 the net flow of funds to and from Washington drained 2 percent of New York State's income; by 1994 that had risen to more than 4 percent, with dire consequences for the city, which was far and away the largest source of the money extracted by Washington.

The city's financial rescue—through a consortium of bankers led by Felix Rohatyn of Lazard Freres and of labor leaders led by Victor Gotbaum of the American Federation of State, County, and Municipal Employees—restructured the debt but left the structure of a wildly overextended government, the crumbling economic base, and the dysfunctional relationship with Washington untouched. The biggest myth, explained Richard Ravitch, Economic Development Board chair, after the "rescue," is that "things have fundamentally changed in the way the city does business. We haven't yet seriously examined the pension system, or the Health and Hospitals Corporation, or how federal dollars are used, or the range of services the city still performs."

Ravitch was right. Though the city decreased its workforce by 22 percent during the first three years of the fiscal crisis, total labor costs (half the city budget) decreased by only 1 percent because of growing salaries and pensions for the workers who remained. None of the labor practices that had driven the city down—the (at best) thirty-five-hour workweek, the absence of medical copayments (common in the private sector), the ban on part-time employment even for school bus drivers who worked only for a few hours in the morning and then again in the afternoon—none of these practices had been reformed. Looking on the city's decline, the Liberal Party leader Alex Rose, the man who had twice made Lindsay mayor, noted sorrowfully before he died that the "Little Wagner Act" had been a "mistake." "Workers," he explained, "are not extracting a share of the profits but rather a share of taxes."

The city's financial rescue made labor leader Gotbaum into a force to be reckoned with. "There is no question about it," Gotbaum boasted. "We [the municipal labor leaders] have the ability to elect our own boss." Gotbaum's next boss and the new mayor in 1978 was Ed Koch. Once a liberal reformer, Koch made all the right noises when he won the mayoralty against a crowded field that included Mario Cuomo, who later won the governorship, and Bella Abzug, who went on to obscurity but whose old left ideas lingered on. Koch was, noted a member of the Municipal Assistance Corporation, which had been created to keep the city on the financial straight and narrow, "the first mayor in memory to promise to do more for less."

Koch tried at first. He insisted that "the main job of city government is to create a climate in which private business can expand in the city to provide jobs on the public payroll." He fought for civil service reform. New York City in 1978 counted more than thirty-nine thousand civil service job titles in 243 occupational groups. The federal government has only 22 occupational groups, but because of union opposition Koch couldn't get a single State Assembly Democrat to sponsor a reform bill.

Halfway into his first term, Koch looked to leverage his popularity into a run for governor and gave up on reform. Fortunately for the city, in the short run at least, it was saved from a return to ruin by President Reagan's deregulation of the financial markets, which set off an economic boom on Wall Street. The boom meant that Koch as mayor and, later, Cuomo as governor were like guys playing the tuba while it was raining gold; for a while they couldn't help but do well.

During his mayoralty of New York, from 1978 to 1989, Koch entertained the city with tough talk that blinded friend and foe alike to his traditionally liberal practices. Koch, whose top staff was mostly old Lindsay retreads, loved the sound of his own voice. Ranting about "poverty pimps," he inflamed the minions of the righteous while wasting his political capital to little effect. Soon enough, though, he made peace with "poverty pimps" like Raymon Velez in the Bronx and Samuel Wright in Brooklyn. He found that he could use the new patronage inherent in "third party government" to win black and Latino political support. So while social service spending both by government and by nonprofit contractors declined in most cities during the Reagan years, it kept on expanding in New York through boom and bust.

The budget for the city's social service agencies grew from $3.6 billion in 1980 to $9.5 billion in 1994, a 260 percent jump, while the city's overall budget grew only by 140 percent, from $13.9 billion in 1980 to $31.9 billion in 1990. Human service contracts grew from $1 billion in 1985 to nearly $3 billion in 1993. Social service jobs in the city more than doubled, from 62,000 in 1980 to 134,000 in 1994, according to the Bureau of Labor Statistics, while manufacturing jobs dropped from 450,000 in 1982 to 290,000 in 1992.

The expansion of both directly delivered and government-subsidized third-party social services set off such a scramble for space that agencies began fighting with each other and private business for good locations. In one case a minority-owned copy shop was forced out of business, putting ten people out of work so that the misnamed Volunteers of America—95 percent of their funding is from government—could open up yet another social service operation on the already saturated Upper West Side of Manhattan. Not coincidentally, the VOA's well-paid executive director, Richard Salyer, was the adviser on homeless policy to the city council.

There are today so many social service agencies in New York City that they trip over each other to "service" clients. There are, for instance, so many AIDS prevention programs run by both the city and the state that, as Heather MacDonald of the Manhattan Institute's *City Journal* points out, the city can't even keep count of them, although it thinks there are somewhere between four hundred and eight hundred, not including those run on a largely private basis by AIDS service organizations. There are so many programs to service teen mothers that in 1984 the state legislature passed the Teenage Services Act (TASA). It added no new programs except that it "authorized a new category of social worker whose sole purpose [was] to guide teen welfare mothers to other services—in particular, to entitlements."

By tracing the hypothetical case of a teen welfare mother who had first received Healthy Start, Heather MacDonald describes the web of programs available to aid failed families. Healthy Start is a case management program to help young mothers receive Medicaid, WIC (Women, Infants, Children), emergency assistance, rent supplements, or drug treatment, as needed. Besides workshops on self-esteem and life skills, Healthy Start also trains tenant organizers and encourages young mothers to consider careers in social service, while providing guidance to other social servers on how to deliver "culturally sensitive services." If there is a danger of child abuse, a housekeeper or a provider of some other support service can also be made available.

But suppose that despite these early interventions the child has emotional problems. The services available to such a child, according to MacDonald, are as follows:

> If he starts disrupting classes and falling behind in school he will likely be placed in special education, where he will be assigned a school-based support team of psychologists and social workers. He may qualify for Supplemental Security Income disability payments for "age inappropriate behavior." But if he still suffers from "adjustment disorder," he may enter a "home-based crisis intervention" program. Social workers from five agencies will visit the child's home for eight weeks of intensive "skills building," parenting, and problem-solving training for the family. If despite all this the child then robs someone, the child may be sent to the Family Ties program, another attempt at family preservation which takes juvenile delinquents who are "at risk of placement" and gives them and their families eight weeks of cognitive restructuring, behavioral modification, anger management,

> and rational-emotive therapy—in short the same kind of family preservation services that had already been given

The upshot is, in the rare instance, rehabilitation. Still, the success of failure is in the many jobs it sustains along the way.

In 1973 economist Charles Brecher concluded that the effects of antipoverty investments were "mixed and modest." In 1996 there was no longer any ambiguity. Despite unparalleled spending, poverty had grown; more important, it had deepened as shorter and shorter generations of dysfunctional family fragments reproduced themselves. The young women in family homeless shelters today, notes Ralph Nunez of Homes for the Homeless, are younger, less educated, less experienced, and more damaged than those of five years ago. New York City spends over one-fifth of all local social service dollars in the country; it spends six times the local government average on Medicaid, welfare, homeless services, and foster care while spending less than the national average on such traditional municipal functions as education, sanitation, parks, and roads.

The failure of antipoverty programs has not ended the debate, however, since a new—and in some ways a more plausible, if equally destructive—argument has arisen. Today advocates and their allies defend social spending as essential to the New York economy. And they're right. After mainlining federal subsidies for thirty years, New York is hooked.

This is more than a metaphor. "The largest industry in my Community Board [Lower East Side] is drugs," explains Charles King, the director of Housing Works, the largest provider of housing to the HIV homeless; he says that "the second largest is social services." That combination is all to the good, he argues, because "social services bring benefits, bring jobs, because helping people who need help trickles down to the rest of the community." King's Housing Works helps keep the connection between drugs and jobs in play. Addicted HIV homeless people who enter the Housing Works facilities are not required to try to become drug free. Instead, they are asked to practice "harm reduction." That is, they are asked to reduce their drug usage, but if they feel they have to continue to smoke or shoot up, then they are asked to do so away from common areas and in the privacy of their rooms and only after they have made provision for their children. In other words, the highly respected King runs a state-sanctioned, tax-supported "enabler" for druggies, if not a drug den.

A more sophisticated version of the jobs argument is the old standby that says that welfare serves as the best possible Keynesian multiplier because welfare families quickly spend almost all they have. Welfare, argues antipoverty advocate Liz Krueger, is "woven into the fabric of the city economy." Food stamps sustain bodegas and grocery stores in low-income neighborhoods; welfare rent subsidies sustain the landlords; Con Ed, the electric utility, depends on special welfare subsidies for utility payments; and jobs in the nonprofits and in Medicaid depend on public hospitals, which are the primary employers for many minorities. Concludes Kreuger, "Welfare is a revenue producer for the city." "In the crassest of federal transfer terms . . . the poor and the subsidized attendants to the poor," wrote the *Village Voice*'s Wayne Barrett, "may be our primary cash crop."

By this logic, the absence of jobs and affordable housing are arguments for expanding social support rather than for asking if prior policies helped produce those conditions. This is the economics of slow, continuous decline. Offering a partial answer to these arguments, Richard Schwartz, a senior adviser to Mayor Giuliani, referred to the fact that municipal hospitals have about three times as many workers per patient as the city's private hospitals. Schwartz attacked what I described in chapter 7 as the "leaky bucket" approach to economics. Our municipal hospitals, he explained, "are probably the most inefficient job creation program known in America today." Schwartz described the steps of this program as follows:

> You take someone's dollar from a paycheck, you send it to Washington, Washington sends it to Albany, Albany sends it to New York City, the city matches it with 50 cents, Albany matches it with 50 cents. Then New York transfers that money to the corporate headquarters of the HHC [Health and Hospitals Corporation], which then transfers the money to the HHC hospital. Then, finally, that money translates . . . into a [make-work] job.

The side effects of municipal Keynesianism in one city are (1) a permanent inflation (so that New York's price levels are almost always well above the national average), (2) a workforce accustomed to make-work jobs and prepared only for other make-work jobs, and (3) neighborhoods overrun with social service facilities that destroy the quality of life. The ugly reality is that New York is trapped in more than one cycle of dependency. The city is dependent on an artificial economy that has grown out of control and prospered at the expense of the city's overall well-being.

Social services have become both big business and the key to a politics that revolves around serving and expanding the social service industry. In 1993 alone New York City awarded thirty thousand social service contracts worth nearly $3 billion. State and federal contracts brought in another $4 billion to the social service industry. It's a $7 billion-a-year industry that employs a growing percentage of the workforce in the U.S. city with the fewest workers proportional to the general population. While the city's job base shrank by 10 percent between 1984 and 1994, social service jobs increased by 60 percent, to 150,000, a growth of 55,000 jobs. Overall, publicly funded jobs in government, health care, and private social services account for one-third of all employment in Brooklyn and just under half in the Bronx. More than one million people in the city—one-third of the workforce—work in government, health, and social services.

Described in *Crain's New York Business* as "the new Tammany," the social service sector is represented by the 40 percent of the city council that either comes from or has strong ties to the industry and by the plurality of Democrats in the New York State Assembly, where they are in a near-permanent majority. The difference between the old and the new Tammany is that the old dispensed jobs that were regularly accountable to election outcomes, and most of those jobs were in essential sectors like roads and sanitation. The new Tammany, by contrast, is organized around what Jane Jacobs described as "transactions of decline." Its many antipoverty programs—there is not one but many programs for any problem—serve largely to substitute for the functions once performed by the family.

Poverty programs that were created to bring minorities into the economic mainstream have over the years metastasized into an alternative economy. The supposed means to aid the poor, namely, social services, have become an end in themselves. New York no longer produces many private sector entrepreneurs, but its many public sector entrepreneurs have discovered that pathology, both social and medical, can be packaged, marketed, and sold like a commodity once the city, state, and federal governments have set themselves up as buyers.

17. The Rudy Deal

True story: Two men are standing outside a Queens voting booth handing out palm cards for the 1988 election. The older man, a Democratic Party regular, turns to the reformer and asks suspiciously, "So what are you? Who do you represent?" The reformer replies, "I'm a Democratic Socialist." "That's okay," the regular responds, "just as long as you're not a goddamned liberal."

New York's old-line liberals, the "old believers," had a great many chuckles in the early 1990s when perfervid followers of Menachem Schneerson claimed that the Lubavitcher Rebbe was the messiah. When Rabbi Schneerson died, psychologists warned of the danger of failed prophecy for the mental health of his Hasidic followers. Fair enough, but what can we say about the mental health of those old believers, the city's old-line liberals, who keep expecting secular salvation to come by way of Washington and the welfare state?

A great deal was riding on the Clinton presidency. The claim that twelve years of Reagan-Bush were responsible for everything from poverty and unemployment to AIDS and intolerance was repeated so often by local politicians like Governor Cuomo, Mayor Dinkins, and members of the city's congressional delegation that it took on an almost liturgical quality. In the topsy-turvy world of New York City politics, the 1970s, when the Bronx burned and the city almost went bankrupt, are remembered fondly as an era of federal support. By contrast, the boom of the 1980s, when minority families made major gains in income, was decried by Manhattan Borough President Ruth Messinger and Public Advocate Mark Green as the decade of greed because federal subsidies failed to keep pace with the city's exploding budget.

I've traveled extensively among the old believers, attended their meetings and even occasionally debated them. They are a curious bunch. Whenever I noted to the elders assembled that Mr. Clinton had continued the bipartisan tradition, despite expectations to the contrary, of transferring New York money to the Sun Belt, I was met with civil-rights-era cries of "What about Mississippi?" When I pointed out that poverty in New York State and Mississippi was roughly on a par, when adjusted for the cost of living, I was met with cries that Newt Gingrich was an "evil man." Maybe so, but what I never encountered was a willingness on the part of the old believers to come to grips with the failure of the New York City welfare state. The evidence of their eyes dissolved before the ideology they had inherited.

The city and state of New York are different. Other parts of the country are subject to international, national, and even regional business cycles. But the people of New York are special: they're subject to their own business cycle as well, a cycle driven by state spending. It works like this: In boom times, like the 1960s or the 1980s, when the sky is raining gold, government expands wildly. It takes on new tasks and expands old programs (whether they work or not). But, like the harvest of the first farmers, everything collected in these flush times is immediately consumed; nothing is put away for the inevitable economic winter. When the economy goes bust, as it did in the early 1970s and early 1990s, the city and state raise taxes to maintain the enlarged government instead of scaling back. The higher rationale elaborated by former governor Mario Cuomo is that since private investment falls short of public needs, the state has to step in and make up the difference. In New York City and New York State, that has meant the proliferation of job and economic development agencies, enterprise zones, loan guarantees, and subsidized development schemes, all of which generate their own constituency.

So-called development schemes repeatedly ratchet up the size, cost, and reach of government. They generate a vast array not only of public employees but of government contractors and vendors who live off the public sector and who vote for the city and state officials who hired them. This includes Wall Street, which has done very well on city debt even as New York's bond rating sinks to just above junk bond status. The tax-free Industrial Development Authority (IDA) bonds, which allow companies to borrow at below-market rates, require a great deal of oversight and paperwork. They generate mountains of work for lawyers and bond houses. "It's a dirty little secret in the world of corporate welfare," explains a Wall Street insider, "that the convoluted process of awarding public subsidies to private business has been an enormous cash cow for the city's financial and legal elite, turning the IDA's vast regulatory apparatus into a lucrative economic pipeline."

Economists of almost all stripes warn against raising taxes in the teeth of recession; it only makes things worse. The pols in New York City and State know better. Council members and legislators of both parties raise taxes in a recession rather than lose votes by reducing government spending. This then sends the economy deeper into recession, producing a fiscal crisis, temporary layoffs, and, in due course, more government. After all, if business that is strapped by high taxes and hard times can't put new investment into the economy, the government, as Governor Cuomo was only too happy to explain, has to step into the breach.

With each new turn of the cycle, the city and the state sink down a notch. New York City has never recovered from the last national recession, which began in 1989 and ended in 1992. In New York the recession began seventeen months earlier and the city has yet to fully recover. All in all, 329,000 jobs (about 12 percent of total employment) were lost. In the years since the end of the national recession, only about 25 percent of the jobs lost in New York City have been recovered, despite a booming stock market and a surge in tourism fueled by the declining dollar, even though millions of jobs were created nationally.

In the mid-1980s, Ed Koch had the benefit of a booming economy to cover not only his addition of fifty thousand vote-enhancing jobs to the city payroll but also a healthy growth in the unions' fringe benefits packages. David Dinkins, who came to office just as the recession arrived, tried to do the same but wasn't so lucky. Dinkins, a social democratic hack who had never administered much of anything beyond the office of borough president, was bewildered by what had befallen him. A political rival quipped that Dinkins tried to run the mayor's office as if he were still borough president—by filling his day with ceremonial functions. On these numerous occasions, Dinkins, a far more pleasant man than his predecessor, continuously complained about the declining federal support for the city. It's true that the federal contribution to the city budget had dropped from 18 to 9 percent over the course of the 1980s, about the same percentage as for other cities, but that drop came in part because the federal contribution, which increased in absolute terms, didn't keep pace with a city budget that tripled over the course of the 1980s, from $10 billion to $30 billion a year.

Stuck in a time warp, Dinkins, like Mario Cuomo, knew only that the "future once happened here." That was enough. Passive before the problems of the city and acting on an old script, Dinkins hoped to be rescued by Washington. New York's liberals reacted to Bill Clinton's election with chords of FDR's theme song, "Happy Days Are Here Again." One headline read OFFICIALS COUNTING THE DAYS TILL THEY COUNT CLINTON AID. So sure was *Newsday* of the imminent arrival of federal manna that under the headline WHAT'S IN IT FOR US it ran a collection of wish lists compiled by urban experts.

An ecstatic Dinkins aide announced that the mayor wanted to follow in La Guardia's footsteps and "set the urban agenda." La Guardia went to FDR's Washington with a wish list; David Dinkins could do no less. A jubilant Dinkins, his own 1993 reelection possibilities seemingly enhanced by Clinton's 1992 victory, waited less than a half a day after the election before sending off a twenty-page wish list to the guy going to the White House. He asked for help with everything from infrastructure to the arts.

But a lot had changed since La Guardia formed a political partnership with FDR. New York no longer has the clout to call the shots in Washington. When La Guardia was mayor, New York City had twenty-two representatives in Congress; today, population and power having shifted to the South and the West, it has only twelve. And as the city has been diminished, so too has the state. In the 1992 congressional elections New York State lost all three of its seats on the powerful House Appropriations Committee and two of its three seats on the Ways and Means Committee. "We are a hurting state," said the director of New York's Washington office.

Clinton was never able to give New York much. The president's proposed \$19.5 billion stimulus program, based largely on the U.S. Conference of Mayors' "ready to go" construction and infrastructure projects, was soundly defeated even though the Democrats controlled both houses of Congress. But Clinton was able to take away a great deal. A Marine Midland Bank study found that half the families hit by Clinton's tax increase lived within ninety miles of the Empire State Building. Because of New York's high incomes (made necessary in part by high price levels), \$19 billion in taxes were extracted from the region, explains economist Leslie Hunt of HSBC Holdings.

Dinkins himself was no piker when it came to taxes. One place where he was willing to act on his own was in raising revenues. In the teeth of the recession, Mayor Dinkins not only raised a billion dollars in taxes and fees to maintain government spending in the face of a declining economy, but also began to extract additional revenues from small business by ordering the Departments of Sanitation, Buildings, and Consumer Affairs to issue more citations. While this policy meant the annoyance of more parking tickets for many motorists, it was a threat to the viability of small businesses buffeted by the recession. At its worst, this meant gun-toting sheriffs in Rambo-like raids on supermarkets that failed to pay dubious litter fines. The bureaucracy was literally feeding off the city.

Up in Albany, Mario Cuomo faced his own massive budget gaps and responded similarly; he raised fees and nuisance taxes by $1.5 billion. But when Cuomo, alarmed by the city's growing budget gaps, talked of bringing the Financial Control Board, created in the 1970s collapse, to straighten things out, Dinkins responded with unconcealed anger. The mayor warned that if Cuomo invoked the FCB to straighten things out (an achievement that would have enhanced a Cuomo bid for the presidency), he would "bring in Jesse Jackson and make this a real black–white thing."

Meanwhile, big business continued to decamp. In 1989 Exxon followed Mobil, J. C. Penney, Texaco, Shell, Cities Service, and many other Fortune 500 companies in fleeing New York. All told, 102 of the city's 131 Fortune 500 companies merged or left between 1969 and 1994, taking five hundred thousand jobs with them. Moreover, the burden imposed by the loss of old jobs was compounded by the city's inability to generate new ones. In 1992 Merrill Lynch moved twenty-five hundred back-office jobs across the river to Jersey City. A year later, as the Dinkins administration wound down, Lehman Brothers followed suit with nearly a thousand jobs. Jersey City did not offer financial incentives specially created to lure these companies. A spokesman for Mayor Bret Schundler explained, "We have no city payroll tax, no city income tax, no corporate tax; we don't even have an unincorporated business tax or tax on commercial leases."

New York will never be a low-tax area; it will never be able to compete on the basis of taxes. If New York had high taxes and a high level of public service, it would be in far better shape. What's deadly is its combination of extremely high taxes and its low level of public services. When you add the cost of private school to city, state, and federal taxes, little room is left for upwardly mobile families, who can vote themselves a tax break by moving to the suburbs and using suburban public schools once their children reach school age.

What remains is something new under the sun. New York has the first economy to be based on the export of services, in this case, high-end financial and legal services. The Big Apple's roughly $250 billion gross city product is about the size of the Danish and Swedish economies combined, but it lacks their balance. Almost on its own the booming stock market is keeping New York afloat even as the city continues to lose manufacturing and routine service jobs, but it's also producing a dangerous bifurcation. Mean incomes continue to grow because of the financial sector even as the median and modal incomes decline along with the number of unskilled jobs.

While New York has been slow to adapt economically, it has undergone a vast demographic transformation. Many natives are as desperate to leave as immigrants are desperate to arrive. New York in the 1980s received the largest influx of immigrants, 854,000, since the closing of Ellis Island in 1924. Of the city's 7.3 million people, 2.1 million are foreign-born; 40 percent of the city's households speak a language other than English at home.

New York City has become a giant exporter of native talent. Between 1985 and 1990, almost twice as many people left the city for other places in the United States as were drawn to New York. Of the 860,000 who left, half a million left the region altogether, many of them moving to Florida; of those, three-quarters were not retirees but people thirty-five and younger who were looking for opportunity.

Many of the new immigrants, black and white, are making it in this new economy. As of 1994, Filipinos, at $47,000 a year, are the ethnic group with the highest median household income. American-born whites are a distant second with $38,382 and are followed by immigrants from India. In 1990 median family income for American-born blacks, more than a third of whom work in government, was $22,000, compared to $30,000 for African-born blacks and more still for blacks born in Jamaica. American-born blacks had a higher poverty rate than any largely black immigrant group except Dominicans.

The new immigrants are succeeding not because the low-end jobs they largely occupy are growing but because between 1970 and 1990 New York lost unskilled white workers faster than it lost unskilled jobs. African-Americans, however, never competed for those "dead-end jobs." Labor force participation rates for blacks plummeted while the opportunities were taken by the new arrivals, including African immigrants, instead. Native-born black workers either moved up into better-paying public sector jobs or got out of the labor force altogether. The taxi, restaurant, hotel, garment, and cleaning jobs, once major sources of employment for native-born black workers, have been taken over by immigrants.

While middle- and upper-middle-class Americans, black and white, left for brighter horizons, immigrants kept arriving all through the recession. In the nineties the native out-migration of better-educated and higher-income residents undermined the tax base even as arriving immigrants placed increasing demands on the hospitals, schools, and social welfare budgets.

In sum, the Gotham Rudy Giuliani inherited when he became New York's 107th mayor in January 1994 was a city that had gone through thirty-eight months of recession with no recovery in sight. Two out of every eleven New Yorkers were on welfare of one form or another, the highest total since the Great Depression, and New York's average income had been dropping at .08 percent a year since 1989. Giuliani inherited an operating deficit of $2.8 billion, a sum larger than the budget of four states—but, then again, New York City's budget itself is larger than that of forty-eight states.

Rational people were planning their exits. At the time, it was hard to attend a meeting with or talk privately to middle- and upper-middle-class New Yorkers without getting into a discussion about how best to cut one's losses in leaving. A 1992 *New York Times* poll found that 60 percent of the adult population hoped to leave within four years and 51 percent actually planned to do so. Peter Vallone, the city council Speaker, warned that the city's tax base, already resting on a "precariously small number of people," was sure to crumble if the middle class continued to leave. New York had a total of roughly 3.1 million private sector jobs in 1961; today it has about 2.7 million, a loss of approximately four hundred thousand private sector jobs, but its overall population is roughly the same. Chicago, by comparison, has the same number of jobs as in 1968 but with nine hundred thousand fewer people.

In the week of his first State of the City Address, Mayor Rudy Giuliani made sure to pay homage to history. He attended a reprise performance of the 1959 musical *Fiorello.* There is a simple rule in New York City politics: When you want to invoke leadership and innovation, refer to New York's revered depression-era mayor, Fiorello La Guardia, as often as possible.

New York's new mayor, nominally Republican, invokes Fiorello as often as possible, but his rhetoric sounds far more like New Democrat than New Dealer. His targets are sometimes the very bureaucracies built by La Guardia and his Great Society heirs. What began as the successful response to one crisis has ended up producing another, as yesterday's innovations have become today's encrustations.

Giuliani is an immoderate centrist. What he brought to the job was his prosecutor's zeal for taking on the bad guys and his La Guardia–like reformer's outrage at ongoing injustices. Giuliani can see both sides of an issue in alternation, but he defends whatever position he assumes at the moment with absolute certainty. It may be that he thinks that as mayor he can embody the higher purposes that transcend ordinary contradiction. This is not a quality that endears him to other politicians. Even his few potential allies in an overwhelmingly liberal and Democratic city find him hard to bear. Explained former schools chancellor Frank Machiarola, "Giuliani hasn't enough friends; Dinkins had too many friends." Giuliani has little of La Guardia's ability to woo and schmooze, to cajole and glad-hand enemies, making them into allies. Rather, he has a talent for the opposite. But in a city like New York, where it's hard to get anything done—where even the offer of free public toilets was blocked by the bitter opposition of homeless and handicapped rights groups—bullheadedness can be more than a mixed blessing.

Giuliani's take-charge style, his efforts to hold the line on runaway spending, his willingness to face down racial racketeers, and his remarkable success in pushing crime back to pre-crack levels have made him a standard-bearer for the "new mayors." When it comes to fighting crime and maintaining order, Giuliani has been such a successful "reinventor" that he and his first police chief, William Bratton (who was on the cover of *Time*), became objects of international adulation.

From his inaugural on, the Mayor has been a relentless booster of the city, touting New York as the "capital of the world," the "greatest city in the world," and so on. But Giuliani has had limited success in reducing taxes and in reviving the economy—except when it comes to completing the job he began as a prosecutor, namely, reducing the city's crime tax.

Crime is an economic issue in New York, a city where the five strongest Mafia families in the United States have had a stranglehold on trash hauling, the city's convention center, and its food distribution markets. David Gallagher of the Brooklyn-based Center for Neighborhood Economic Development estimates that crime drains at least $1 billion a year from the city's economy—not including the cost of businesses driven out by crime and of investments not made. The "mob tax" adds 40 percent to the cost of trash hauling for the private sector, so that New York companies pay twice the Chicago and three times the Los Angeles rates.

Giuliani, along with Manhattan District Attorney Robert Morgenthau, has begun to break the mob monopoly on garbage hauling by bringing in outside companies, like the nationally prominent Brown and Ferris. Similarly, he has begun to undermine mob control of the Fulton Fish Market, which has been losing market share to Philadelphia and Boston, and he has been the beneficiary of Governor Pataki's cleanup of the Javits Convention Center, which during Cuomo's governorship was run by the mob, a situation that began even before its doors opened.

The Javits Convention Center, quips a high-ranking official who insisted on anonymity, "has never been in the convention business." The Javits Center, which has structural problems, was completed two years behind schedule, after a bid-rigging scandal, and was $111 million over budget. Building the center was, like so many other public "authorities," a jobs program, for architects, bond underwriters, consultants, vendors, and mob-connected unions—all beneficiaries of New York's tradition of large-scale public works. Even in the city of pseudo work, the Javits Center construction rules, which required three workers for the job of one, stood out. Worse yet, the three underworked guys often insisted on being further overpaid by shaking down the exhibitors for bribes at every point where the rules required that even the simplest tasks had to be done by the Javits Center's mob-connected unions. A show manager anonymously explained that while "Chicago is no labor paradise, . . . at least the politicians and unions there realize they have to stay competitive. In New York the unions did what they wanted, and until this year [referring to the efforts of Giuliani and Pataki] we couldn't get anyone at city hall or Albany to stand up for us."

The expectation when he ran for mayor in 1993 was that Giuliani's interest in innovation stretched beyond law-and-order issues, important as they are, to the economy and the organization of government. Giuliani's rhetoric about downsizing, privatization, and reinvention set off shivers in David Dinkins and in many of those who voted for him. In an unprecedented mayoral farewell speech delivered to the city council, Dinkins, fearing the worst, urged the members to defend his social programs and "the most proudly progressive government on God's earth" from the coming onslaught. He asked the council to "make sure that New York's working people—the union members who bailed us out of the fiscal crisis—do not become scapegoats for the city's ills." For his part, Stanley Hill, the leader of District Council 37 of the American Federation of State, County and Municipal Employees, warned the incoming "If you are reinventing government . . . you are talking about city workers."

Neither needed to have been quite so worried. The police aside, Giuliani has, under intense budgetary pressure, engaged in more retrenchment than restructuring, let alone reinvention. After a promising start, his efforts at privatizing the school custodians stalled, as did his attempt to prune back regulations that make it difficult for companies to grow in New York's bureaucratic thicket. His major privatization initiative, selling off some of the public hospitals, has been dramatically scaled back.

The Giuliani administration is run by a very small circle of close advisers, almost all of whom are longtime comrades from the battles fought against organized corruption when Giuliani was a federal prosecutor. It's a talented group, but as City Council Speaker Peter Vallone, a thoughtful middle-of-the-road Democrat, points out, the city can't always be run, much less reformed, by a half-dozen people, almost all of whom are lawyers. Vallone, noting the narrowness of the Giuliani staff, teased, "On health care the mayor has been very good on crime. On the issue of the schools the Mayor has been very good on crime," and so on.

Despite the depths of the recession the city suffered under Dinkins's lethargic reign and despite the riots and racial incidents that marred Dinkins's term in office, Giuliani was able to win only a very narrow victory. There was no broad constituency for reform, let alone the wrenching changes needed to make New York's economy competitive again. Giuliani's failure to lay out a positive vision for schools in the new economy parallels a larger failure to explain why the budget cuts he was imposing could be a down payment on a better future.

Giuliani's lack of a mandate left him several options. He chose an approach that melded fundamental reform with political practicality. He began cutting money to those services largely unique to New York in type or generosity. For instance, he substantially reduced the subsidies to the city's public hospital system while tightening up welfare eligibility standards. Both policies still left New York with the most generous social provision in America. However, when it came to the politically potent public employees, whose salaries represent almost half of the city's $32 billion budget, Giuliani moved in an uncharacteristically cautious and conciliatory manner, that is, by reducing the workforce through attrition and buyouts. Furthermore, he never asked for either fundamental work rule changes or co-payments for medical insurance.

Giuliani was betting that a combination of crime reduction and conciliatory collective bargaining would win him the time he needed until an economic upturn could ease the pain of transition to a smaller government and larger private sector economy. It's a bet he's largely winning, with considerable consequences for the city's future. When he took office, like Dinkins before him, Giuliani was caught in a dilemma. Since recessions simultaneously reduce revenue and increase welfare outlays, the result is either layoffs, higher taxes, selling off city assets, increased debt, or reduced spending. The mayor chose a mix of all five.

Giuliani imposed some minor tax cuts on hotels and on New York's unique commercial rent tax, but the mayor has made the "temporary" income tax surcharges imposed by Dinkins his own. He has increased the city's long-term debt in a repeat of the worst practices of yesteryear, namely, by borrowing money from capital budgets to pay for current operating expenses. He is engaged in an ongoing assets sale and has auctioned off the city-owned TV station, a good idea, and has tried to sell off the city's upstate reservoirs, a terrible idea that would have left New York unable to protect its watershed from pollution. Rudy the reformer spoke of saving New York from the acute embarrassment of owning the city's Off Track Betting Corporation, the world's only bookie that loses money. Under Rudy, OTB is no longer in the red. But rather than sell it off for a pretty penny, Rudy the regular has held on to OTB because it's the city's best patronage pit, a natural spot to stash campaign workers for the next election.

There have been no layoffs, but Giuliani has reduced the mayoral workforce by almost twenty thousand workers by attrition. But because the compensation package for the workers retained continues to grow faster than either productivity or the city economy, total labor costs continue to increase both relative to the total budget and in real dollars. Under Giuliani, overall spending rose at 5.6 percent a year while revenues grew at about 1.6 percent. This means a growing deficit, one that will reach $5 billion in 2000—if the city gets that far without a fiscal crisis, which could be easily set off by either the next economic downturn or a sustained drop in the stock market.

Finally, in the case of the schools, Giuliani has sharply reduced spending, although not at the expense of the teachers' unions. One of the first places he looked for savings was the city's $8 billion school budget. New York's schools were organized on accounting principles that would have been familiar to Mr. Micawber. Its thirty-five divisions, thirty-two local school districts, and eleven hundred or so schools had 277,000 different ledger accounts to track spending. The school board, like the city of Washington, D.C., couldn't even tell the mayor's office how many people it had working for it, though certainly Dinkins had added thousands in his bid to be reelected. Finally, Schools Chancellor Raymond Cortines announced in February 1994 that he had "discovered" thirty-five hundred hitherto unaccounted-for employees, most of them working at the offices of the central board of education, the infamous 110 Livingston Street. The same day the lost continent of bureaucrats was discovered, Councilman Herb Berman announced that local school boards, always a bottomless pit of patronage, had spent $2.2 million on conferences in Hawaii, Las Vegas, and Puerto Rico.

You can get a sense of the byzantine bureaucracy behind the city's educational make-work programs from the introduction to a fourteen-page memo regarding an obscure office of three. The memo was addressed to the following:

> Community school board presidents, superintendents, UFT and CSA [teachers' and administrators' unions], district representatives, principals, UFT chapter leaders, district business managers, directors of personnel, district directors of instruction and professional development, MTIP liaisons, SBM/SDM

district liaisons and facilitators, deputy chancellors, executive directors [and] heads of office.

Giuliani promised a "relentless" campaign "to cut the living daylights out of the overhead" in the school system and get the dollars down into the classroom. This looked like a made-for-success situation, a feisty mayor forcing bureaucrats to fess up. But it didn't work out that way. Instead, there was widespread criticism of Giuliani's performance. Why? First of all, Giuliani, who is expert in the art of turning would-be allies into enemies, came off as a bully when he insisted on pounding likable but ineffectual Raymond Cortines, the Hispanic schools chancellor, in personal terms. Just as important, Giuliani, driven by budget deficits as far as the eye could see, spoke only of how to cut the educational fat; he never laid out his own vision of what he wanted from the city's education program except to belatedly point to the Catholic schools as a possible model. Early on, a report done for Giuliani suggested school decentralization, an idea supported by a wide range of political figures, including the city's most formidable left-liberal, Ruth Messinger. But the plan, like all suggestions for decentralization in the tightly controlled Giuliani administration, was dropped quickly.

Giuliani's cuts of more than $2 billion have had, as many will admit privately, strikingly limited effect (except for relieving some student overcrowding). But Giuliani refused to draw the parents into a dialogue on what the cuts might mean and refused to honestly acknowledge that there would be even limited pain, so that every instance of newly overcrowded classrooms was seized upon by anxious parents as evidence of some broader deception they felt but couldn't identify.

Had the parents looked more closely, they would have seen a deception of sorts in the contract that held the politically potent teachers' union harmless. Salaries make up half the city's education budget, but teachers are not overpaid. Rather, they are, as a group, underworked and unaccountable. New York City teachers who are in the classroom (and only half are there at any given moment) spend less time in teaching than their counterparts in any other major city, while one teacher in six in any given year is on sabbatical. Worst of all, the sixteen-step contractually agreed-upon grievance procedure makes it virtually impossible to discipline incompetent or dysfunctional teachers. Instead, they are passed around from school to school.

But dependent as he had been on the teachers' union's neutrality to win in 1993 and dependent as he expected to be two years hence, Giuliani proceeded to negotiate a "we don't do windows contract" that left the disciplinary procedures and sabbaticals intact while relieving the teachers of hall monitoring duty. The contract guaranteed there would be no layoffs, although raises would be delayed for two years. The teachers, inspired by a newly emergent militant faction, rejected the contract, only to later change their minds when the mayor hung tough.

No place in America has resisted welfare reform more ferociously than New York City and State. The 1988 federal Family Support Act, the major welfare reform legislation of the 1980s, tried to push the states into both more job placement and, failing that, more job training. Other states (like Wisconsin, which took the lead in welfare reform by implementing various strategies for job placement) assumed that there was no substitute for work itself. In New York City and in the state, the number of welfare recipients placed in jobs actually went down, even as the social service industry became a vast job training apparatus that succeeded in creating jobs for the job trainers but little else.

The concept of a job being demeaning and dead-end, a concept so crucial to the growth of welfare in the first place, has a death grip on the minds of the city's social activists. Placing welfare clients in low-wage jobs, complains Megan McLoughlin of Federation of Protestant Welfare Agencies, "merely shifts people to the ranks of the working poor, trapping them in dead-end jobs." From the social activists' point of view, the city's training programs for welfare recipients had to be extensive and elaborate if they were to prepare people for jobs that were, as was their due, financially and personally satisfying to start with. Dedicated to ending not welfare but welfare reform, activists like Maureen Lane insisted that low-end "work is not a substitute for welfare because it either pays too little or takes jobs from union members."

"The problem," explained Senator Moynihan, the principal author of the 1988 welfare reform legislation, "was that hugely influential voices were invariably raised against [reform] efforts, calling them punitive, coercive, mean." In practice, this meant that the same antipoverty lawyers (or their heirs) who had done so much to create the welfare explosion of the 1960s fought, along with their many friends in the courts and the legislature, to limit work requirements for welfare recipients. By 1993, New York State ranked forty-third in the percentage of adult welfare recipients with jobs, thirty-second in paternity established, but second in the percentage of participants in vocational or skills training.

Until the mid-1990s the Democratic majority in the New York State Assembly, dominated by members of the social services industry, blocked any welfare reform. As one disgruntled member put it, "People up here just don't think there's a problem." They had good company. While he was governor, Mario Cuomo resolutely insisted that female-headed teenage families just weren't a problem. Here's the governor at his balmy best: "If you took a fifteen-year-old with a child, but put her in a clean apartment, got her a diploma, gave her the hope of a job . . . that would change everything." It would? If we did all this, concluded Cuomo, "the fact that she had a baby at fifteen wouldn't produce *any* disorientation at all, and the hope that comes from a new context would solve the problem." In other words, according to the governor, the teen mother is a victim not of her values and choices but of economic and governmental neglect. But if government spending is likely to offer the hope that Cuomo refers to, New York should already be reaping the benefits, since New York leads the country in per capita social expenditure and is spending more than ever before. Our problem, though, is not public disinvestment but private disinvestment, the personal choices that lead to single-parent homes.

The election of Giuliani as mayor in 1993 and the defeat of Cuomo by George Pataki in 1994 opened up reform possibilities. The social welfare industry had vehemently opposed both men. Since neither man was beholden to the social welfare industry, each was free to make it more difficult to get on and stay on welfare, as Blanche Bernstein had suggested twenty years earlier. The social welfare advocates who had run Blanche Bernstein out of office lost credibility and control of the debate by insisting that there were no entry-level jobs in New York even as they were being filled by successive waves of immigrants.

Reducing the welfare rolls can take place either by making entry onto the rolls more difficult, bumping people off the rolls, or placing people in jobs. Giuliani made a rhetorical commitment to placing Aid to Families with Dependent Children (AFDC) clients in private sector jobs. Speaking before America Works, the for-profit placement agency that has had a remarkable record of getting people off welfare and into long-term private sector jobs, Giuliani described the organization as the model for what should be done. In a return to what was, in a sense, La Guardia's approach, Giuliani emphasized reciprocity, that is, the need for welfare clients to give something back in return for what they have received.

But perhaps because he was squeezed by budgetary consideration, Giuliani has trimmed the rolls almost entirely at the front end. He has tightened up eligibility requirements and has created a workfare program that, first of all, screens out people who are already working and, secondly, pressures people to take a private sector job rather than work for their welfare grant. The program has, on its own terms, been an enormous success. From early 1995, when the city began both workfare and more careful eligibility checks, to late

1996, the welfare rolls dropped 18 percent (from 1,160,000 to 950,000 people)—this in a period of slow economic growth.

New York's workfare program, the largest in the country, has the virtue of replacing laid-off city workers (particularly in the Parks and Sanitation Departments and in hospitals) with less expensive labor. The old-style sanitation workers of the pre-union 1950s, who went around with a spiked stick to pick up litter, kept the city clean, but they disappeared under the weight of rising costs. Now that basic cleanup work is being done again. Workfare has made a real difference in cleaning up city parks and highways; this is no small matter, as anyone who has walked New York's often trash-ridden streets knows. But it appears that few workers have graduated from WEP (Work Experience Program) into regular jobs, and those few have largely ended up with city jobs. Workfare seems to have done little to wean workers from government dependence.

Workfare is part of a short-term solution to the city's welfare burden. It provides the warranty of employability employers need to have if they are going to hire people off welfare. But some of its initial benefits, like its relatively low cost compared to the more expensive America Works placement programs, turn negative over time. According to senior mayoral adviser Richard Schwartz, workfare costs the budget-strapped city about $3,000 per workfare enrollee a year—others say the cost is closer to $5,000—compared to a cost of $5,400 for the highly successful America Works. But if the workfare recipient stays more than two or three years, it starts to cost more—and not just in budgetary terms.

The city's public employee unions initially accepted workfare because it elevated some of their employees into supervisors. But in the long run the practice of having city employees and workfare enrollees working side-by-side—with one group making at least three times more than the other, plus benefits—makes both groups uncomfortable. The experience with the Comprehensive Employment and Training Act (CETA), a temporary federally funded work program in the 1970s, suggests that mixing permanent and temporary workers embitters the short-termers. WEP workers, particularly those with better skills, who are stuck in workfare for any length of time are bound to become resentful and sullenly angry at the turn of luck that has led them to do the same work as others but for much less. This can only inflame labor militants, who are right to see that workfare is in part a return to the old-fashioned kind of contingent labor force that did most of the city work in the pre–La Guardia, pre-union days.

Giuliani has been able to balance the budget (1) by substantially reducing spending; (2) by resorting to so-called one shots, that is, by selling off city assets; and (3) because of the extraordinary revenues generated by the long Wall Street boom. But the city is running out of assets to sell, the Wall Street boom can't last forever, and the city faces projected budget deficits as far into the future as the eye can see.

There *is* an alternative strategy. When I was a senior member on the Giuliani transition team, I warned that you can't jump a chasm in two leaps. I argued that no economic recovery was in sight and that New York was suffering not from a cyclical downturn but from a secular decline, meaning that Giuliani could succeed both politically and in restarting the stalled economy only if he was willing to quickly make the budget cuts that would both restore fiscal balance and make targeted but substantial business tax cuts possible. By this logic Giuliani should have governed as though he expected to be a one-term mayor; only by so doing might he have gained both his own political success and the city's salvation. If he had taken this path, he would have used his inaugural, as he did not, to outline the depths of the city's economic difficulties and present the two unpalatable alternatives the city faced: slow but sure decline or wrenching change with the promise of economic rebirth.

Would my approach have worked? Maybe not. Minority voters who occupy the vast majority of unskilled city jobs would have been hardest hit by large-scale restructuring. Many minority voters—indeed, the entire black political class—are still smarting from Giuliani's defeat of the city's first African-American mayor, David Dinkins. The great majority of black and, importantly, Hispanic swing voters have come to dislike Giuliani so much that they believe the city was safer under his predecessor even though the decline of violent crime in minority areas has been palpable.

To win some room for a radical restructuring, Guiliani would have had to get past the racial bitterness engendered by the brutal 1993 election in order to draw minority voters, if not their leaders, into an ongoing dialogue on the relationship between the city's future and their own. And to do that, it would have been necessary for him to gain more minority trust by showing a greater willingness to bring minorities into his administration. Similarly, Giuliani and his virtually all-white staff could have won some trust and softened the blows of the coming transformation if they had increased minority hiring on city construction projects and in the Police, Fire, and Sanitation Departments, which are to a great extent still all-white preserves. But even if he had done all this, the city's fiscal straits would have left very little room for him to maneuver.

New York went into the recession before the rest of the country and came out six years after the national recovery. By quickly making deep budget cuts, Giuliani could have not only offered substantial tax cuts targeted to small businesses but also avoided the continuous cutting that has left city agencies demoralized by ongoing uncertainty. But deep cuts in the public sector economy would not in the short run have necessarily produced a private sector revival. There's bound to be a considerable lag time between reform and revival, and the pain of the transition might have been unbearable, both politically and for those individuals and neighborhoods dependent on government.

New York is caught in an intractable dilemma. To revive, it needs to restructure, but without an economic recovery it can't pay for the heavy costs of easing such a transition. The problem is not just that if a temporary recovery comes, as one did in the 1980s, people will lose interest in the long term; it's that unless New York restructures, a full recovery is unlikely.

18. After the Revolution

In March of 1995 I wandered into a time warp when I went to a Columbia University conference on "Liberalism and New York." From the speakers I heard little in the way of a reconsideration of liberal policy. Many of them just groused. Several pointed to relatively successful programs, like Head Start, and decried the lack of adequate federal funding. None could name a social program that had failed and deserved to be cut; not even job training, a four-star example of expensive failure, rated a passing criticism.

While I was sitting in the audience, my mind drifted to an earlier conference in which one brave liberal—I think it was New York magazine columnist Mike Tomasky—acknowledged that New York liberalism, whatever its earlier solidaristic impulses, had degenerated into little more than a patronage system. The liberal reformers defeated Tammany, it seemed, only to imitate what they had once decried. As I tuned back into the present conference, I heard another speaker eloquently defend the Ocean Hill–Brownsville community control fiasco as part of a "golden age" for the black community in New York. It was enough.

There was no surcease when I wandered out to the corridor for some fresh air. There, speaking just a few blocks from the devastation of Harlem, yet another bien-pensant *held forth on why any attempt to compare Southern black in-migrants with earlier immigrants was so morally reprehensible that it had to be "defeated." New York's economy, he went on, has to adjust to black needs, not the other way around. For these old believers, too much money had been bet on losing hands to fold now.*

In nearby Harlem, the losing hand was being played out with deadly consequences.

The past and the transition to the future, if not the future itself, were on display in mid-1990s Harlem. The past was in full display at the Abyssinian Baptist Church, made famous by one of its preachers, the late congressman Adam Clayton Powell. In October 1995 a jubilant crowd of sixteen hundred greeted Fidel Castro as he arrived at the 136th Street church, where the Cuban dictator had made a famous visit thirty-five years earlier. Castro, dressed as always in his military fatigues, entered the church to choruses of "Fidel! Fidel!" and marched to the podium, where he was given a ten-minute standing ovation.

For most of those who saw the event on TV, Castro was a cold war relic, an antique from the age of decolonization, when the "big men"—like Kwame Nkrumah of Ghana, Gamal Abdel Nasser of Egypt, and Julius Nyerere of Tanzania—totally dominated their newly independent countries. In the more successful African economies, like Ghana and Tanzania, the big men are now derided as "extractors," people whose semisocialist experiments left their countries in economic ruin.

But for those in the audience raised on Marcus Garvey, Malcolm X, and Che Guevara, Castro was an enduring example of the armed struggle against white colonialism, the hope that the Third World might still redress the balance of the first. He was an incarnation of an old longing evoked by Ralph Ellison in *The Invisible Man.* Here's Ellison describing a fictionalized version of the 1943 Harlem riot.

> They moved in tight-knit order, carrying sticks and clubs, shotguns and rifles, led by Ras the Exhorter become Ras the Destroyer upon a great black horse. A new Ras of haughty vulgar dignity, dressed in the costume of an Abyssinian Chieftan . . . a figure . . . out of a dream.
>
> "Come away from that stupid looting," he called to a group before a store. "Come join with us to burst into the armory and get guns and ammunition."

Three New York members of Congress—Charles Rangel, José Serrano, and Nydia Velázquez—were there at the C-Span-televised event at the Abyssinian Baptist Church. Also attending were Farrakhan's lieutenant Conrad Mohammad; C. Vernon Mason of the Tawana Brawley hoax fame; and Angela Davis, the famed sixties radical turned tenured professor. Rangel greeted Castro with a warm hug, and Powell's successor at Abyssinian Baptist, Calvin Butts, introduced Castro as "one of the great leaders in the world" and spoke of his inspirational qualities. In a sense, Butts was right. As I well remember, Castro had been an inspiration for the young Marion Barry, for the militants of New York's Ocean Hill–Brownsville fight, and for the "political" gangs that emerged from the Watts rebellion.

Castro spoke with assurance about the bright future of state socialism. He insisted that Cuba would never change, because its path had been and still was the right one. To prove his point, he offered to send medical help to Harlem, as he had to Nicaragua. His promise of aid brought cheers, as did his mentions of Nkrumah and Nasser.

During his 1960 trip to Harlem, Castro, the hero of the Third World emerging from colonialism, was visited by his allies, the Soviet Union's Khrushchev, India's Jawaharlal Nehru, Egypt's Gamal Abdel Nasser, and Ghanaian strongman Kwame Nkrumah. Since then, the Soviet Union collapsed; India turned toward capitalism; Egypt, its economy ruined by Nasser, became dependent on the U.S. treasury; and Ghana descended into decades of civil strife.

While some of those present for Castro's appearance at the Abyssinian Baptist Church might have argued that Cuba would have been an economic success but for the American boycott, for most of those cheering the guest, economics was beside the point. It was Castro's steadfastness, his unwillingness to yield to American society, that they identified with. Their cheers spoke to the appeal of Frantz Fanon, whose ideas about Third World revolution were closely linked with Castro's. When Castro told the audience that their church's very name was suggestive of the Ethiopian struggle against Mussolini's imperialism and rhapsodized about how Cubans had "shed [their] blood to fight against colonialism," he was reiterating Fanon's central message of social salvation by collective violence. In places like Harlem, South Central Los Angeles, and Anacostia, nationalists embraced what Bayard Rustin described as an angry "racial chauvinism" to eradicate the traces of "racial shame that might be lurking in their souls."

The Harlem of 1995 had changed considerably since Castro's last visit. While half the stores on the main shopping stretch, 125th Street, were now black owned, Central Harlem, for so long the symbol of black aspirations, had lost a third of its population and a great deal of its vitality since 1970. For some, the arrival of new, nationally known businesses offered the promise of renewal, but for others, like record store owner Shukulu Shange, soon to be a key character in a Harlem tragedy, they were a threat to both his small store and the 1960s promise of community control. Shange explained, "All of the big corporations that have come to Harlem—the Duane Reade, Foot Lockers—they come here to milk us down, and when there is no more money, they will leave the community and all those black people . . . won't be able to get back in business."

Shange, who thought of himself as a model black businessman, was, even as Castro was speaking, faced with more immediate problems than those brought about by the arrival of big business in Harlem. Eleven blocks away from Abyssinian Baptist, on 125th Street, protesters organized by Morris Powell, a vendor of pies and oils who dressed in African garb, were marching on his behalf. Shange was involved in a dispute with his landlord, a Syrian-Jewish businessman, Fred Harari.

Shange had gone to Powell, a lieutenant in the Reverend Al Sharpton's National Action Network, for help in a complex landlord–tenant dispute. Technically, Shange's lease was held by Harari, but Harari himself was renting his space from the United Pentecostal House of Prayer, the black church that owned the building where Harari and Shange were tenant and subtenant, respectively. After the church raised Harari's rent, he tried to pass on some of the additional costs to his subtenant, but Shange balked. Shange was well aware that the United Pentecostal House of Prayer, one of the largest landlords on 125th Street, intended to undertake a multimillion-dollar renovation and in search of higher rents had already evicted a number of longtime tenants, both black and white.

The United Pentecostal House of Prayer had offered Shange a new store, but he had refused because he thought the rent was too high and the terms too restrictive. In most of New York, landlord–tenant business disputes end up in court or in the tenant moving into a vacant location, of which there were many near Shange's store. But Shange intended to turn a contractual matter into an issue of race and community control.

Downplaying the church, Shange pitched the issue to Powell as a case of a white landlord trying to force a black merchant out of business in Harlem. Powell, an escaped mental patient who had been thrice accused of attempted murder, had come to prominence of sorts as a spokesman for Harlem's street vendors. Shange found a sympathetic ear in the gray-bearded Powell, who adorned himself with big buttons that read BUY BLACK and MARCUS GARVEY.

When Powell and Shange decided to picket Fred Harari's clothing and variety store, Freddy's Fashion Mart, there were numerous promising precedents. In 1989 the Church Avenue Korean deli boycott had occurred, an action that helped undermine the Dinkins administration but served as a success for Sonny Carson, who was famous for the Ocean Hill–Brownsville community control clash and the Crown Heights rioting, for Carson succeeded in driving the deli out of business. And earlier in 1995, Norman "Grand Dad" Reide, vice president of the National Action Network, during a speech delivered before a public school audience and broadcast over WWRL had accused "bloodsucking Koreans" of "reaping a financial harvest at the expense of black people." Sharpton had followed up this expression of sentiments by announcing a strategy of attacking "economic disrespect" by sanctioning those who show disrespect.

Sharpton's economics, their primitive notions of wealth by forcible extraction aside, rests on the assumption that leaders like Sharpton himself have a privileged status within an isolated black economy. Separatism erects a kind of tariff barrier behind which second-rate ideas, like second-rate goods, can be sold at a high price in the name of community control. For example, Sharpton, Reide, Powell, and Raymond Harris, a prominent player in the 125th Street picketing, had accused the Korea First Bank, which has no branches in Harlem and conducts most of its business in Korean, of antiblack hiring practices. Reide told his supporters that he had demanded "jobs, mortgage loans, [and] business loans for blacks from the bank." The shakedown ended when the bank wrote Sharpton's National Action Network and WWRL checks for $2,000.

Emboldened by his success, Powell, who had long threatened "There will be war [against white merchants]" and "This street will burn," was an intimidating figure to many on 125th Street. Supported by Harlem's leading newspaper, the *Amsterdam News*—which asked "Could this be the beginning of a systematic attempt to drive viable black-owned businesses out of Harlem?"—Powell organized a daily boycott of Freddy's Fashion Mart. As in the earlier Korean deli boycott, the protesters shouted racial epithets, this time "Jew bastards" and "bloodsucking Jews"; they referred to other whites in the store as "crackers" and to black customers as "traitors."

Conrad Muhammad, Farrakhan's man in Harlem, said the struggle "symbolized the plight of black people in Harlem and their inability to find safety nets and support." A man who called himself Shabazz was one of the protesters, as was the Reverend Al Sharpton. Shabazz forced his way into the store shouting, "I will be back to burn the Jew store down."

On December 8, 1995, after more than three months of demonstrations but before a restraining order could be issued, protester Roland Smith, who had renounced his American citizenship and preferred to be known by his African name, Abubunde Mulocko, took action. Mulocko, who was a devout reader of Marcus Garvey, of the "bible" (Fanon's *Wretched of the Earth*), and of all varieties of Afrocentric mysticism, imagined himself a warrior for black dignity. Apparently angered by the mistaken assumption that the store had hired Hispanics instead of blacks, Mulocko, who had a long criminal record and whose paranoia was "goosed by the protests," noted Jim Sleeper, burned the store down.

When he entered the store, Abubunde, who had cast himself as the hero in a Fanonesque drama that was about to reach its climax, shouted, "It's on now!" Armed with a .38, he shot three whites and a Pakistani in cold blood—he had mistaken the light-skinned Pakistani for a Jew—and then set a fire that killed five Hispanics, a Guyanese, and a black, the security guard whom the protesters had taunted as a "cracker lover." The dead killed by the fire, which Abubunde started with a can of paint thinner, were mostly off-the-books immigrant employees who had found a small niche in New York's service economy.

All of this occurred a few feet from the offices of Harlem's elected officials, like Congressman Charles Rangel, who said nothing although he has a long history of sniffing out racism in the most unlikely places. Rangel, who spoke at Farrakhan's Million Man March, has denounced both tax cuts and interracial adoption as "racist," but he saw no problems worth mentioning on 125th Street until after the massacre, when he then proceeded to both express sympathy for the victims and attend the press conference organized by Farrakhan's Conrad Muhammad on behalf of the protesters. For his part, Assemblyman David Patterson spoke of Morris Powell's "good intentions," allowing that Powell could sometimes be "too strident."

The day after the fire, the protesters were back in business at another Jewish-owned store, Bargain World, handing out leaflets that read NOW WE WILL DRIVE BARGAIN WORLD OUT OF BUSINESS.

In the Harlem massacre, as in the L.A. riots and in Reverend Wilson's Anacostia boycott in Washington, D.C., the logic of community control and the riot ideology were joined in a self-destructive embrace. Black nationalism and the accompanying assumptions of community control and the riot ideology have proven to be knives without handles; they're certain to rip the bearer, whether or not the presumed enemy is injured as well. They carve out a double game: if whites leave, they're accused of racist disinvestment, and if they stay, they're accused of colonialist extraction.

Like the Vernon Hawkins episode in D.C. and the Los Angeles riot, the Harlem massacre represents the end of a political cycle begun more than three decades ago. The Reverend Sharpton wants to be seen as the heir of Martin Luther King, but while the forms of protest are often the same, the substance has been subverted. The great causes of thirty years ago have degenerated into a squalid series of shakedowns at a time when white guilt isn't what it used to be and the marks aren't always paying up.

During the 1992 March on Washington for Urban America, attended by only thirty-five thousand, many of whom were New York City public employees, Baltimore's Kurt Schmoke, mayor of a city with some of the highest crime rates in the United States, expressed the bankruptcy of the old ideas. Demanding more help from Washington, Schmoke told the crowd, "*We don't want to have to burn down our cities* [to get more aid]." And what if cities were burned down? More money isn't coming from Washington, where rural and suburban representatives are firmly in command and the growth of entitlements guarantees that politics will be about dividing up a shrinking pie for everything else.

For a quarter of a century Harlem's "big men"—Rangel and his allies, David Dinkins, Percy Sutton, and Basil Patterson—controlled the flow of state, city, and federal antipoverty money into Harlem through the Harlem Urban Development Corporation (HUDC). The monopoly on antipoverty money, like foreign aid money in the Third World, was translated into a political monopoly. As in Curley's Boston, the politics the big men supported reproduced the resentments that kept them in power.

Much of the antipoverty money flowing into Harlem was dispensed as patronage, producing a public sector economy: 43 percent of the jobs in Harlem are held by people directly employed by government or by largely government-funded nonprofit agencies. Like Third World foreign aid, the antipoverty money was channeled into grandiose proposals for never-completed showcase projects, like the planned twenty-two-story Harlem International Trade Center for 125th Street, where Third World leaders like Castro were to have come to conduct business. After twenty-five years in business and $100 million in antipoverty money, some housing aside, the HUDC had very little to show for its efforts except the copy machines and telephone banks that helped keep Rangel and company in office.

In some ways, Harlem wasn't that different from New York State under Mario Cuomo, who similarly looked to funnel the economy through his political operation. The business of Rangel, Dinkins, et al. was to keep Harlem in the public sector, if not in poverty. When Blockbuster Video tried to open a store on a site controlled by the HUDC, they were told, reports *New York Magazine*'s Craig Horowitz, that local minority interests had to be cut in. "Well, everybody knew what that meant," says a state official who was involved in putting the final deal together. "National chains don't take local partners. That's why you haven't seen any up on 125th street." When the Empowerment Zone legislation recently brought in more money from the federal government, Rangel and company wanted more government spending on social services, spending that would have to pass through their hands.

Rangel wanted another branch of the City University of New York (CUNY), government offices, and drug rehabilitation centers—anything but private sector development.

Before the massacre at Freddy's Fashion Mart, it seemed as if the Harlem Empowerment Zone might end up the same way as HUDC despite pressure from Governor Pataki and Mayor Giuliani, both Republicans, to produce tangible results. In the wake of the massacre, Rangel was forced to accept a highly talented and private-sector-oriented director for the Empowerment Zone. The new director, Debby Wright, one of a number of new people trying to wrest Harlem from its old ways, worked at First Boston and in the Giuliani administration before taking the post. She was initially forced to reassure would-be investors in Harlem that there would not be another massacre.

For the moment, the most important new opportunities for inner-city employment and revitalization are in retailing. With the overbuilding of suburban malls, developers and retailers are increasingly turning toward the untapped inner-city market. With the aid of the Local Initiative Support Corporation (LISC), a new shopping center and movie complex for Newark and a new Pathmark in East Harlem are being planned. In forlorn New Haven, developers are competing to build a million square feet of shopping space in a city that's only twenty-one square miles.

The older cities are, to use a horrible neologism, "underretailed." From 1967 to 1992, explains sociologist Jan Rosenberg, New York lost more than 4 percent of its retail stores and more than fifty-two thousand retail jobs as high taxes and excessive regulation pushed, and prices at suburban superstores pulled, city people to shop outside the city. More than two-thirds of the people who live in Harlem shop elsewhere because there are so few local stores. Reports the city's planning commissioner, Joe Rose, New York exports about $3.1 billion of retail activity a year because one-third of households do major shopping outside the city.

In recent years Ben and Jerry's, Rite Aid, and Blockbuster Video have opened in Harlem, and the Gap, Disney, Sony, Home Depot, and Caldor are looking for sites. The Harlem manager of Ben and Jerry's sees the new stores and the managerial and entry-level positions they can provide as the community's shot at a piece of the American dream.

For most, upward mobility begins with the sort of entry-level job long derided as dead-end. At a time when one American in eight has worked at McDonald's at one point or another in his or her life, notes journalist Amity Shlaes, "fast food outlets have replaced the army as the primary source of secondary socialization for people with limited skills." Pizza Hut's chairman, talking about his stores in South Central L.A., explained, "We teach people team building, time management, basic math, even how to assimilate."

The success of the new immigrants demonstrates that mobility must be pursued rather than provided. Whatever our desires for recompense, success has to be a matter of effort and accomplishment, not a gift of government. What local government can do, as it has to some extent in L.A. but less so in New York and D.C., is encourage the economic conditions that allow people to pursue their personal progress.

Now, a century after the end of the Reconstruction period, when Southern blacks were resubjugated under new forms of servitude, and twenty years after it was made clear that a second reconstruction was shunting the sons and daughters of servitude into a genuinely dead-end welfare and social service economy, it's time to acknowledge that inner-city America will never be economically integrated until it fully participates in and benefits from the wealth-creating market economy.

The promise of inner-city economic development draws on the now forgotten arguments for capitalism, arguments that antedate its actual development in the Enlightenment of the nineteenth century. Bernard de Mandeville, the British satirist and philosopher, argued that the virtue of capitalism was that it could serve as a substitute for the endless warfare of early modern Europe by channeling the aggressive passions of ethnic and national conflict into the more benign channels of commercial competition.

19. By Way of a Conclusion (to an ongoing story)

Modern liberalism was born in the big cities and died there, a suicide of sorts. Liberals lost their birthright to govern big-city America not so much because they were overwhelmed by a well-armed foe but because their sense of moral superiority was so suffocating as to make it impossible for them to either adapt to new conditions or learn from their critics.

Urban liberalism died not because the federal government was insufficiently generous but because the money that was sent for social services sowed the seeds of self-destruction. "There is a wistful myth," wrote Jane Jacobs, "that if only we had enough money to spend . . . we could wipe out all our slums . . . [and] reverse decay. But look at what we have built with the first several billions. This is not the rebuilding of cities, this is the sacking of cities." But then in the perverse logic of the sort that has obtained in Harlem, South Central, and Anacostia, the devastation wrought by misguided policies was adduced as proof that even more money had to be spent on those same policies.

Liberals lost not only political control of New York, Washington, and Los Angeles but the debate over urban issues as well. Says Senator Moynihan of his fellow Democrats, "We were never able to confront the social decline of our cities. We were in denial and learning disabled." That left urban reform in the hands of moderate Republicans like Giuliani in New York and Riordan in Los Angeles or the nonpartisan professionals in D.C.

If these three cities are in the midst of at least partially undoing the errors of the 1960s, it's not because they've imposed a full-blown ideological alternative. Rather, their success to date comes from starting to repair the damage done by the great gambles of the 1960s.

"In much of inner-city America, 1995 will be remembered as the year of demolition," wrote Rob Gurwitt in *Governing* magazine. No fewer than thirty-two housing projects around the country were slated for total or partial demolition in 1996. But it was more than buildings that were being dismantled; the whole intellectual apparatus erected in the 1960s to deal with urban issues was being dismantled as well.

The cities had lost confidence in themselves. Explained one official, "Cities want to start over." If we could restore our older cities to the conditions they enjoyed before Lyndon Johnson declared 1965 "the year of the cities," before *Newsweek* proclaimed John Lindsay "the hero of the cities," and before the Watts riots transformed the urban landscape, it would be considered a historic achievement. Yet there is some reason for optimism. Broadly speaking, city governments are moving from redistribution to economic growth; from social services to private sector jobs; from a belief that poverty causes crime to the reverse; and, in general, from reliance on government to attempts to revive markets.

The two major Los Angeles riots of recent years have been turning points in the life of America's big cities. The 1965 Watts riot and the upheavals that followed in Detroit, Washington, Newark, Cleveland, and a hundred other cities produced a politics and policy designed to buy off further violence. The riots themselves ceased but were followed by the rolling riot of crime rates rising to unprecedented levels. The cities have never recovered. In the 1960s there were three cops for every crime; by the early 1990s the ratio had reversed.

Inflamed by the Rodney King verdict in August 1992, the City of Angels erupted again. But the 1992 South Central riot has, in unexpected ways, proven strikingly beneficial to American urban life. First, the 1992 L.A. turmoil was the beginning of the end of the riot ideology. The 1960s riots had produced new money for the cities as a form of riot insurance. The 1992 L.A. riot and the smaller riots it tripped off in Las Vegas, Seattle, and Atlanta produced a vast volume of rhetoric, but no new aid was forthcoming. No longer able to hawk the failings of their residents, the cities had to think about reintegrating the ghetto into the larger economy. Second, the L.A. riot broke the stalemate over policing produced by two untenable alternatives. Root-cause liberalism, which said that working people of the cities, white and black, would just have to bear the cost of a world bent to menace until full justice could be achieved, had already been rejected. But before the riot get-tough policing was still a live option.

Before the 1992 L.A. riot, conservatives tried to strengthen the paramilitary hand of police departments, many of which modeled themselves on the L.A.P.D. But conservatives had been passing get-tough measures since the mid-1960s to no good effect. Tough, "war on crime" policing served in L.A. to turn all inner-city civilians into "the enemy." The stark choice, as Johnny Cochran summed it up for the jury in the Simpson trial, seemed to be between fighting racism or giving the police free rein. Or so it seemed.

It was not until the L.A. riots that get-tough policing, like liberalism, was also discredited. This left the rest of the country receptive to the reforms instituted by George Kelling and William Bratton, first in the New York subways and then in the city as a whole, under Mayor Giuliani. In the April 1997 mayoral election in L.A., incumbent Richard Riordan and challenger Tom Hayden battled over who could be more Giuliani-like when it came to crime. "Giuliani is real," said Hayden. "Giuliani is tough. There's no comparison. He's better than Riordan in every respect." For his part, Riordan, who had announced his candidacy for reelection by insisting that "public safety must always be our number one priority," called on Los Angeles to adopt what he described as New York's "highly sophisticated system of [police] accountability." Los Angeles took a step in that direction when in a reassertion of civilian authority the police commission chose not to reappoint Chief Willie Williams for a second term, despite what amounted to an all-out political campaign by the chief to keep his post.

The success of the Kelling-Bratton-Giuliani strategy was a great moment for urban America, because for the first time since the dark days of the 1960s a great American metropolis made significant headway in dealing with a major problem. Just as important, its underlying approach suggested a more general strategy for redeeming the cities from the damage wrought by the gambles of the 1960s.

In a sense, urban America wants to return to the past, but one leavened by the lasting reforms of the civil rights era. While there is no going back to an older concept of community that was too often racially exclusive, there is wide support for a reassertion of common standards of public behavior. Antonio Pagan, a Puerto Rican city councilman representing the Lower East Side of Manhattan, explains that in his district "the people asking for the laws to be enforced are the minorities themselves." Pagan is disdainful of the constant attempts to "cheapen the discussion" by past references to racially discriminatory enforcement. Civil libertarians, he argues, "try to turn it into a black–white issue to avoid the issue" of the social breakdown afflicting our neighborhoods.

The transformation Pagan describes is encapsulated in the story of an

African-American tenant activist: Mrs. Jones (a pseudonym) has lived in Brooklyn's Red Hook Houses, the biggest single public housing project in New York, for thirty-six years. She and her husband raised six kids there. When the Joneses first arrived, there were five-dollar fines for small violations of project rules. Minor vandalism, littering, loitering, keeping dogs in apartments—all these brought fines. But the absence of due process recourse gave management enormous discretionary authority, which it sometimes abused. Like many tenants, Mrs. Jones resented the arbitrary manner in which fines were sometimes imposed by a white manager. As a tenant leader, she fought to strip the manager of his authority to levy fines, yet this is something she now regrets. Those small rules, she says today, once set the tone for projects that are now overwhelmed by crime and violence. Mrs. Jones argues that the revival has to begin with a restoring of the standards of behavior she and most of her neighbors still share. Her conclusions, I would suggest, are shared by an overwhelming majority of urbanites, who recognize that the very heterogeneity of city life imposes a premium on moral reliability.

The return to old assumptions regarding public order applies to issues of social mobility as well. There are few urban observers who speak explicitly of the immigrant analogy, although the success of recent immigrants is never far from the minds of almost anyone who thinks about the cities; but smart local activists have given up the idea of state-sponsored group mobility and have turned to assumptions once associated with the immigrant ascent.

The practical effect of the state-sponsored group mobility approach was the generation of hostility toward those individuals who "made it" before the group as a whole did, a result that led some to conclude that it was better to fail than to desert your people. The practical effect was to help turn the inner cities into "complex poorhouses," to use Camilo Vergara's felicitous phrase, in which the only thriving business was social services. But today the make-work–social-service economy is being questioned as never before. It is increasingly derided as "Poverty Inc.," a lucrative business for those who directly benefit by peddling pathology to a willing buyer in the federal government but death for the cities and neighborhoods that encourage it.

What was left when the heady wine promised by the growth of social services evaporated was the vinegar of liberal pity and condescension, sometimes dressed up in the language of multiculturalism, toward sad people and sad places. As Councilman Art Feltman of Hartford explains, "There's a paternalistic view in the social services community that the poor will always be poor . . . and that if not for us do-gooders everyone is going to die. I think we have to have confidence that, given the right opportunity, people can do more for themselves and take more responsibility."

Feltman is seconded by Joe Hall of the Banana Kelly Community Development Corporation, which has helped rebuild parts of the South Bronx. "The only way to get back where we were before the Destruction," Hall explains, "is to make sure we never again have a reliance on government funding built on social service models—those that create dependency." Hall continues, "Revival can be built on home ownership, retail revival, private sector jobs and community self-help that minimizes the role of 'credentialed professionals.'" What Feltman and Hall have rediscovered is the time-honored means by which generations of immigrants moved and continue to move up the social ladder.

The theme of immigrant incorporation was central to Richard Riordan's landslide reelection as mayor of Los Angeles. Both Riordan and Tom Hayden had Latino campaign managers; both concentrated on winning Hispanic voters who for the first time were a larger part of the electorate than African-Americans. But while Riordan, a businessman, appealed to these new voters as citizens who needed jobs, Hayden invited Latinos to think of themselves as victims who needed social programs. Riordan won with 60 percent of the Latino and 62 percent of the Asian vote.

Hayden's militant opposition to economic growth, and his sixties-style talk about "community control" of economic development were badly out of synch with "immigrant aspirations to make it into the American middle class," explained Gregory Rodriguez. Equating brown skin with 1960s black politics, Hayden wanted Latinos to take the protest path African-Americans took in the 1960s.

Five years after the 1992 L.A. riots, that path looks more forlorn than ever. If there was an underside to Riordan's reelection, it was in the political isolation of the African-American community. They alone voted for Hayden's protest politics, by a margin of four to one.

Writing in the late 1960s in the wake of the Ocean Hill–Brownsville *Kulturkampf,* Columbia sociologist Herbert Gans penned an influential article, "We Won't End the Urban Crisis Until We End Majority Rule," defending the concept of community control. Gans argued that African-Americans should have the right to "secede, establishing [their] own institutions without being financially punished by the majority." For nearly the thirty years that's pretty much what happened. The inner cities partly seceded from the larger culture but continued to be subsidized with various forms of social support. Welfare reform brings that to an end as well.

Just as the declining influence of the European welfare states is a result of their failure to both reform themselves and respond to the new challenge from Asia, so too is the decline of big-city liberalism a product of the unwillingness to both reform welfare when the Democrats controlled Congress and adapt to the rising challenge of the South and West. The 1996 Welfare Reform Act melded anti-immigrant and anti-welfare sentiments into an anti-urban package. The legislation might have been better titled the Anti-Los Angeles, Anti-New York, Anti-Marion Barry Act of 1996. The District and its mayor are simply an ongoing embarrassment, a running excuse to ignore or minimize the more hopeful developments in urban America. But the welfare reform bill will drain large sums from both L.A. and New York, since most of the cuts in federal spending are for legal immigrants and these two cities represent the highest concentration of legal immigrants in the United States.

It would be foolish to try and predict the consequences of the 1996 Welfare Reform Act, which is 250 pages of legislation accompanied by a 250-page House–Senate Conference report explaining its intentions. Some of its provisions, like eliminating AFDC and Medicaid for most legal immigrants, should and will be fought in court. Other provisions, like the work requirements for a progressively increasing percentage of the AFDC adult population and a lifetime limit of five years on welfare, will be subject to game playing, rules fudging, court challenges, and the sheer administrative challenge of keeping track of people, not to mention placing them in work situations.

In all three cities, attempts to create or expand city workfare programs will also face challenges from public sector unionists, who rightfully fear for their positions, and from "living wage" campaigns. In 1993 local legislation gave the District the highest minimum wage of any city in the country. In New York and Los Angeles, campaigns to create a higher local minimum wage for government-related work have gained considerable momentum. Although justified on some grounds, their success would make it all the more difficult to create the large number of low-wage jobs needed for people pushed off AFDC.

What is clear, though, is that welfare reform, along with coming cuts in federal housing and health care subventions, will place enormous, perhaps unbearable, pressure on the old ways of doing business in the cities. All three cities face a challenge to their fundamental sense of themselves.

Welfare reform will help force all three cities to confront their basic weaknesses. Take the District, which lost thirty thousand jobs during President Clinton's first term. The anti-Washington mood of the country, reflected by both the tenor of Clinton's reelection campaign and the return of a Republican Congress, means that federal employment is going to continue to decline, albeit gradually. Once immune not only to competitors but also to the business cycle, D.C. is facing challenges both from plans to privatize government entitlements and from the resurgent influence of state governments, which have taken the lead on welfare reform. Looking at the rise of Republican governors relative to legislators in the national government in Washington, one wag asked the residents of the District to think about how Detroit must have felt when it saw the first Toyota or how Akron must have felt at the first glimpse of a Michelin tire.

Assuming the best of intentions, never a good bet in Barrytown, how will the D.C. government be able to place a growing number of people in jobs when the nearly bankrupt District (which had, compared to the states, the worst job creation record in the United States over the past decade) has to lay off thousands of city workers? The answer in part is that the District is going to have to reach outside itself to the booming Greater Washington metropolitan area for the jobs needed. This will be no small task. For one thing, members of the middle class of the nearby regions of Maryland and Virginia take great pains to distance themselves from D.C.—according to a recent survey, even to the point that 60 percent refuse to identify themselves as coming from the Washington metropolitan area when they travel. This means a humbling end to the "chocolate city" dream celebrated in the 1975 funk-rock tune of that title. Rather than becoming a black quasi-state government providing the full array of welfare state services, D.C. will shrink back into being a federal district that's forced to concentrate on the efficient delivery of basic services.

For Los Angeles County, with its relatively low AFDC rates (compared to New York and Washington), welfare reform may produce a fierce debate on immigration. Welfare reform means a new influx of workers into a low-wage market already hard hit by sharply declining pay. The cost–benefit ratio of the immigration that fueled twenty years of economic development is likely to turn increasingly negative. If mass immigration does come to a close, L.A.'s dynamic decentered economy is likely to rise to the challenge even if its civic culture will not.

Like the District, New York faces a challenge to its very self-concept. The social and political arrangements of the past sixty years are imperiled by both economic and political decline. New York is faced with not only welfare reform but a whole series of shocks to its make-work economy. In addition to welfare reform and the reduction of federal housing subsidies, the move to managed health care will curb the number of people who can be employed by way of New York State's outsized Medicaid budget. Similarly, the pressures from Republicans in Albany to eliminate rent control and, finally (after an uninterrupted series of scandals), the dismantling of the local school patronage networks put in place after Ocean Hill–Brownsville means an end to the system of subsidies that defined New York City's social and political arrangements.

In New York City the entitlement economy can't survive the combination of federal budget cuts, sharp cuts in the state tax rates (and, hence, revenues), and the city's spiraling budget deficits. Temporarily buoyed by Wall Street revenues, the Big Apple is on the brink of a wrenching transformation. In the early years of the Giuliani administration liberals cried wolf. Every time the ax was taken to a bloated agency, they insisted the sky would fall. It didn't. In the coming years they may have more reason to duck. The danger to the fabric of the city is not only in cuts to the poor. According to the Citizens Budget Commission, only thirteen cents of every social service dollar goes to the needy; the rest goes to those who administer the programs. That vast army of antipoverty and health care delivery workers, sometimes only a few years away from poverty themselves, are the backbone of numerous lower-middle-class neighborhoods, neighborhoods that will be hard hit by the decline in social service and health care cuts.

For New York, the old game of extracting an increasing share of a declining pie is at an end. Still, the central and not unreasonable fact is that for many, given the misshapen structure of New York's economy, slow decline is preferable to the promise of capitalism's "creative destruction." Slow decline will, at least for the short run, provide a sort of security against the dangers posed by full-scale reform.

If New York were a city better able to break free of the gravitational pull of its past, Giuliani would campaign not only to win but to force his Democratic opponents, all of whom have ducked the reasons for the city's decline, into a debate on how to face the unavoidable transformation ahead. And, with luck, it would be a debate that would at last offer up at least the outlines of a new social contract.

The contract would have to be based on the trade-off between a declining public sector and a rising private sector. The possibilities are there. In a city that will probably be only 35 percent white by the turn of the century, job growth comes from small, and many times immigrant-owned, businesses that increasingly drive local employment. These are the companies in everything from computer graphics to specialty foods; companies that, if the city can be made more business friendly, may well remake Gotham, along with the promise of a global economy, for the next millennium. Even welfare reform, as sweaty as it will be in the short run, offers some hope for the future. Welfare policy has been tax and economic policy. To the extent that the welfare rolls can be reduced, taxes can be cut, creating the possibility for business expansion and new jobs.

New Yorkers need to be reminded that theirs was a great commerical city before it was a welfare state, but this will be a difficult task in a town still bathed in New Deal nostalgia. In Gotham we tend to remember the future even as we imagine a past that obscures the city's commercial roots.

At the end of Evelyn Waugh's *Brideshead Revisited,* the novelist's elegy for a dying order in aristocratic England, the narrator visits a previously forgotten chapel on the grounds of a boarded-up English manor during World War II, now occupied by the British army. He is surprised to find that the soldiers of his unit have been quietly rediscovering the estate chapel. Such is the role of cities in the new economy. Lining city streets are vestiges of a world that *worked.* As we look for the future, we may be increasingly surprised to see it gazing back at us from an unexpected corner of the past.

The future did once happen here, and it will again, although it will be a smaller, less imposing future in an information age economy that disperses and decentralizes everything from capital markets to car manufacturing. Great cities like New York, Los Angeles, and Washington are far more than what the would-be technoprophet George Gilder describes as "leftover baggage from the industrial era."

Whether industrial or postindustrial, cities nurture the face-to-face contact within creative communities that drives the advanced sectors of the economy. The dynamism that once drove the advertising industry in New York and the film industry in Los Angeles has flowed into new channels.

The multimedia revolution in communications and entertainment is taking place largely in three cities—Los Angeles, San Jose, and New York—while Vienna, Virginia, just outside the District, has become the capital of the telecommunications industry. Creativity in cyberspace, like creativity in the older industries, is the product of the intellectual energy and intensity of interaction found in places like the multimedia shops of West L.A. and New York's Silicon Alley (located just a few blocks from my office at The Cooper Union).

New York and Los Angeles, almost as much as Washington, think of themselves as capitals. Mayor Giuliani talks of how New York is the "capital of culture," the "capital of finance,"and the "capital of the world"; Los Angeles mayor Tom Bradley spoke of his city as the "capital of the Pacific Rim"; and

Washington will remain the capital of the United States. But caught, like the rest of society, in the centrifugal currents of the new economy, none of these cities will be able to dominate the landscape as it once did. Yet even after being taken down a notch or two, they will remain, by virtue of their concentrations of energy and intellect, at the center of the American political imagination. These great cities will continue to shape our future, just as the future continues to shape itself within them.

Acknowledgments

I have accumulated many debts in writing this book, but none greater than that to my wife, Jan Rosenberg. In addition to helping me develop the arguments in this book, she often took on the full burden of household chores to give me time to work. If this book gains even a small measure of success, it will be due in large part to her efforts. My sisters- and brothers-in-law, Jeanne Rosenberg, Max Trumpower, Joni Rosenfeld-Naft, and Howard Naft, helped out with accommodations and clippings. My teenage sons, Harry and Jake, got me sources, ran errands, and generally helped out.

No one, other than my wife, has helped more than my friend Jim Chapin, who, while disagreeing with much of what I wrote, sharpened the argument at key points. I also owe a considerable debt to Joel Kotkin in Los Angeles and Jeff Itell in Washington, whose generosity and willingness to discuss the issues at length at almost any time of day or night were an enormous help.

Let me also thank, in Los Angeles, Harold Meyerson, Peter Dreier, and Gregory Rodriguez for giving me insights as well as their own personalized tours of L.A.. David Abel, Roger Waldinger, Warren Olney, Eric Shockman, Rafael Sonenshein, Steve Erie, Luis Caldera, Mark Horowitz, Rick Tuttle, Marc Haefele, David Ayon, Richard Katz, Rick Orloff, Camilo Vergara, and Xandra Kayden were kind enough to share their time and writings with me.

In Washington, Steve Diner, Charles Harris, George Grier, Dwight Cropp, Jonetta Rose Barras, Mark Plotkin, Carol Johns Gray, Mathew Watson, Tom Edmonds, Sam Smith, Virgil Thompson, Harry Jaffe, and David Plotz generously shared their time and writings with me.

My friends Sol Stern, Jim Sleeper, Julia Vitullo-Martin, and Ed Costikyan were invaluable in allowing me to talk through important elements of the New York story. My friend and neighbor Ian Smith was the computer whiz whose efforts allowed me to read the L.A. and D.C. newspapers on line every morning.

My dean, John Harrington of The Cooper Union; Al From, Will Marshall, Chuck Alston, and Tom Mirga at the Progressive Policy Institute; and Scott McConnell at the *New York Post* were generous in giving me the time I needed to finish this book. Will Marshall also helped sharpen my understanding of urban issues in our ongoing conversations and in the article "Markets and Empowerment: Helping Cities Help Themselves" that he and I wrote together.

Suzanne Strickland, Peter Skerry, David Seifman, Morley Winograd, Wally Katz, Rob Tier and Ken Cummins, Ben Haimowitz, and Pat Hurley helped with specific sections of the story. Cooper student Nick Popolo aided my research.

Jack Schwartz and my agents Glen Hartley and Lynn Chu read the entire manuscript for me. My editor at The Free Press, Mitch Horowitz, not only encouraged me to write this book but also did a terrific job of emending the manuscript. It's been a pleasure to work with him. Thanks also to my copy-editor, Toby Troffkin.

Finally, special thanks to my friend Eric Foner, whose kindness kept me engaged in academia when I was about to give up on it, and to Julius Rubin, who sparked my interest in studying cities.

Needless to say, none of the above-named are responsible for the arguments and errors herein. And I greatly appreciate that many people who helped knew fully well that we disagreed on important issues, but were so decent as to help anyway.

Index